The Japanese Police State

The Japanese Police State

The Tokkô in Interwar Japan

Elise K. Tipton

UNIVERSITY OF HAWAII PRESS
HONOLULU

To the memory of my father,
Wilfred H. Kurashige, M.D.

© Elise Tipton, 1990
This book is copyright under the Berne Convention.
No reproduction without permission. All rights reserved.

Published in North America by
University of Hawaii Press
2840 Kolowalu Street
Honolulu, Hawaii 96822

First published in 1990 by Allen & Unwin Australia Pty Ltd
8 Napier Street, North Sydney, NSW 2059 Australia

Library of Congress Cataloging-in-Publication Data:

Tipton, Elise K.
    The Japanese police state: the Tokko in interwar Japan/by Elise K. Tipton.
      p. cm.
    Includes bibliographical references and index.
    ISBN 0-8248-1328-6
    1. Japan. Kaishichō. Tokubetsu Kôtō Keisatsubu. 2. Police—Japan—History—20th century. 3. Internal security—Japan—History—20th century. 4. Political crimes and offenses—Japan—Prevention—History—20th century. 5. Japan—Politics and government—1912-1945. I. Title.
HV8257.A45K458 1990
363.2'0952'09041—dc20   90-46765
                                                            CIP

CONTENTS

Introduction   1
  Studies of the police in prewar Japan
  Studies of the police in general
  The political and social roles of the police
  The Tokkô in prewar Japan: factors to consider
  Totalitarian, fascist or authoritarian
  The concept of a police state

Chapter 1 The suppression of the left   17
  The suppression of the Meiji socialist movement
  The emergence of a new suppression policy
  The development of the suppression
  Explanations of the suppression

Chapter 2 The police tradition   35
  The police tradition from the Meiji period
  The political police within the police tradition
  The origins of the police ideology

Chapter 3 Rule by law   52
  The Tokugawa legacy
  The Meiji legacy
  The Peace Preservation Law
  Rule by law during the 1930s

Chapter 4 Professionalism   74
  A professional people's police
  A professional emperor's police
  Internal divisions
  Problems of professionalism

Chapter 5 The emperor's police ideology   105
    Conflict with the Justice Ministry
    Conflict with the Kenpeitai
    The origins and functions of the emperor's police ideology
Chapter 6 The Japanese police state   134
    The domestic context of the Japanese police state
    The Japanese police state in comparative perspective
Appendixes   154
    I   The Tokkô chain of command in the 1930s
    II   Disposition of Peace Preservation Law violations
    III Disposition of right wing related cases
Notes   159
    Introduction
    Chapter 1
    Chapter 2
    Chapter 3
    Chapter 4
    Chapter 5
    Chapter 6
Bibliography   188
Index   207

ACKNOWLEDGEMENTS

I would like to express my appreciation for the assistance of various people and institutions which have made this book possible. Thanks go to George M. Wilson, Richard Mitchell, Lawrence Olson, and David Titus for reading the original dissertation and making many comments and suggestions for revising the manuscript. In Japan research was made possible by affiliation with the Institute for Social Science at the University of Tokyo. There I benefited from the expertise of Professor Okudaira Yasuhiro. Nakahara Hidenori and the staff of the International Service Section of the National Diet Library were very helpful.

Financial support came from a Fulbright-Hays Dissertation Abroad Fellowship and a Comparative History Research grant from the University of California at Santa Cruz. Appreciation also to Julie Manley for typing the manuscript and to Fiona Inglis and the editorial staff at Allen and Unwin Australia for seeing the manuscript through publication.

It is customary to thank children and spouses last, although, as in this case, they often deserve first acknowledgement. Lee and Christine need to be thanked for their patience. Special thanks must go to my husband, Ben, who has acted as a sounding board through the years and whose critical reading of the manuscript was invaluable for the revisions.

Note: Japanese names have been rendered according to the customary Japanese order of surname first.

INTRODUCTION

'If you say "Tokkô", even a crying child falls silent.'
Takagi Takeo, 1954[1]

Spectres from the prewar period continue to haunt Japan. Central to the image of prewar Japan is the brooding sense of menace inspired by the Special Higher Police (Tokubetsu Kôtô Keisatsu), commonly known as the Tokkô. In 1954 memories of Tokkô terror remained fresh, but in 1975 the editors of a multivolume documentary history of the Tokkô ominously warned that the Tokkô still lived.[2] In 1984 the author of a history of the Tokkô worried that today's security police was becoming the Tokkô of the future, and a popular NHK television series introduced another generation of Japanese to the picture of Tokkô brutality. Even more recently in 1990, an *Asahi shinbun* article noted that police intervention in certain high schools over teachers' statements about the January general election reminded some people of the prewar Tokkô.[3] This continuing nervousness about a resurrection of the Tokkô derives from analogies made between the Tokkô on the one hand and Hitler's Gestapo and Stalin's State Political Administration, better known as the GPU, on the other. Discussion of the significance of political repression is therefore premised on moral judgements rooted in the shock of defeat 45 years ago.

The Japanese political system suffered a moral as well as a military defeat in 1945. In attempting to explain this double failure, both Japanese and Western scholars have utilised terms such as 'authoritarianism', 'fascism' and 'totalitarianism' to describe the prewar order. However, they have disagreed over both the meaning and appropriateness of these designations. The term 'totalitarianism' arose in the Cold War atmosphere of the 1950s to link the Soviet Union with Nazi Germany. Although historians still use it at times descriptively, political scientists in general no longer find it a useful analytical concept. As monolithic views of prewar and even wartime Japan disappeared, the term seemed progressively less appropriate to the Japanese context.

The term 'fascism' has continued to enjoy wider currency than 'totalitarianism' among historians of both Europe and Japan and of both Marxist and non-Marxist persuasion. Nevertheless, after decades of research and debate there is still no consensus on a definition of fascism. Moreover, none of the many definitions can be used to describe Japan without major alterations. If there was a 'Japanese fascism', it differed significantly from European fascism to the extent that theories of fascism lose their explanatory power when applied to prewar Japan.

Dissatisfaction with the concepts of totalitarianism and fascism has led some Japanese specialists to prefer 'authoritarianism'. However, although a suggestive descriptive term, authoritarianism is even less satisfactory than fascism as an analytical concept for it lacks any specific content. Unlike fascism, authoritarianism does not suggest concrete categories of analysis, such as ideology, political organisation or social structure, that could be used to erect an explanatory framework.

The one element that the idea of authoritarianism does suggest is domestic political repression. This seems to be the aspect of the notion that has recommended it to scholars. Indeed the repression of political dissent and the pursuit of political dissidents form the common elements of all the terms used to describe the prewar Japanese political system. This suggests that repression is the key element that must be explained. Yet scholars have not looked closely at the police, particularly the Tokkô, nor attempted to analyse its role in the political system as a whole. Until recently studies of the problem of political control tended to focus on individuals and groups that suffered under the prewar regime rather than on the repressors themselves. This served to document abuses, but not to tell why they occurred—to describe the tragedy of prewar Japan, but not to explain why it happened.

Studies of the police in prewar Japan

Considering the importance assigned by contemporary observers and Allied Occupation authorities to the role of the police in prewar Japan, it is surprising that so little Western scholarly attention has been directed to the police.[4] Americans writing in popular magazines, journals and books during the 1920s and 1930s viewed police activity as an important element in prewar Japanese society. They reported the increase in political police activities and growing restrictions on freedom of speech and press, and they speculated on the implications of these developments for the establishment of fascism in Japan.[5] At the end of the war an American intelligence report argued that its political activities made the Tokkô 'a potent political force' and 'in large part responsible for the creation of obstacles to the democratic development of the Japanese people'.[6] General MacArthur accepted this view, describing the police as the 'strongest weapon of the military clique', one that had enabled the military 'to spread a network of political espionage, suppress freedom of speech, of assembly, and even of thought, and by means of tyrannical oppression to degrade the dignity of the individual'.[7] This evaluation of the political role played by the prewar and wartime police became the impetus behind Occupation policies to purge all political police officials immediately and reform the police system as a whole, in order to prevent restoration of a 'police state' and to remove obstacles to democratisation.[8]

Histories of the Japanese Communist Party (JCP) and other leftist groups by Western scholars all refer to suppressive activities carried out by the police; they consider these activities a major, if not the main, factor in the failure of the Communists and other leftists to sustain an organised opposition movement against the existing political order and elites.[9] However, the focus remains on the leftists themselves; no analysis of the police is made. Richard Mitchell's studies of the Peace Preservation Law administration and of political censorship have begun to fill the gap in our knowledge of the evolution of the government's thought control policies during the 1920s and 1930s.[10] His consideration of the Justice Ministry clearly shows the complexity of the system and points to the need for an analysis of the workings of the key repressive agent in the system, the Tokkô.

In Japanese scholarship the problem is not one of neglect, but lack of impartiality and dispassionate analysis. This is a manifestation of a general problem that until recently has plagued Japanese scholarship concerning the prewar period. Events of that period have been too close—whether abhorred or embarrassing—to be treated from any emotional and intellectual distance. The Tokkô is often made the supreme example of the 'dark valley' that is supposed to characterise Japanese history in the 1930s and 1940s. It attracts attention in all histories of repression and repressive legislation as well as in studies of the police in general, and it also figures in some studies of administration and bureaucracy.

Interpretations may be described as either 'official' or 'opposition' viewpoints. The opposition viewpoint prevails among most scholars and the general public as well as among the socialist and communist parties. It has much in common with that of Occupation authorities, for it also regards the Tokkô as the Japanese counterpart of Nazi Germany's Gestapo and the Soviet GPU and as a central element in Japanese 'fascism'. It emphasises the omniscient and completely centralised nature of the Tokkô's organisation and activities.[11] Japanese critics, like Occupation leaders, call the Tokkô a weapon or tool of the ruling group. In their terms the Tokkô was established and used by the ruling class and its absolutist emperor system to suppress the non-ruling class. Through use of the Tokkô the ruling class checked the contradictions that accompanied the rapid development of capitalism.[12]

The viewpoint defending the Tokkô may be called the 'official' interpretation because it is generally put forth in official and semi-official government histories of the police, as well as by former police officials. It takes pains to refute analogies between the Tokkô and the Gestapo or GPU, arguing that, unlike the German and Soviet police, the Tokkô was a public administrative agency no different from other branches of the police, with its personnel publicly recorded and performing their tasks openly and based on public laws and regulations. Therefore, the Tokkô was by no means a secret police. Moreover, the argument continues, while some Tokkô officers used extreme methods, most were only faithfully enforcing the laws—strictly controlling both extreme right wing elements and the left wing Communist Party and thereby preventing illegal acts.[13]

Since the second half of the 1970s Japanese scholars have begun to move more comfortably between these polemical extremes. Aside from the publication of numerous Tokkô-related documents, there have been attempts at a less partisan treatment of the Tokkô.[14] In 1984 Ogino Fujio published the first detailed chronological history of the Tokkô. His focus is institutional, and Ogino himself says that he has not fully considered the links between the expansion of the Tokkô and developments in social movements.[15] In addition, this approach leaves open the question of why the government reacted so strongly to such obviously weak movements, lacking in mass support. Equally important, it tends to treat the Tokkô as a passive instrument of the government rather than seek explanations in the internal dynamics of the Tokkô itself. Ogino does not consider the Tokkô's position in the police institution or prewar political system as a whole.

Studies of the police in general

In Western scholarship a similar trend can be seen in studies of police in general. Those concerned with political police have sometimes been limited to moral condemnations of police brutality, terror or 'totalitarianism'.[16] Although more historical studies of police now take an analytical approach, there are still only a few that consider the political and social role of the police.[17] As in the case of the Tokkô, the police elsewhere in the world has usually been portrayed as an obedient agent of the existing regime, as a mere reflection of the political system.[18] Police histories are often institutional histories; they focus on the police as a purely administrative agency and concentrate on organisational and functional developments.[19]

Many criminologists and sociologists have recognised the active social role played by the police, but their concerns have not usually been historical or comparative.[20] Police studies have been dominated by case studies with particular national or historical preoccupations. Consequently, although their interest in police–public relations unveils problems common to the police in many countries, it often leads to hypotheses and conclusions too specific to a given culture or time period to be useful in the interwar Japanese context. Research since the mid 1970s has begun to look across national and cultural boundaries, but comparative police analysis, like police history, remains in the pioneering stage.[21]

Political scientists specialising in modernisation and political development in South and Southeast Asia and Africa have carried out the most helpful and suggestive studies for the historian. A few have analysed the role of the police in these social, economic and political processes.[22] They have argued that the police acts as an agency of political socialisation, meaning that it participates in the process of transmitting political values and behavioural patterns to individual citizens. Children's experiences with police officers are often their earliest contacts with government officials and can condition their way of viewing the political world.[23] Political scientists are just beginning to realise this, however. Most specialists in political socialisation and development concentrate their attention on schools, churches, the military and the mass media; they exclude the police.[24] One would also expect theories of political communication such as Karl Deutsch's to include the police as an object of research, since police officers have close contacts with citizens and provide a channel for information to flow between citizens and higher levels of government. Again, however, the police has been overlooked.[25]

The police does more than passively reflect the political system. It interacts with its political, social and cultural environment. David Bayley has explored the relationship between police development and historical circumstances in a comparative study of police systems in Britain, France, Germany and Italy. While he still treats the police development primarily as a reflection of external circumstances, he finds that the four police systems did not change in any uniform or automatic way in response to historical events, but rather demonstrated considerable stability or 'impermeability'. He cites the continuities in the French police system before and after the revolution as an example. However, the systems did change, and Bayley recognises the complex interaction that takes place among historical events, police institutions and political life.[26] This tends to reinforce James Q. Wilson's conclusions from his study of eight American urban communities.[27] Wilson suggests a correlation between police work style and political culture. However, he adds that, while police officials are keenly sensitive to their political environment, they are not governed by it.

The political and social roles of the police

Historically, the nature of political systems and their police have often but not always coincided. An outstanding example of a non-coinciding case is the coercive and authoritarian approach taken by the British in nineteenth-century Ireland.[28] Moreover, while instances of police action and policies independent of the government have been more rare than those of the military, the police's role in Ghana during the late 1960s demonstrated the possibility. There the police split and the two factions played separate political roles, the uniformed police allying with the military against Nkrumah and the political police.[29]

The police possesses several traits that endow it with influence in political and social life. Like the military, police power derives from its control over coercive forces. Unlike the military, police officers are usually the sole wielders of force against members of their own society.[30] Consequently, they are expected to use that force with maximum restraint. The more they rely on it to fulfil their assigned tasks, the less effective they appear to be. The police also differs from the military in its position as the initial point of contact between citizens and the law enforcement machinery. The police derives its strength from possession of authority as well as raw power. That authority carries moral overtones, for laws express the interests, values and beliefs of the ruling socio-political elite.[31] Crimes are actions declared undesirable according to prevailing norms.

Wide visibility enhances police effectiveness. In contrast with most other government officials, police officers wear uniforms setting them apart from ordinary citizens. Moreover, their diverse responsibilities bring them into more contact with individual citizens.[32] Maintenance of domestic order and stability heads the list of responsibilities. However, police officers perform administrative tasks beyond crime prevention and detection even in societies such as Britain and the United States, which have adopted a narrow definition of police work. In interwar Japan, where a broad definition of police work was accepted, police officers performed a multitude of tasks that brought them into daily contact with citizens. Consequently, they and other low-ranking officials, rather than remote members of the Diet, cabinet and higher civil service, came to personify political power for ordinary Japanese people.[33]

While perhaps more political 'agents' than 'principals', police officers may be significant in political socialisation. The manner in which they carry out their responsibilities influences their environment as much as the nature of the responsibilities themselves. As Wilson has emphasised, police officers are supposed to have minimal discretion, but in practice discretion is inevitable since laws require interpretation to be applied. Police officers decide whether or not to enforce a law and how to enforce it. In sharp contrast with most other large organisations, discretion within a police organisation increases as one moves down the hierarchy.[34] How police officers exercise discretion can affect people's attitudes towards their government and the political process in general. Do they operate openly or secretively? How do they treat individuals in their public contacts? Do they act impartially or in the interests of a particular group or groups? As an important element in all citizens' direct political experiences, relations with the police therefore shape their conceptions of law and political authority. Gabriel Almond and

Sidney Verba appreciated this in their study of civic culture when they used people's expectations of treatment by the police as an indicator of 'output affect' in the five countries surveyed.[35]

Finally, the police may be influential because it develops into a corporate entity.[36] However closely the police is associated with the regime, it also develops its own public and self-image, its own aims and ideals, and its own norms and style of operation. Its recruitment and training needs often lead to establishment of its own educational institutions and publications or may stimulate other institutions to meet these requirements. A police organisation also socialises its own members. The self-image developed influences individual police officers' views of their society and the role they should play in it. This includes their attitudes about the extent of a political role that the police should play.

The police official thus combines many roles. Balzac elevated police work to the noblest profession because it encompasses the work of three other noble professions: the soldier, who is guardian of society and protector of citizens; the priest, who is guardian of morality; and the artist, who seeks to explore motive and understand the human condition.[37] A New York police officer put it in contemporary terms:

> 'Cops aren't just crime fighters—we're in the aid business. Each time I answer an emergency. I have to think, "What am I on this one—minister, psychiatrist, social worker, marriage counsellor or law–enforcement agent?"' [38]

Both views demonstrate an insight into the involvement of the police in some of the most fundamental problems of society. Its responsibilities necessarily make its role more complex and influential than that of a 'nightwatchman'.[39] Depending on circumstances the police may contribute to maintenance of political stability or to processes of social change. A focus on the Tokkô's role in the suppression of the interwar Japanese left can therefore contribute to a reassessment of police roles in general as well as to an understanding of interwar Japanese politics and society.

The Tokkô in prewar Japan: factors to consider

The complexity of both the police officer's role and the specific and non-specific factors of time and place that shape this role suggest that a broad range of factors would need to be considered in an explanation of the position and actions of the Tokkô. Certainly, the interwar Japanese police, both as an institution and as a group of individuals, interacted with the specific historical circumstances of the 1920s and 1930s. The shift in government policy towards the left from repression to vigorous and systematic suppression was in part the political authorities' response to a sense of crisis popularly expressed by many individuals and groups during the late 1920s. The widespread feelings of social, economic and political dislocation pervading Japan were closely linked with the decline of Taishô democracy and with a shift in the balance of power elites in favour of the military. The suppression of the left was one aspect of authorities' response to this increasingly insecure and anxiety-ridden situation.

However, the fact that the Japanese government had followed a repressive policy towards socialism since its inception as an organised political movement in 1901 suggests that the suppression of the late 1920s and 1930s was not prompted by immediate circumstances alone. Moreover, from an external point of view there seems to be little justification for a sense of political danger on the part of government authorities. Despite the popularity of leftist ideas among intellectuals, students and industrial workers, no leftist organisation ever became a major political force; certainly none ever threatened the takeover or overthrow of the existing government or imperial system. As JCP specialist George Beckmann concludes, the Japanese communists 'never became a serious threat to the modern synthesis that was being built by Japan's dominant conservative forces. The Communists, like the Socialists, were only dissidents on the fringes of society; they never became a mass force.'[40]

It is important to explain the contribution of the police to this failure of organised leftist movements in the interwar period. However, since the left never posed an objective threat to the government or political system, there arises the more broadly significant question of why it was perceived by the police as a profound challenge—a challenge not only to the established political and economic system, but even to the foundation of the so-called national polity. One must go beyond the immediate events and conditions of the 1920s and 1930s to answer this question, for the answer depends in part on an understanding of conditions derived from the Japanese past and traditions before the 1920s, in part on an appreciation of the ideology of the police, and in part on a consideration of Japanese political culture as a developing set of patterns of attitudes and behaviour. Beyond the national context, characteristics that the Japanese police shared with all police and bureaucratic institutions also can be seen to contribute to a systemic and cultural explanation of Tokkô repression.

Three basic questions account for the order of topics. What were the perceptions and policies of the police towards the left during the 1920s and 1930s? What were the reasons for those perceptions and policies? Finally, what were the consequences and implications of those perceptions and policies for the left, the police and the political system as a whole? Explanations of Tokkô repression must be set against the background of the government's policies. The history of police perceptions and policy towards the left and the problems the left posed during the 1920s and 1930s highlights continuities and identifies changes in policy. It also shows areas of disagreement among scholars of the suppression and the problems with some of the previous explanations of the suppression and the role of the Tokkô.

The reasons for the way in which police officials perceived the leftist problem and carried out policy in a particular manner fall into four categories: history and traditions of the police; the legal framework; police recruitment, socialisation, ideology and other internal elements; and relations between the police and its external environment. The history and traditions of the police institution, especially the position of the political police in that institution, provide a good starting point. Setting the interwar police into its historical context is particularly important for understanding its repressive role. Inheriting essentially unchanged the organisation established during the Meiji period, police officials continued to look for inspiration to the conceptions enunciated by the founder of the modern Japanese police, Kawaji Toshiyoshi, regarding their role in Japanese society. The police tradition therefore supplied models for attitudes and behaviour for Tokkô officers during the 1920s and 1930s.[41]

Most political police laws and regulations were also part of the historical legacy received by the interwar Tokkô. They are important for understanding Tokkô actions because they designated political tasks and responsibilities and defined the scope of police operations. The interwar police, including the Tokkô, repeatedly insisted on the importance of law as the basis of their authority. At the same time the Tokkô was notorious for abusing the laws. A resolution of this apparent inconsistency lies in police officials' concepts of the role of law in Japanese society. Since the laws in any country are always subject to interpretation, such concepts and other fundamental political values undergirding the legal framework are as important as the specific content of laws for understanding police behaviour.

Recruitment, training, ideology and rewards constitute another cluster of factors affecting police attitudes and behaviour. Their social, economic and educational backgrounds and the criteria by which they were recruited partly determined the qualities of Tokkô officers. The kind of training and socialisation they experienced after entering the police strongly influenced their attitudes. Training and socialisation mean not only the knowledge and skills taught to police officers, but also the self-image and ideology promoted by police authorities. The latter includes the purpose and aims of the police, views of law and the relationship of the police to the people and the state. Japanese police leaders made strenuous efforts throughout the 1920s and 1930s to professionalise the police but met with limited success. Appreciation of this failure to achieve professionalism contributes not only to an understanding of the suppression of the left, but also to an understanding of the functioning of bureaucratic structures during the interwar period.

Relations between the police and other institutions, particularly the Justice Ministry and Kenpeitai (Military Police), not only shaped policies and the nature of their execution, but also changed the actual scope of police operations and stimulated redefinition of the police's role in Japanese society. This redefinition of role, embodied in an ideology of the emperor's police (*tennô no keisatsu*), also had its source in the larger external environment of the police. It was both a response to the shared sense of general social and political crisis and the outcome of competition with other institutions.

The police response to the leftist problem illuminates the functioning of the political system as a whole. The Japanese police was not simply a dependent variable nor merely a passive instrument in the hands of the ruling elite. The police institution interacted with other elements of the system in a complex and changing manner, particularly in its relationships with the Justice Ministry and the Kenpeitai. From the outside the government appears to be a single-minded monolith in its response to the leftist challenge, but from the inside it appears as a more complicated structure, affected by philosophical as well as bureaucratic rivalries. Throughout the evolution of the thought control system, however, the Tokkô remained a crucial element, and police leaders helped to shape as well as to administer that system. Consequently, the elucidation of the Tokkô's internal and external developments offers a new perspective on the problem of defining the prewar Japanese political system. It also provides terms and conditions useful in comparisons with other countries.

Totalitarian, fascist or authoritarian?

Was Japan totalitarian, fascist or authoritarian? There are problems with all these labels when they are applied to Japan. As indicated at the beginning of this Introduction, the term 'totalitarianism' has become outmoded because of its now obvious Cold War biases. In addition, detailed study of the Nazi and Stalinist states has revealed that the term gives a crude and misleading picture of even Germany or the Soviet Union. 'Totalitarianism' was at most an ideal of those regimes but certainly never a reality. Still less does it describe Japan of the 1930s and 1940s.

Since the revival of interest in the concept of fascism in the 1960s a whole literature has developed on the subject, but theoreticians have not even approached a consensus on a definition of the term.[42] There is not even unanimity over whether or not both Mussolini's Italy and Hitler's Germany should be considered fascist. Marxists may be less divided than non-Marxists, but even here there are internecine disagreements. Recent writers such as Nicos Poulantzas have criticised the Stalinist conceptions of fascism in the Comintern theses of the 1930s as being too economistic, but they still view fascism as the process in which monopoly capital establishes its dominance over society.[43] Examination of Japanese police leaders' image of their communist enemy indicates that Marxists have exaggerated the degree of capitalist control over repression policies, oversimplifying the situation by portraying a manipulative relationship based on purely class interests. The police did not always act in strict accordance with economic class interests. They developed an independent ideological rationale for their approach to social problems, a rationale rooted in part in a critique of the abuses of the capitalist system. Moreover, the existence of serious differences between police and Justice Ministry officials over peace preservation policies shows that the government was far from being united on these issues. Marxist works may be valuable in directing attention to the relation between fascism and class, but as they stand they provide inadequate explanations of prewar Japanese domestic policies.

Interpretation of prewar Japan as fascist according to non-Marxist definitions is also misleading. More than one attempt has been made to discard the term as a description of the prewar state, without denying the existence of fascist movements or ideas.[44] The reason is that, even setting aside the problem of a common definition, none of the many definitions available fits the Japanese situation without the omission of one or more crucial elements. Elements commonly found in definitions of fascism include a radical, often anti-modern ideology, a mass movement centred on a party, and a charismatic leader. Many individuals and groups in Japan during the 1920s and 1930s expressed anti-communist and in addition, anti-modern and anti-capitalist ideas. However, none sought mass support. In particular, the movement of young military officers, which is usually viewed as fascist, consisted of a small segment of the ruling elite. Moreover, none of these radical anti-modernist groups were able to put their ideas into practice. Aside from the young officers' movement, another example would be the New Order movement of 1940. Even with Prime Minister Konoe's support, the movement could not overcome opposition from Diet politicians, big business and the bureaucracy to its proposals for eliminating the Diet and drastically restructuring the capitalist system.[45] As for a charismatic leader, by the 1930s the potential of the Japanese political system for such a leader had been absorbed by the routinised charisma embodied in the imperial institution.

Maruyama Masao's formulation of a special kind of Japanese fascism has been very influential in both Japan and the West. He has rejected the necessity of fascism being established by a mass movement from below and argued that Japanese fascism was imposed from above.[46] However, qualifications such as this and a preoccupation with pointing out distinctive features of Japanese fascism render his definition problematical as a comparative concept. If the establishment of fascism meant no change in the social basis of political elites or in the institutional structure of the political system, what is to distinguish the 'fascist' government from what came before it? European fascist movements invariably described themselves as revolutionary, but Maruyama's definition precludes a revolutionary transformation in the political structure.

In the search for alternative labels and analytical concepts, scholars have often turned to 'authoritarian' or 'highly authoritarian'.[47] However, these seem unsatisfactory as well. The main problem is that they cover a very broad spectrum of regimes, too broad for making meaningful comparisons. Almost any repressive state may be described as authoritarian, regardless of the nature of its ideology, or the socio-economic basis of its support or the stage of its economic development.

The concept of a police state

Was Japan a 'police state'? The notion of a police state offers a useful supplement, if not an alternative, to the time-worn and much debated terms 'totalitarian', 'fascist' and 'authoritarian'. It has the obvious advantage over these of relating directly to the agents of repression and of corresponding in important ways to the ideals and self-image of the police. However, its primary utility and interest come from its being a general term that links specific Japanese phenomena with similar phenomena in European history. It is a comparative term that offers a chance of increasing our understanding of both phenomena. As is the case with other general terms, such as 'fascism', the concept of police state must be carefully defined. In the twentieth century, specifically since the German and Soviet regimes of the 1930s and 1940s, the term has taken on the emotional and derogatory meaning of a government that exercises power arbitrarily through the police, dominated by a political police, in disregard for the rights of citizens. It has also become a popular term of abuse applied to a wide range of regimes that differ in terms of their level of economic development, social structure and political ideology but have in common their suppression of opposition by means of a secret police.

However, 'police state' has not always carried these pejorative connotations. Prior to the 1930s it was the translation of *Polizeistaat*, a neutral technical term used to designate the type of 'regulative state' that emerged on the European continent during the eighteenth century.[48] 'Police' referred to civil administration—to government regulation of any kind, such as supervision of trade. 'Police state' therefore referred to order imposed from above by a sovereign.[49] Prussia under Frederick William I (1713–40) and Frederick II (1740–86) represented the first *Polizeistaat*. It was a state under an absolute monarch dedicated to the protection of the people, to the welfare of the state and its citizens and to the improvement of society through the rational division of labour within society and administration. Based on police power legally inherent in the state, it sought to regulate the activities of the individual for the welfare of the state. Advocacy of absolutism and the interventionist state derived from the seventeenth century cameralist and mercantilist belief that a strong independent government and a powerful ruler were preconditions of the spiritual and material welfare of the subjects. The subjects' welfare would increase productivity, which in turn would redound to the benefit of the state.[50] Mercantilist and cameralist doctrines therefore buttressed the emphasis on economic improvements and on the development of the political community for the augmentation of state power. The state did not neglect individual welfare but regarded it as a byproduct of the power and economic prosperity of the state, rather than as an end in and of itself.[51]

With Emperor Joseph II (1780–90) of Austria the *Polizeistaat* continued to be a paternalistic, rationally organised state devoted to mobilisation and development. However, it relied not only on extensive use of police regulatory powers, but also on the use of police forces as the state's supervisory censor. Recognising the importance of public opinion and seeing a need to control it, Joseph centralised the police and developed it into a complex and pervasive state apparatus that did not confine its surveillance to his officials or potential rivals, but extended it to all classes in society. The police forces included a secret police that operated according to Joseph's most secret instructions.[52]

In France the *Polizeistaat* reached its height as an interventionist state when Joseph Fouché became Minister of Police under the Directory and Napoleon I. Fouché showed his concern for political matters over day-to-day public order by making the 'high' police the heart of the police system. Before the revolution police duties had possessed a strongly paternalistic flavour. The police had also carried out much secret work, but this was designed to prevent private disorder and scandal among prominent families and the court. It was not essentially political intelligence work.[53] Fouché assigned the high police the 'double mission of uncovering and dissolving coalitions and legal opposition to the established authority as well as the murky plots of royalists and foreign agents'.[54] The high police's secrecy and information-gathering activities had the purpose of forestalling and preventing crimes, including 'any which the law has not yet foreseen'.[55]

During the nineteenth century the institutional and theoretical bases of the *Polizeistaat* were destroyed in France. Police powers gradually devolved from a single ministry controlling all internal administration to other ministries. The political police remained important but lost the primacy that Fouché had given it, and police authorities in general came under political and judicial control as the notion of sovereignty itself changed from sovereignty of the state to sovereignty of the nation and its delegated representatives. In comparison with the police of common law states, such as Britain, the French police remained more strongly centralised and endowed with greater powers over a wider range of responsibilities, but it operated under public scrutiny.[56] The fact that these changes occurred to a much lesser extent in Germany and Austria underlies the development of another kind of police state during the 1930s and 1940s.

The police states of Nazi Germany and Stalinist Russia, often described as 'totalitarian', became the source of the derogatory connotation now associated with the term 'police state'. However, stripped of the emotional and non-analytical elements, the term may yet be useful in our understanding of prewar Japan. The analogies made between the Tokkô and the Gestapo and GPU rest on their similar terroristic behaviour, centralised control, secret modes of operation and, perhaps most dreaded of all, preoccupation with political re-education or thought control.[57] Nevertheless, a rigorous comparative analysis of these three police institutions has not been made. Aside from examining the Tokkô itself, the concept of police state can set the Tokkô in the context of the political system as a whole by comparing its organisational status and independence, its relation to law and its purpose with those of the political police in Nazi Germany and Stalinist Russia. This in turn will help to delineate the composition, dynamics and ideological foundations of the prewar Japanese state.

1

THE SUPPRESSION OF THE LEFT

'The communist movement is now in a state of decay. This is the perfect moment for its eradication.'
Commissioner Nagano Wakamatsu, 1935[1]

The government's antagonism to leftist organisations began during the Meiji period. Rekindled after the First World War, that inherited antagonism developed into a policy of systematic suppression from the late 1920s onward. By the early 1930s the small Japanese Communist Party (JCP) had been virtually obliterated, but precisely at this moment the suppressive apparatus of the state expanded still further. Its field of operations widened to include not only leftist agitators but also radical right-wing groups and even religious organisations. From detecting specific political crimes police officials came to see themselves as responsible for surveillance of all thought that might disturb the national polity. From punishing offenders they came to see their role as re-educating individuals and reintegrating them into the national polity. For police officials police work had become central to the role of the state itself. The expansion of the police and of the Tokkô in particular suggests that significant groups within Japan's ruling circles shared their vision.

The suppression of the Meiji socialist movement

The Home Minister ordered Japan's first socialist party dissolved within hours of its formation in 1901. That dissolution order exemplifies the Japanese government's policy and methods regarding leftist movements from their meagre beginnings in the Meiji period until the end of the Second World War. When industrial workers began to form labour unions and conduct wage strikes during the 1890s, the Meiji government demonstrated its intolerance of disturbances to the social, political and economic order by responding with police repression backed by increasingly restrictive legislation. The 1900 Public Peace Police Law declared organisation by workers to be a disturbance of the public peace, thereby making unions and strikes illegal for all practical purposes and crippling the labour movement for over a decade. Socialist intellectuals motivated by Christian humanism, such as Katayama Sen, had previously been active in the labour movement, hoping to make it the vehicle of social and economic reform. The legal blow to the movement induced them to turn to political means in the form of a socialist party to achieve a solution of social problems.[2] When the government blocked that avenue as well by banning the Social Democratic Party, socialist activity reverted to that of study groups.

Repression had the effect of crystallising differences among socialists and radicalising some participants in the movement. One group led by Kôtoku Shûsui wanted to pursue political goals, while Katayama's group sought primarily social and economic reforms.[3] After a brief period of cooperation in early 1906 when the Saionji government permitted formation of the Japan Socialist Party, these differences hardened and evolved into a bitter schism between social democrats and anarchists. Several incidents of spontaneous worker violence contributed to the appeal of Kôtoku's call for direct action at the party convention in February 1907. Although not endorsed by the convention, Kôtoku won considerable support. Consequently, when authorities learned about the convention through the *Heimin shinbun*, they ordered the party dissolved.

Katsura Tarô became Prime Minister in January 1908. Supported by the conservative oligarch Yamagata Aritomo, he instituted an all-out effort to destroy the socialist movement. In response to Katsura's instructions to destroy all subversive literature and to arrest anyone who publicly advocated socialism, the police broke up a demonstration by some of Kôtoku's followers carrying flags inscribed with the words 'anarchism' and 'anarchism-communism'. Many were arrested in this Red Flag Incident, and fourteen received two-year prison sentences.

The climax of Katsura's suppression policy and the demise of the Meiji socialist movement came with the Great Treason Incident. The police arrested Kôtoku and a number of his followers in 1910 for plotting to assassinate the Meiji emperor, his family and ministers of state. Kôtoku and eleven others were convicted of treason and executed in January 1911. The incident shocked the public and aroused fear of socialism. It led not only to an intensification of police activities, but also to an expansion of the police organisation, notably the establishment of the first Tokkô section in the Keishichô (Tokyo Metropolitan Police Board) in August 1911. A Tokkô section was established in the Osaka police department the following year, and higher police sections proliferated in other prefectures.

The emergence of a new suppression policy

Only a few individuals attempted to resuscitate the socialist movement during the First World War, and their efforts remained fruitless until the postwar period ushered in the more open intellectual and political environment of 'Taishô democracy'. As the Allied victory stimulated the rise of Wilsonian democratic ideals, the Russian revolution spurred a renewed interest in socialism. Conditions of the industrial working class made it receptive to both democratic and socialist ideas. Wartime demands for Japanese goods had created an economic boom that swelled the industrial labour force and fostered the growth of labour unions. Labour organisations flexed their new muscles in an increasing number of labour disputes, accompanied by arrests, which leaped to a high of 1965 in 1919.[4] They also joined anti-establishment groups in a movement for universal manhood suffrage. The end of the war brought a collapse in demand and, subsequently, economic recession. On the one hand this pushed labour unions on the defensive, but on the other hand it turned some workers towards radicalism. The Hara government's rejection of a universal manhood suffrage bill also contributed to some loss of faith in parliamentary means. Anarcho-syndicalist influence among workers reached its peak.[5]

Conditions in the countryside had also created unrest. Dissatisfaction over shortages of consumer goods and spiralling rice prices erupted in the spontaneous 'rice riots' of 1918. As the disorders spread to cities, towns and villages throughout the entire country, the government proclaimed martial law and was later forced to resign. The rural violence of 1918 accompanied the growth of tenant farmer associations, which continued during the 1920s.

The labour movement and tenant farmer movement were part of a mushrooming of what government officials called 'social movements' or 'thought movements' because they all sought to rectify defects in the social system. Ironically, police authorities, like Marxists, viewed their emergence as the 'natural' result of various 'contradictions' that had developed along with modern capitalism and industrialisation. However, this did not necessarily mean that they were revolutionary; in fact the tenant farmer movement remained unreceptive and even hostile to communism and socialism.[6] All such 'social movements' continued to suffer from lack of mass participation, but their emergence helped to raise issues on behalf of the masses, such as universal manhood suffrage, labour legislation and tax reform. Some scholars also consider the exceptional mass character of the rice riots as the stimulus for the reorganisation of the peace preservation system during the 1920s.[7]

During the riots the police made many arrests and administrative detentions and imposed an absolute ban on newspaper articles about the disturbances. However, the Home Minister also instructed officials that the riots were not the product of a few agitators but the expression of discontent of people from all walks of life, with whom officials should sympathise and whom they should treat kindly.[8] Nevertheless, the riots exposed the limitations of the existing political police machinery, which centred on the surveillance of individuals. This system was inadequate for dealing with mass movements. Consequently, in 1921 and 1923 the Home Ministry expanded and reformed the police surveillance system, bringing organisations as well as individuals under its watchful eye.[9]

These Home Ministry measures were mild compared with those sought by Justice Ministry officials. The Justice Ministry favoured strong suppression of the rice riots and of any movements that might disturb the public peace.[10] The arrest of Kondô Eizô in 1921 and discovery of his attempts to organise a communist party precipitated the drafting of a new law to control radical social movements; this was introduced into the House of Peers in February 1922. Although jointly sponsored by Home and Justice Ministries, the bill enjoyed far more enthusiastic support from Justice than from Home officials.[11] The proposed law was directed primarily against propaganda activities of anarchists and communists. It failed passage after meeting harsh criticism for the ambiguity of its wording in both the committee and floor debates and after provoking considerable opposition among liberals, scholars and journalists outside the Diet.

While the Justice Ministry continued to advocate a new peace preservation law, several events stunned the public during 1923. In June the police exposed the existence of the JCP for the first time to the public by a series of arrests in Japan and Korea. Three months later a disaster of enormous proportions hit the Kanto area. An earthquake and the fires that followed it destroyed over half of Tokyo and took about 60000 lives. As a result of rumours that Korean nationalists and Japanese communists had started fires and plotted a revolution, mobs and gangs hunted and killed many Koreans. Martial law was declared, and the police rounded up known anarchists, communists and other leftists. Incidents of brutality and murder by police officers and soldiers occurred. Among these the murders of ten labour leaders at Kamedo police station, and of anarchist leader Ôsugi Sakae, his nephew and feminist Itô Noe by Kenpeitai officers, became the object of public outcry and official investigation. The investigation committee of the Kamedo Incident concluded that the military and police officers involved had taken measures proper under martial law conditions and therefore required only an apology for the slayings.[12] The courtmartial of Kenpeitai Captain Amakasu Masahiko and others for the Ôsugi and Itô murders resulted in a prison sentence of ten years with hard labour for Amakasu, a three-year sentence for Sergeant-Major Mori Keijirô and acquittal for the rest. Amakasu was released from prison after three years and later held high government and party positions in Manchuria.[13]

Pak Yol (pronounced Boku Retsu in Japanese), a radical associated with Ôsugi, and his Japanese wife were among those Koreans put under 'protective detention' by the police during the earthquake disorders. Following a delayed release, they were again detained and questioned about possession of a bomb and eventually prosecuted and convicted of high treason. Evidence of this crime was tenuous, and one postwar scholar considers the conviction a fabrication woven by the judge's leading questions.[14] Nevertheless, the trial left the impression that there had been an assassination plot against the emperor and the crown prince. Still more shocking, therefore, was an actual assassination attempt against the crown prince in December 1923 by Nanba Daisuke, whose father was a member of the House of Representatives. During his trial Nanba insisted that he had acted out of his communist convictions.[15]

This so-called 'Toranomon Incident', coming in the wake of the earlier disturbing events, reinforced sentiments favouring an expansion of police forces and powers as well as new peace preservation legislation. After the arrest of Communist Party members Tokkô sections were established in Hokkaido, Kanagawa, Nagano, Aichi, Kyoto, Hyogo, Yamaguchi and Fukuoka, making a total of ten throughout the country. In the Keishichô the number of Tokkô section members rose from 80 to 90 between 1923 and 1924, compared with an increase of five between 1922 and 1923. Of the ten additional members, six went to the Tokkô subsection and four to the Korean higher police affairs subsection.[16] The Keishichô as a whole expanded by about 2000 new officials, and reform of the police surveillance system continued.

Justice Ministry officials now redoubled their efforts to obtain passage of a new peace preservation law. In February 1925 they again introduced a bill to the Diet jointly with the Home Ministry. Like the 1922 anti-radical bill, the proposal for the Peace Preservation Law generated considerable discussion about its phrasing. However, it excited less opposition outside the Diet than had the 1922 bill, and many opponents within the assembly were converted into supporters.[17] As a result the bill passed both houses easily in March. However, Article 17 of the Public Peace Law, which had made strikes illegal, was repealed soon after.

There remain some questions of why the law passed almost unanimously just three years after an anti-radical bill had been rejected and of how it could have passed while the Protect-the-Constitution coalition controlled the cabinet. Some scholars, as well as opponents of the law at the time, link the Peace Preservation Law and universal manhood suffrage law to account for the conservative Privy Council's approval of expanding the electorate and for the relatively liberal Kenseikai's support for a new repressive law. Others offer their coincidental passage as an example of a 'carrot and stick' policy that, they say, characterised the Japanese government's handling of political opposition.[18] However, not only have former Home Ministry officials denied any cabinet–council agreement connecting the two laws, but also it is clear that bureaucrats had been working for some time on the two bills separately.

A key reason for the 1925 bill's success was the united support it received from both the Justice and Home Ministries, in contrast to the lukewarm support received by the 1922 bill from the Home Ministry. Home Ministry officials had changed their minds about the need for a new peace preservation law. The Kenseikai and individual Diet members also reversed their stances after 1922, and *Asahi shinbun* editorials criticised them for this while debate over the bill proceeded.[19] One reason for these shifts in position lies in the events between 1922 and 1925, which heightened the government's fears of communism. Another lies in compromises worked out between Home Ministry and Justice Ministry officials over the form and terminology of the 1925 bill, which resolved their differences of opinion on measures considered necessary and proper for dealing with social movements. Even after Home Ministry support for the bill was won, further compromises were required to accommodate objections in the Diet.

The form and terminology of the 1925 Peace Preservation Law

are important for understanding its relationship to previous laws and legal traditions, particularly as it affected police powers and functions, and for explaining the expansion of police repression during the 1930s. In certain respects the 1925 Peace Preservation Law grew out of tradition and past developments, but it also possessed new and perhaps unique qualities. The use of the term '*kokutai*' (national polity) was one of these new features. While in fact not unprecedented its usage as a statutory concept was not generally known. Partly because of that it posed problems of interpretation for the police officers charged with applying the law. Even more important was the existence of broad psychological and spiritual meanings associated with the term that could be confused with narrower legal definitions.[20] The lack of definitions, specific explications or exemplification of terms such as '*kokutai*', 'confer' and 'agitate' left the police with great discretionary power.

The development of the suppression

The 1925 Peace Preservation Law is often regarded as spearheading development of the prewar thought control system, particularly in providing the legal basis for expansion of the Tokkô. Its first application in late 1925 against 38 students belonging to the Kyoto branch of the radical national student organisation Gakuren presaged its use against not only organised and direct revolutionary activities, but also activities involving discussions, meetings and propaganda.[21] It marked a shift in government policy towards student activities, which had previously been under close police scrutiny but seldom interfered with even off campus.[22] In addition it shows the emergence of Justice Ministry officials, especially procurators, as leading actors in thought control, for they had insisted on the arrests when the Home Ministry had taken a wait-and-see attitude.[23]

The first large-scale organised application of the Peace Preservation Law against communists came with the well-known March 15 Incident of 1928. References to the mass arrest in popular songs suggest its widespread impact on the public mind.[24] For a long time Tokkô officials and procurators had been paying close attention to all activities that might be related to rebuilding a communist party. In early 1927 Inspector Môri Moto of the Keishichô's Tokkô section received an anonymous phone call concerning rumours of an important meeting held at the Goshiki Hot Springs in Yamagata prefecture in December 1926. Môri, together with Tokkô Section Chief

Kôketsu Yazô and Subsection Chief Urakawa Hideyoshi, set to work investigating the meeting. As a result of this investigation and other reports received by the Tokyo and Osaka police, police officials confirmed the formation of a second JCP and watched for an opportunity to carry out arrests.[25] This came shortly after the first general election held under the new universal manhood suffrage law in February 1928.

In implementing the new course established by the Comintern's 1927 Theses, the JCP had in fact stepped up activities, put up candidates under the names of proletarian parties and, for the first time, used its own name on propaganda materials distributed publicly. Despite widespread police interference in the election, for which Home Minister Suzuki Kisaburô was later censured, the proletarian parties garnered half a million votes. This provided added incentive for the mass arrests of 15 March. In contrast to past practice Tokyo District Court Procurator Shiono Suehiko and a few Justice Ministry bureaucrats took the lead in planning, organising and supervising the operation.[26] Beginning at 5 am Tokkô and other police officers in Hokkaido, Tokyo, Osaka, Kyoto and 27 prefectures swept over 100 places and made 1568 arrests. They seized numerous documents, including a list of 409 party members, four times the number previously estimated.[27] Arrests multiplied during the following months, and on 10 April the police banned the Labour-Farmer Party, the All-Japan Proletarian Youth League and the Council of Japanese Labour Unions.

The Tanaka cabinet favoured a policy of strong suppression. It introduced a harsher revised Peace Preservation Law, which would have made attempting to change the *kokutai* a capital offence but failed to get Diet approval. In June, however, it secured Privy Council approval for an emergency imperial degree having the same effect, and the Diet later assented to the revised law after heated debates.

Expansion of the police accompanied the Tanaka cabinet's harsher suppression policy. In July the Tokkô was extended to police departments nationwide, and the number of Keishichô Tokkô personnel jumped from 100 to 129.[28] In the Home Ministry Keihokyoku (Police Bureau) not only was the specialised staff for political matters increased, but also a new system of central administrative officials with judicial police authority was initiated to direct prefectural Tokkô officers.[29] The number of agents residing in Peking, Shanghai and Harbin rose, and new agents were sent to Berlin, London, New York and Chicago.[30] By the end of the 1920s there were over 63 000 police officials in the entire country.[31]

A general strengthening of internal police communications and contacts accompanied the organisational changes. Two monthly publications began: *Special Higher Police Materials*, to report on conditions of social movements and their control in all prefectures,[32] and *Publications Police Reports*. The 55th Diet censured Home Minister Suzuki for election interference but approved an expanded police budget of over 2 million yen. Almost half of that amount was slated for new or extended police telephone lines to speed communications among police departments throughout the country.[33] The Diet also granted the Justice Ministry 320 000 yen for thought investigation. 'Thought procurators' were appointed in all appeals courts and major district courts. The military also undertook efforts to formulate and intensify thought countermeasures in the army and established a thought subsection in the Kenpeitai.[34]

The expanded and reorganised police immediately went on the offensive. From documents confiscated during the March raids and questioning of arrested communist suspects, the Tokkô and procurators learned for the first time in detail about the party's organisation and membership. On the discovery that many party leaders had escaped the March sweep, a second mass roundup was planned and executed on 16 April 1929 (the so-called April 16 Incident). Periodic arrest waves continued during the 1930s, reaching a peak of 14 622 in 1933. The police arrested a total of 64 844 leftists for alleged violations of the Peace Preservation Law between 1928 and 1943.[35] Police censorship activities also increased after the March 15 Incident. Between December 1928 and May 1929 the police prohibited 56 books related to political or social subjects. This represented 20 per cent of all books published in those fields.[36] Large scale raids made it impossible for communists and their sympathisers to publish legally; their publications were driven underground. Meanwhile arrests had broken the JCP's international communications and links to foreign sources of financial support. Hard-pressed on all sides the party turned more to the use of violence. During 1930 24 Keishichô police officers were wounded and one was killed by communists.[37] In addition to stimulating an increase in the Tokkô's defence armament,[38] communist violence provoked more severe police action against communists, mainly in the form of torture.

Defenders and critics of the police, especially the Tokkô, disagree over the existence and extent of police brutality and its 'trampling of human rights'. Critics contend that the Tokkô carried out organised torture and terror, making it comparable to the Gestapo or GPU (State Political Administration).[39] Defenders, such as former Tokkô officials, protest that use of torture was the exceptional act of individuals, not the policy of Tokkô leaders.[40] The actual extent of police brutality lies somewhere between these two extremes, but certainly there are too many recorded cases of torture to be able to deny its frequent use by Tokkô officials.

The case of novelist Kobayashi Takiji's death in 1933 is the most famous example of Tokkô brutality, since it has been the subject of numerous novels, plays and movies. The police announced the cause of death as heart failure and denied use of torture.[41] Kobayashi's family was unable to find any hospital in Tokyo that would agree to do an autopsy, probably because of pressure from the police. Several reports by people who saw the corpse described the wounds on the body in such detail as to leave no doubt that Kobayashi was tortured. Besides wounds from beating and kicking, there were traces of hot tongs on his forehead, over a dozen holes in his thigh as if made by a nail or drill, broken fingers and numerous other gruesome injuries.[42]

Kobayashi's murder was by no means the first blamed on the police. Since the March 15 Incident leftists had been making charges of police torture and murder, including that of JCP leader Iwata Yoshimichi in 1932.[43] Labour-Farmer Party representative Yamamoto Senji had even described cases of torture in an interpellation during the House of Representatives Budget Committee meeting in February 1929.[44] Therefore there were more than isolated cases of police torture. As for other violations of human rights, such as prolonged detention, even former Tokkô officials admit that they were widespread.

Despite constant raids and the imprisonment of party leaders arrested in the 1928 and 1929 roundups, the communist movement reorganised and gained 400 members by the end of the summer of 1932.[45] However, this was a short-lived revival, ended decisively and permanently by the arrest of almost all party leaders in late 1932. This destruction of the party and its front organisations terminated the history of the JCP as a political organisation in the pre-1945 period. Thereafter the communist movement consisted of only small groups.

Communist reorganisation attempts were dealt a stunning blow by the defections of imprisoned party leaders Sano Manabu and Nabeyama Sadachika in 1933. Sano and Nabeyama's conversions, called '*tenkô*' in Japanese, started a stream of others.[46] Tokkô spy operations reinforced the conflict and distrust among the remnants of the party. A former Tokkô official traced the beginning of large-scale spy operations to the Tokkô decision to release workers as well as students who seemed repentant, using the method of 'prosecution withheld'. He claims that the initiative to become spies often came not from the Tokkô, but from the suspects themselves, those with a weak ideological commitment who wanted to give up their communist activities.[47] The importance of spy operations was reflected in the increase of more than 660 000 yen in the secret funds category of the 1932 Tokkô budget.[48] The effectiveness of Tokkô infiltration of the party was evident in what the press called the 'Red Lynching'. Central committee members Oizumi Kenzo and Obata Tatsuo were tortured in late 1933 by their Communist Party colleagues during investigation of suspicions that they were police spies. Obata died as a result of the torture. Oizumi escaped, turned himself in to the police and, during his subsequent trial, revealed that he had indeed worked for the Tokkô.[49] The communist-dominated National Party of Japanese Labour Unions split from the party over the incident, but soon after it too was destroyed by the police. Even the shell of a party organisation was annihilated when police captured the last central committee member, Hakamada Satomi, in March 1935.

While the Tokkô completed the suppression of the communist movement, right wing disturbances of the public order and threats to government officials forced the Tokkô to direct its operations against rightists as well as leftists. With the Manchurian Incident and economic depression as background factors, the upsurge of rightist coup attempts and direct action deepened the sense of national crisis that had been spreading since the late 1920s. It is this crisis atmosphere that lies behind the expansion of the police in general and the Tokkô in particular.[50] Drawing conclusions from the 15 May 1932 assassination of Prime Minister Inukai (the so-called May 15 Incident), the May 1932 issue of *Tokkô Monthly Report* announced the necessity of making secret investigations into some religious and educational organisations that previously had been competely outside the sphere of police observation. Now, however, they were considered revolutionary and their actions unlawful due to the influence of nationalist ideology.[51]

Also in 1932 a reorganisation of the Keishichô raised the Tokkô section to the status of a division and created a Tokkô subsection for right wing movements as well as one for left wing movements. An increase in Tokkô personnel brought the number of Tokkô department staff members to about 310, supplemented by about 400 subsection staff in police stations throughout the city.[52] Police authorities attempted to curb rightist violence by stricter enforcement of the laws controlling firearms and explosives. They made two wholesale roundups of swords, guns and explosives in 1932.[53]

Censorship measures also intensified. Keishichô statistics relating to newspapers, magazines and communications show that the number of bans on sale and distribution climbed from 488 in 1931 to 964 in 1932. In 1932 the Tokyo police ordered 39 articles removed, compared with ten the previous year, and gave warnings regarding 1591 articles, compared with 430 in 1931.[54] Home Ministry statistics similarly show the upsurge in prohibitions, which peaked in 1932. Such measures drove legal left wing publications completely out of business by 1935.[55]

The arrest of elementary school teachers in Nagano prefecture in 1933 marks the beginning of the period when the Peace Preservation Law was applied to persons without any relationship with the JCP or other communist organisations.[56] This incident occurred in an atmosphere of deep anxiety about the nation's future and amidst a flurry of activity seeking proper and effective countermeasures against radical thought. The Minseitô and Seiyûkai both presented proposals to the Diet and asked the government to act on them.[57] Consequently, after the Diet session ended the Prime Minister set up the interministerial Thought Countermeasures Committee. Based on recommendations submitted by the Home and Justice Ministries, the committee decided on proposals for thought control policies in September 1933.[58]

The government tried to enact the committee's thought control proposals in 1934 when it introduced bills to revise the Publication Law, to consolidate and strengthen the system of submitting copies of new books to censorship authorities, and to revise the Peace Preservation Law. Key elements in the proposed revision of the Peace Preservation Law were establishment of a system for maintaining surveillance of converts from Marxism (*tenkôsha*) and a system of preventive detention that police could use against persons who did not convert. Only the revised Publication Law received approval in 1934. The revised Peace Preservation Law failed passage primarily because of opposition to the preventive detention system.[59]

The proposals for the *tenkôsha* surveillance system and the preventive detention system reflected the shift in actual use of the Peace Preservation Law from a criminal law to an administrative law since the late 1920s. Between 1928 and 1941 only about 5000 out of more than 74 000 suspected Peace Preservation Law violators were prosecuted. Instead, police and Justice Ministry authorities came to apply the law as a means of making conversions from Marxism and other ideologies considered threatening to the *kokutai*.[60] Since few cases reached the trial stage, the police and procurators played a more important role than the courts in making the law effective. Simultaneously, *tenkô* rather than judicial punishment became the object of its application. These shifts are evident in the increasingly frequent use of stays of execution and probationary release without prosecution during the early 1930s and in the attempts to establish an observation system for *tenkôsha* in 1934 and 1935, which finally achieved success in 1936 with passage of the Law for Protection and Observation of Thought Criminals.

The shift in emphasis from criminal punishment to *tenkô* suggests that government authorities were not solely interested in eliminating political opposition by force. One American sociologist proposes that, because communism and socialism threatened to break the social bonds uniting the Japanese people, *tenkô* was necessary as a mechanism for maintaining social integration.[61] Other reasons relate to traditional legal practices and attitudes, police perceptions of communism and other social movements, and the views of certain influential Justice and Home Ministry officials regarding methods of controlling social movements.

The Thought Countermeasures Committee also made proposals for social policies and 'guidance of thought into proper channels'. This indicates the expansion of the aims and scope of the thought control system during the 1930s. The Tokkô no longer limited its operations to suppression of communist and other extreme leftist movements or even to violent right wing movements, but expanded its field of operations to include observations of conditions and trends of all social and thought movements. Students, intellectuals and religious organisations became objects of Tokkô control, and the Tokkô began to arbitrate tenant farmer as well as labour disputes. At the same time right wing nationalists clamoured for 'clarification' of the *kokutai* and attacked Tokyo Imperial University professor Minobe Tatsukichi for his theory that the emperor was an 'organ' of the state. A series of forced resignations of liberal university professors followed the 'organ theory affair'.[62] Changes in the *Tokkô Monthly Report* reflected these political developments and the broader range of Tokkô targets. During 1935, for example, the 'movement against the organ theory' and the arrest of members of the Ômotokyô religious sect received more attention in the *Tokkô Monthly Report* than did the communist movement.[63]

Once Japan became embroiled in war with China, police, like all military and civilian officials, threw their energies into mobilising the entire country and its resources for war. This included efforts to secure public support for the war and to develop an ideological foundation for it.[64] Individuals and organisations supporting the Popular Front movement against the war were arrested or banned. Under these conditions the Diet finally approved revision of the Peace Preservation Law in 1941. This revised law authorised actions that police and Justice Ministry authorities had been practising for years. In general it broadened the law's scope and added heavier punishments. Specifically, it established a preventive detention system for those who refused to convert, explicitly brought religious movements within its jurisdiction and provided special judicial procedures for thought crime cases.

A comparison of the 1941 revision with the original Peace Preservation Law indicates the changes and development in thought control policies and the Tokkô's role during the 1920s and 1930s. The original Peace Preservation Law was a criminal law providing judicial punishments as a means of suppressing communism and anarchism, but it became an administrative law used by the Tokkô and procurators to reform the thinking of individual scholars, students, intellectuals and members of various religions as well as communists and anarchists. The conception that police officials held of their role in the state apparatus and in society had changed dramatically. Corresponding to the changed view of the police role there occurred a change in activities and methods. From being a subordinate agency charged with discovering specific illegal acts and apprehending the perpetrators, police officials came to view themselves as an institution charged with the protection of the well-being of the whole of society.

Explanations of the suppression

Analysis of the Japanese 'police state' and the scale of repression requires appreciation of their relative dimensions. Despite the personnel increases, Japanese police forces did not become as large as might be expected in a period that has been described as the prelude to fascism. The ratio of police officials to population in Japan was similar to ratios in Europe and the United States at the same time. Tokyo in the late 1920s had about 12700 police officials for a population of about 4.5 million (28.2 police officials per 10000 population). New York, with a population of 5.6 million in 1920, maintained a force of 12000 police officials (21.4 per 10000); Berlin under the Weimar Republic had 14000–16000 police officials for 4 million inhabitants (35–40 per 10000); and Paris had about 12300 police officials for a population 4.6 million (26.7 per 10000).[65] In 1931 county districts in England averaged 10.2 police officials per 10000 population. In Japan in the rural prefectures of Aomori, Kagoshima and Nagano there were respectively 5.6, 5.2 and 5.5 police officials per 10000 people in 1920. In 1930 these ratios remained almost the same at 5.5, 5.2 and 5.9 per 10000 population, so increases in personnel only kept up with population growth despite the frequency of tenant disputes. On balance, the numbers of police officials in Japan during the 1920s do not appear disproportionate.[66]

Further, Tokkô terror did not approach the proportions reached in Nazi Germany or the Soviet Union under Stalin. Certainly, many persons became objects of police attention. In 1929 there were 269 000 detentions under the Administrative Enabling Law; in 1931 there were 473 000; and in 1933, also the peak year for arrests under the Peace Preservation Law, they reached 1.2 million.[67] The pervasiveness of Tokkô activities implied by these figures helped to give the Tokkô its dreaded image. However, the figures do not mean that millions of individuals were being detained, for the totals include repeated detentions. Police frequently pressured suspects by 'detaining' them over and over, in effect holding them in custody without formal charges. The practice was well-known and has been admitted by former Tokkô officials. Some were held in this way for as long as two years. Such prolongation of detention constituted an infringement of civil rights, and those detained no doubt underwent duress if not brutality. Nevertheless, the actual number of detainees was considerably less than the total number of detentions. They were held in ordinary police stations; there were no special camps set up for political prisoners or suspects. They were subject to ordinary police procedures; detainees were not to be interrogated, and eventually they had to be either charged or released.

As for those victims of the Peace Preservation law, some 65 000 were arrested between 1928 and 1943 but only about 6000 prosecuted. Of those arrested, some hundreds suffered from torture and some dozens died in police custody. These figures are horrifying but nevertheless remain orders of magnitude fewer than in states where violence against both individuals and groups became a systematic feature of state policy. Without condoning it, one must still conclude that there was a significant difference in scale. The mass terror generally defined as central to totalitarianism was not carried out in prewar Japan.

The shortcoming of both the defenders' and the critics' positions on the role of the police, use of torture and other abuses of power is the failure to make any attempt to explain those abuses that occurred. Defenders deny the existence of officially approved torture therefore feel no need for an explanation. Critics, almost all of whom are Marxists, simply assume that police brutality and disregard for people's rights are natural tools of a fascist state. They thereby ignore several areas that may be examined to shed light on the reasons for police brutality, its extent and its possible recurrence in the future. Background factors may be found in the tradition of police techniques and the traditional relationship between police officials and the people. As for immediate circumstances, important factors include not only the actual policy of the police leadership as manifested in specific instructions on use of torture and other abuses, but also police training and the system of rewards and punishment. Tokkô officers' attitudes towards the objects of their control and the types of crimes that they dealt with may be traced at least partially to their education and training. The Tokkô's particular image and standing within the police institution may also have influenced Tokkô officers' behaviour. Moreover, the fact that the actions of all police officials were largely beyond recourse for ordinary citizens also played a significant role.

According to Japanese Marxists, the government's repressive policies were the reaction of the ruling class to the new social phenomenon of an organised, class-conscious and revolutionary proletariat created by the contradictions of the capitalist system. They were the domestic policies consciously hammered out by the absolutist emperor system in the stage of monopoly capitalism to support its foreign policy of aggressive wars.[68] Marxists attribute the Tokkô's widening of the interpretation and application of the Peace Preservation Law and other laws during the 1930s to 'fascisation', to the nature of the absolutist emperor system and to the character of peace preservation laws in general;[69] however, this does not provide a satisfactory explanation of the phenomenon. 'Fascism', 'absolutist emperor system' and 'imperial fascism' are labels imposed on the Japanese government that pursued aggressive military expansionism abroad and suppression of all potential as well as manifest opposition at home. They may define the object of investigation, but they do not explain how and why it came about, and they do not leave any room for seeing differences of opinion within the government. They also lead to a tendency to equate Japan with European fascist states and thereby obscure important differences between them.

Another explanation for the expansion of the Tokkô and the scope of thought control during the 1930s emphasises competition between bureaucratic institutions or groups within them, specifically friction between the Justice and Home Ministries and, within the Home Ministry, between police and other Home Ministry officials. It rests on the assumption that it is the nature of bureaucratic institutions to perpetuate their self-existence and expand. Once the Communist Party was destroyed, the Tokkô and thought procurators extended repression to other movements and individuals in order to justify their continued existence and expansion.[70] The revelation of differences within the bureaucracy marks a break from monolithic views of prewar and wartime Japan and shows the new direction in which scholarship on the prewar period, especially in Japan, has been heading. However, intrabureaucratic rivalries should not be emphasised to the exclusion of other factors. Factors external to the institutions and the ways in which they impinged on the institutions also played an important role. In addition, an overemphasis on bureaucratic rivalry runs the risk of seeing policies as the outcome of purely personal infighting and power struggles. Other elements, such as philosophical differences, police training and ideology, particularly attitudes towards law and the image of the communist enemy, also were important in the determination of policy.

Many government officials in fact considered social movements necessary for social progress. However, they were worried about the 'striking' influence of anarchist and communist ideas and their permeation through the mass of the people. These worries became arguments for expansion of the police and were embodied in the Peace Preservation Law.[71] The law did not expressly state that communism and anarchism were the objects of repression, but there was no doubt that they were.[72] As anarchist influence waned, communism came to be singled out as the chief danger to both the fundamental organisation and principles of the Japanese national polity and the capitalist socio-economic system. The introduction of the death penalty for the crime of seeking change in the *kokutai* in the 1928 revision of the Peace Preservation Law leaves no doubt as to the seriousness and hostility with which the government viewed communism. This is also clear in the single-mindedness and persistence of the police suppression. The Tokkô continued to hunt down communists even after the movement had been definitively destroyed.[73] During the 26 February 1936 military rebellion, for example, the martial law declaration was explained as necessary not only to preserve peace and order, but also to prevent a Red uprising, and the police went about arresting socialists.[74] In December 1941 the Keishichô arrested 90 *tenkôsha*, looking for traces of a socialist movement.[75] Throughout the war the police tracked down and stamped out every trace of an attempt to re-establish a communist movement.

Government officials undoubtedly perceived a profound communist threat, and Marxists would like to believe that the social movements of the early 1920s represented an awakening of proletarian class-consciousness. There is some truth to these views, to the extent that social movements like the communist movement claimed to represent the people. Non-Marxists and Marxists alike have viewed the suppression policy as a response to resurgence of the left during the early 1920s. This clearly overstates the strength of the left; in retrospect it is clear that no leftist movement, socialist or communist, presented an objective threat to the government during the 1920s and 1930s. Scholars of leftist movements have pointed out, often with regret, that these movements never became a mass force.[76] JCP membership never reached 1000 and was usually less than half that.[77] Given the police and Justice Ministry authorities' notoriously wide interpretation of the Peace Preservation Law, 4059 prosecutions during the height of the suppression from 1928 to 1934 can hardly be evidence for existence of a 'vast revolutionary conspiracy'.[78]

If the left posed no danger to the established political order, why was such a threat perceived? This is the fundamental question to be answered in order to explain the origins and development of the suppression policy. Clearly there occurred a significant process of development and change in thought control policies during the interwar period. From the point of view of the victims of repression, changes in the repressive policies of the government would appear to be simply a matter of degree. However, qualitative changes in policy also occurred, particularly in the shift from detection and punishment to re-education and reintegration of offenders into society. Further, the government was not united behind a single policy. Not only was the direction of policy the outcome of complex negotiations among important interest groups, but also the implementation of policy became an object of contention among administrative agencies. The police considered themselves central to the entire process. Explaining the police's role now requires examination of the police tradition, the role of law, police institutions and ideology, and relationships with other institutions.

2

THE POLICE TRADITION

'Thus, in this society from birth to death, from beginning to end we do the same things in daily life and police life.'
Matsui Shigeru[1]
'Police officials serve as nursemaids for the people.'
Kawaji Toshiyoshi[2]

The case of the modern Japanese police system suggests that historical traditions provide models for attitudes and behaviour of police officials.[3] These may be extremely tenacious and difficult to overcome despite deliberate efforts by authorities to change the police system. Far-reaching police reforms were instituted after the Second World War, yet postwar police officials continued to trace their ancestry to and looked for guidance in the police system established during the Meiji period. This was evident in the plethora of histories of local and national police that accompanied celebration of the hundredth anniversary of the Meiji Restoration. Consciousness of historical traditions was still stronger among prewar police officials, since the organisation and functions of the police system had remained fundamentally unchanged since the late Meiji period. In 1937 police historian Yamamoto Kazuo expressed the importance of past developments in his argument that knowledge of Japanese police history would illuminate people's understanding of the Japanese nation's historical development.[4]

The Tokkô of the 1930s may be seen as the product of development of certain strands in the Japanese police tradition that go back to the Meiji period. It exemplifies the growth of an administrative police system with a wide sphere of operations and authority, including ordinance making and judicial powers. Such a system penetrated numerous aspects of daily life, including politics, and entered the realm of thought with the establishment of the Tokkô. The Tokkô's creation and expansion were part of the multiplication and specialisation of functions that characterised the development of the police as a whole. At the same time police leaders attempted to unify this more and more complex organisation in order to increase its efficiency and direct its energy towards national goals. The Tokkô structurally was the most centralised branch of a centralised national police system. This national orientation and the Tokkô's thought control responsibilities went hand in hand with the 'nursemaid' ideal envisioned for the police in Japanese society by its founder, Kawaji Toshiyoshi. Kawaji's descriptions of the police as the remedy for national peace and nurturer of the people implied tasks of moral guidance and education as well as peace preservation for the police. Such a view seriously affected relations between the police and the state on the one hand and between the police and the public on the other.

The police tradition from the Meiji period

The fundamental structure and major types of functions to be performed by the modern Japanese police were established by the first decade of the twentieth century.[5] Immediately after the Meiji Restoration soldiers from each *han* (feudal domain) carried out police functions, which at this time consisted primarily of maintaining peace and order. After establishment of the Tokyo metropolitan prefecture, the Heibushô (Military Ministry) selected superior soldiers from various *han* to perform police duties under the city government. Other prefectures followed the same pattern.[6] However, the system had a poor record of maintaining law and order in Tokyo. Lawlessness, including broad daylight robberies, plagued the new capital.[7] Consequently, in 1871 a new system based on Western European models was set up in Tokyo. It consisted of 2000 patrolmen enlisted from Kagoshima by Kawaji Toshiyoshi and 1000 from other prefectures, a ratio of one patrolman to every 3000 city inhabitants.[8] The city was divided into six large wards, each divided further into sixteen smaller wards. In the following year 1000 more patrolmen were added to the force.[9]

The police tradition 37

In the meantime, concern for putting down political resistance and securing domestic peace had quickly brought the new central government to the decision to establish a unified national police system adopted from Western models. In contrast to American and British police forces the modern Japanese police system was designed to buttress the central authority against political rivals rather than to control the lower classes.[10] Its objectives from the beginning were political rather than social, making political functions as important as the preservation of public order.

The government began to carry out its intent to establish a national system while it began studies to find the model most appropriate for Japan at the time. In 1869 Fukuzawa Yukichi received instructions from the government to examine European police systems and clarify the meaning of 'police'. The result was a translation of a book entitled *Control Legislation*.[11] In 1872 Kawaji left on a one-year trip to investigate various European police systems. The omission of Britain from the itinerary indicates that Japanese leaders had by this time already decided that a continental type of police system would become the model for Japan's new police system.[12] Meanwhile, with the abolition of the *han* in 1871, all urban and rural prefectures had begun to receive orders from the central government regarding decisions and changes in regulations concerning local patrolmen. Then in August 1872, the Tokyo patrolmen were transferred to the Justice Ministry and new police officials were established in the ministry. This marked the end of military control over the police and the beginning of a clear separation between the military and police, which lasted until the 1930s.[13]

The Iwakura mission returned from Europe in 1873 and immediately clashed with other government leaders over a plan to send a military expedition to Korea. This major government crisis resulted in Saigô Takamori's resignation and return to Kagoshima. Since Saigô had been commander of the imperial guards, his withdrawal from the government seriously affected the morale of the guards' officers. Many also came originally from Satsuma and returned there with Saigô. This alarmed the government and aroused fears that unrest would spread to other military groups and the police, which included many ex-samurai from Satsuma. These anxieties may have prompted the immediate creation of an interior ministry that had wide powers of internal administration, including the centralised police system proposed by Kawaji, and ranked next to the Foreign Ministry in the hierarchy of ministries.[14]

Kawaji owed his prominence in the new Meiji government to Saigô but had become Ôkubo Toshimichi's protégé by the end of the 1873 crisis.[15] After his return from Europe he had proposed an interior ministry with jurisdiction over the police of the entire country, stressing that it would be an agency for preventing disintegration of central authority.[16] He argued that, like a nurse for people, the police was a remedy for national peace. Police officers should protect good citizens and foster national spirit. They were necessary for the prosperity and expansion of imperial power.[17] Kawaji also proposed the establishment of a metropolitan police force for the capital directly linked with the interior ministry and the placement of firefighting responsibilities under police jurisdiction.

These recommendations showed a preference for the French rather than the British or American model of police, reflecting a desire for central control as well as particular concepts of police work and police law. As in the French system, the police would belong to an internal administrative system that was centralised and nationwide rather than local and autonomous, as in Britain and the United States. Defenders of the prewar Japanese police have emphasised its centralised national structure as one of its distinctive qualities. Home Ministry officials of the 1930s pointed out with pride that Japan's police differed from that of other countries in having an extremely unified organisation, which went beyond even its French and German models in centralisation. They considered it a strong point that central command could penetrate the entire country, because the Home Minister possessed authority over all police personnel matters. Furthermore, they valued the efficiency with which all measures and plans concerning matters such as budget, education, pay, and rewards and punishments could be unified.[18]

In line with continental European usage tracing back to the *Polizeistaat*, the Meiji founders employed the term 'police' in the broad seventeenth and eighteenth-century sense of all internal administration rather than the narrow sense of crime prevention and detection, as adopted by the British and Americans.[19] Consequently, the range of police activities was wide, as indicated by names of the major branches of the police: sanitation and health, traffic, firefighting, public morals, peace preservation. Moreover, police powers were great. In Britain police powers were primarily prohibitive and repressive until the passage of progressive social and health legislation during the nineteenth century broadened the concept of police to include preventive measures. However, these new preventive powers were usually given to special national and municipal departments, not to the regular police. Japanese authorities rejected this narrow concept of police power and adopted continental views. On the continent police traditionally possessed preventive as well as prohibitive powers, and the increased state functions of the nineteenth century went to the regular police. In addition, like the

German police, the Japanese police could issue ordinances (supplemental legislation to regulate conduct within its jurisdiction) and perform judicial functions in certain cases, punishing particular types of legal violations, such as minor offences.[20]

The Japanese also chose continental models in drawing up police legislation. Unlike in Britain, where police laws were confined to prohibiting certain actions viewed as detrimental to public welfare, Japanese laws followed the continental conception of laws as rules of conduct not only prohibiting harmful actions, but also prescribing behaviour that would render repression unnecessary. This led to extensive supervisory legislation over elements regarded as dangers to the public.[21] Japan's adoption of German constitutionalism introduced the principle of rule by law (*Rechtsstaatsprinzip*), which requires a legal basis for exercise of police authority. However, law included not only statutes passed by a representative assembly, but also administrative ordinances and imperial decrees.[22] Adoption of French criminal procedures introduced the principle of trial on evidence, accompanied by abolition of use of torture in criminal investigation. In contrast with the British and American systems, however, the French trial system is accusatorial, assuming guilt instead of innocence until proved otherwise.[23] This was in keeping with the past Japanese practice of sending a case to court only after obtaining persuasive evidence of guilt.

The evolution of this kind of police system began with acceptance of Kawaji's recommendations. In January 1874 the police officials of the Justice Ministry were shifted to the newly established Home Ministry, and a semi-independent metropolitan police force (Keishichô) was set up under the Tokyo prefectural government, headed by Kawaji. Thereafter various name changes and reorganisations occurred, but the organisation lasted with only one interruption until 1945. The Home Minister became the official with highest responsibility for police matters in the country. Below him the key person in nationwide police administration, but without an operative police force, was the Director of the Police Bureau (named the Keihokyokuchô from 1881 on). He could issue directives in the name of the Home Minister, formulate general policies and carry out administrative and operational control over all prefectural departments except the Keishichô. His chief means of control, however, was his authority to appoint and transfer police officials in the rank of superintendent or above. His staff consisted of civilian administrators who had passed the higher civil service examination, not police officials who had worked their way up from the position of patrolman. They could be transferred as police officials to prefectural departments or to non-police posts in the ministry.[24]

At the prefectural level, except for Tokyo, the centrally

appointed governor held the highest police authority, but his immediate subordinate, the chief of the prefectural police division, was regarded as the person actually responsible for police matters.[25] Chiefs of police stations in cities and towns came under the prefectural police division. The Director of the Keihokyoku appointed and dismissed officials of superintendent rank and above, but routine management and most law enforcement duties were left to the prefectural police.[26]

The Keishichô's organisation, patterned after the Paris police system, differed. The Superintendent-General occupied a similar status to the prefect of police in the department of Seine.[27] He received instructions and supervision from the Home Minister, not the Director of the Keihokyoku. Below him at Keishichô headquarters was a hierarchy of bureaus, divisions, sections and subsections, and police stations and substations were distributed around the city.

Soon after the founding of this system, internal disorder and financial pressures led to abolition of the Keishichô in January 1877 and to transfer of police duties in the capital to the Tokyo Keishihonsho in the Home Ministry's Keishikyoku. On several occasions prior to this Tokyo police officers had been sent to Saga, Kumamoto, Yamaguchi and Ibaraki prefectures to put down farmers' and samurai disturbances. There was a fear that reliance on the Keishichô would give it excessive power, but the government also felt the need for strong national police power to keep the peace.[28] Some leaders hoped to cut expenses by abolishing the independent police force.[29] However, at Kawaji's insistence the reorganisation was apparently regarded as a temporary expedient from the beginning.[30]

No more than a month after abolition of the Keishichô the Satsuma rebellion began. Led by Saigô Takamori, an army of former samurai from Satsuma attempted to overthrow the central government. Opposing it was the government's still small and untried conscript army. Yamagata Aritomo opposed all plans to recruit samurai forces, which might undermine the new conscription system. Consequently, when the government needed more troops, Yamagata suggested enlisting more samurai into prefectural police forces, which could then be organised into fighting units against the Satsuma rebels. Yamagata's plan won acceptance, and Kawaji became a major-general in the army at the head of a 3600–man police brigade.[31] A total of 9500 police from the Tokyo Keishihonsho eventually went to prefectures in Kyushu and Kansai to suppress the rebellion and maintain public order. During the war 774 died.[32] The conclusion of a song sung among the Satsuma soldiers attests to the significance of their contribution:

'Were it not for the Imperial Guard
artillery and the Police Brigade
we could advance to beautiful Edo.'[33]

However, some people became worried by the increased force and authority of the centralised Keishikyoku system and criticised the police for its arbitrary use of power. Kawaji again advocated re-establishing the Keishichô. Consequently, he was again sent to Europe in 1879 to study police systems for the purpose of reforming the Japanese system to correspond to the new conditions. Kawaji became sick and died before seeing the Keishichô re-established, but other police officials who had accompanied him in his tour continued to promote his recommendation. They argued for the necessity of re-establishing an independent Keishichô as the solution to abuses of centralised police power, which had led to unreliability in police officials and their work as well as to police arrogance, repression and arbitrariness.[34] Official Home Ministry histories explain that the centralised Keishikyoku system had been intended only as a temporary expedient to deal with the internal disorder.[35] Once peace returned, 'restoration of the police organisation to its usual form was natural'.[36] Therefore, while lauding centralisation police authorities during all periods considered a semi-autonomous Tokyo police force the ideal. In addition, a measure of prefectural autonomy accompanied re-establishment of the Keishichô. Prefectural governments obtained power to make decisions on police expenditures and on appointment and dismissal of officials below the rank of hannin (lowest of the three ranks of higher civil servants).[37]

Yamagata Aritomo's term as Home Minister, beginning in December 1883, marked the transition from the French to the German model of police. Since Prussia's victory over France in 1871 Meiji leaders had been fascinated with Prussian forms of government. More governmental changes were necessary to obtain revision of the unequal treaties with Western countries, and many thought that absolutist Germany was a more appropriate model for Japan than liberal republican France with its revolutionary background.[38] Adaptions from Germany, where the institutional and theoretical bases of the *Polizeistaat* had not been eroded as in France, therefore represented a deliberate rejection of decentralisation and democratisation. Aside from such background considerations, the people's rights movement at home provoked conservatives like Yamagata to seek ways to bolster the imperial system. When preparations for establishing a parliamentary system began in 1885 with a reorganisation of the central government, Yamagata took this opportunity to reform the Home Ministry, notably the police and local government systems. In addition to modernising and standardising the police system, he sought to associate the police spiritually with the emperor and to bring the police more firmly under the Home Minister's authority.[39] For Director of the Keihokyoku, Yamagata chose Kiyoura Keigo, who served an unequalled term of seven years and later went on to the prime ministership and the presidency of the House of Peers.[40]

In 1885 a police training institute was founded for police officials with a rank of inspector or above, and the government invited Prussian police officials Wilhelm Höhn and Emil Figaseusky to Japan. Höhn lectured at the new school on German police laws and the role of the police in firefighting. He also inspected the Japanese system, visiting prefectures all over Japan and offering suggestions for reforms. Police educators of the 1930s lauded Höhn's contributions to the police world, equating them with Emile Boissonade's contributions to the judicial world. They regretted that police officials had forgotten about his fame and success and therefore made a point of bringing his achievements to attention.[41]

Höhn's suggestions on the distribution of police officers led to the spread of influence of the police in local areas. Höhn concluded that the existing system lacked a sufficient number of police stations. Police officers were organised in units of 80–100 men stationed at strategic points from where they were sent out on patrols. Höhn pointed out that the areas of jurisdiction were too large to keep under constant observation and that it was inefficient to send men back and forth on patrols taking four or more days to complete. His recommendation to scatter police officers by setting up many substations and police boxes was immediately adopted.[42]

Also adopted in part were his proposals to raise the height minimum for police officers, raise the age minimum and lower the age maximum. According to Höhn, police officers should be taller than average and of sufficient age (past military service) to gain respect and trust from the public, but young enough to be fit for the pressure of police duties.[43] Höhn believed that Japanese police officers should be paid more and treated better to prevent them from giving in to the temptations of corruption. Berlin police officers, for example, earned higher salaries than other officials. Japan's existing monthly salaries of 6 to 10 yen could support an individual police officer but not his family, so he recommended an average increase of 2 yen. He also made suggestions for pensions, extra pay for night patrol and money for meals when patrolling villages.[44]

Höhn criticised Japanese officials for being too lenient in supervising their subordinates, blaming them for the large number of supernumeraries he observed in police stations and especially in prefectural headquarters. He declared that staffs could be reduced by half without losing productivity, for he saw many cases of time wasted in smoking, teabreaks and talking among office workers. As a means of increasing efficiency and learning about office conditions and the skill or performance of subordinates, Höhn suggested calling together group heads occasionally without giving advance notice and asking about conditions and the handling of duties under their charge.[45] A final example of Höhn's proposals is his advice to unify and standardise police uniforms. He admonished authorities to make certain that the uniforms fitted properly, an indication of the continuing unfamiliarity of Western clothing to Japanese at this time.[46]

One serious challenge to the organisational relationships among police agencies established by Kawaji and reformed by Yamagata came at the end of the Meiji period. Criticism of the Keishichô beginning in the late 1890s arose as part of the opposition parties' general attack on Satsuma and Chôshû's domination of the government. Among the 21 Keishichô Superintendents-General up to 1914, 17 originated from Satsuma, and the Keishichô's upper level officials also were almost entirely Satsuma-born.[47] There had been numerous instances of police interference in elections. Opponents called the Keishichô a tool of the '*han* clique' government that was used to suppress opposition parties, not to protect city inhabitants.[48]

The first attempt to abolish the Keishichô followed the Russo-Japanese war in 1905 under the guise of a budget proposal. Advocates of abolition argued that, if ordinary police duties were moved to the urban prefectural governments of Tokyo, Osaka and Kyoto and higher police duties (that is, political duties) were shifted to the Keihokyoku, money could be saved. This motion was easily beaten after speeches by Home Minister Hara Kei and Arai Shôgo.[49] Explicit objections to the Keishichô's large political role and its manipulation as a government tool arose after the Hibiya Park Incident, when the police was criticised for its actions against rioters opposing ratification of the Portsmouth Treaty.[50] A second proposal in 1906 argued that abolition of the Keishichô was necessary to end abuses of power and the political importance of the Superintendent-General of the Keishichô. Keishichô political power was so strong, asserted the opposition, that it could ignore the views of the procurator's bureau and Tokyo government. There was no reason for having an independent government agency, and duties should be unified. Moreover, institutions must change with the times. This proposal was defeated on a straight party vote.[51]

Although the bill failed, the government felt sufficiently pressured by the opposition to make some changes in the Keishichô. For example, it partially revised the division of duties between the Keishichô and city government. The importance of the higher police was also reduced, at least outwardly. In the past the Superintendent-General of the Keishichô had received instructions regarding higher police matters from the Prime Minister and Home Minister. The reform eliminated the Prime Minister from direct control and the name of the higher police from the Keishichô organisation. It also recognised the limits of authority of the Superintendent-General as being the same as those of an ordinary prefectural governor. However, these were only paper changes, for the higher police did not disappear. A higher police section was put in the Superintendent-General's Secretariat with a subsection to deal with laws controlling public meetings and organisations.[52] Perhaps it is not inaccurate to see the Hara reforms as a means of compromise between the government and the opposition parties that was based on a similarity of assumptions, for no further demands for abolition of the Keishichô arose.

The political police within the police tradition

While the basic organisational relationships among police agencies had been fixed by the 1880s, changes in departmental and sectional divisions later occurred, and numerous police-related laws were enacted after that time. These reflected broad and rapid changes in Japanese politics and society and are evidence of the elaboration and specialisation of functions that characterised development of the Japanese police, as well as the bureaucracy as a whole, during the late Meiji and Taishô periods. The organisational development of police with political functions, crowned by the creation and expansion of the Tokkô, illustrates this process.

The first Tokkô section was established in the Keishichô in 1911, but the Japanese police had been performing political functions since the Tokugawa period. Both defenders and critics of the Tokkô define the Tokugawa system as a 'police state' by which they mean that police power was wielded without limitation for the purpose of maintaining Tokugawa political power rather than protecting or promoting the people's interest.[53] The ethos of the police as the pillar of political authority carried over to the Meiji period, as indicated by criticisms directed against the police and the Keishichô in particular. However, the police openly received responsibility for political tasks. In May 1869 the Danjôdai was established with exclusive responsibility for surveillance of political conspirators. In 1871 it was abolished, but its duties and authority moved to the newly established Justice Ministry.[54] They were reassigned again when the Home Ministry came into being but not exclusively to one section of the police.

An 1886 imperial decree used the term 'higher police' for the first time in a public document. It described higher police duties as those related to organisations, meetings, newspapers, magazines, documents and other publications concerned with politics.[55] The designation came from the French system and reflected the belief of Minister of Police Fouché, founder of Napoleon's political police, in the central role of political police activities.[56] A higher police section was organised in Osaka in 1888, but the majority emerged between 1911 and 1920. During the late Meiji period all three sections of each police department, which included a General Police Affairs Section, a Peace Preservation Section and a Sanitation and Health Section, performed higher police tasks. Because these duties required a lot of time prefectural police chiefs often requested governors to create a separate higher-police section, but this brought about only staff increases until the first decade of the twentieth century ushered in a growing number of labour disputes and strikes, anarcho-syndicalist direct action and the Great Treason Incident.[57]

The Great Treason Incident became the main motive for setting up the first Tokkô section in the Keishichô and for expanding and strengthening other political police agencies, such as the higher police. Official police histories usually explain the establishment of a separate section as the natural or even inevitable response to the increased activity of socialist and other social movements during the previous decade.[58] Similarly, they justify the Tokkô's later expansion as a necessary measure to deal with the emergence of diverse social movements during the 1920s and 1930s, including a nationalist movement as well as a communist movement.[59] Tokkô sections extended to Hokkaido, Nagasaki and Nagano between 1922 and 1926, and the remaining prefectures received sections in July 1928. In 1928 the Keihokyoku's specialised staff also expanded, and a new supervisory system of general affairs officials and assistant general-affairs officials with judicial police power was founded. In 1932 the Keishichô's Tokkô section was raised to the status of a division with six sections, and four years later one of these sections split in two.[60]

The Tokkô's name, translated the Special Higher Police, indicates its organisational and functional origins in the higher police. The Tokkô was one branch of the political police, which specialised in controlling social movements. It became the most important and prestigious branch of the political police, though not the exclusive holder of political police responsibilities. The higher police, for example, dealt with election control, and the Book Section also performed censorship duties. The Tokkô's organisational history therefore parallels the general process of expansion and specialisation of functions that characterised the Taishô police institution and shows the growth of centralised national elements within the police.

A few postwar defenders of the Tokkô emphasise that the Tokkô was not totally centralised, but most Japanese police historians of varying political inclinations point out that the Tokkô was the most centralised branch of a centralised police system.[61] For example, Keishichô headquarters appointed and dismissed Tokkô personnel down to the subsection heads in police stations. In contrast to his authority related to other personnel, the police station chief appointed only staff below the head of the Tokkô subsection. Similarly, in other prefectures the prefectural governor appointed all section chiefs except the Tokkô section chief, whose appointment was controlled by the Keihokyoku.[62] In addition, the command structure differed from that of other kinds of police. Instructions and operational funds began at the top with the Prime Minister and passed through the Home Minister, Director of the Keihokyoku, Peace Preservation Chief, Keishichô or other prefectural police department Tokkô division or section chief, to the Tokkô subsection head. Notably, the governor, prefectural police department chief and police station chief were bypassed along this 'Tokkô route'.[63]

This separate and highly centralised structure within the police institution both reflected and reinforced the national orientation of Tokkô purposes. The semi-official *History of the Home Ministry* explains that the Tokkô's strong central control resulted from its role as the most important police branch responsible for controlling movements seeking to destroy the basis of national existence and to disturb the peace and order of society.[64] This shows that the Tokkô was primarily concerned with protecting the interests of the nation and society as a whole, rather than local or individual interests. It was charged with preventive as well as suppressive responsibilities and, unlike most police, acted as both an administrative and judicial police.[65] Because the government placed such weight on these functions the Tokkô became a kind of elite within the police and exercised greater powers than other branches of the police.

The origins of the police ideology

The historical roots of the Tokkô's national character and involvement with thought control go back to the police ideal advocated by Kawaji Toshiyoshi. Police officials during the interwar period often quoted Kawaji, particularly his 1873 petition and 'Hand and Eye of the Police'. One writer described the latter as the sacred book of the police, like the Bible or Koran. Even in the postwar period it has been recommended as indispensable reading for police officials for its 'crystallisation of police spirit'.[66] The 1873 proposal begins with the metaphor of the police as the remedy for national peace, as in the nurturing of people. It states that police officials protect good citizens and foster national spirit. Therefore, those who want imperial power to expand and flourish are urged to pay attention to his recommendations.[67] In 'Hand and Eye of the Police' Kawaji emphasised the nurturing role of the police, portraying it in the role of 'nursemaid' to the people. He likened a country to a family with the government as parents, the people as children and the police as nursemaid. He stressed that the Japanese people were still unenlightened and therefore particularly childish. He reiterated the family metaphor in another petition, declaring that it is the government's duty to teach the people, just as it is parents' duty to teach their children even if the children dislike it. Kawaji always emphasised that the upbringing of the people must rely on the care of the nursemaid-police. He admonished police officers to 'render kindness with reason and above all, be patient', even when people act unreasonably and unjustly.[68] One of his mottoes for police officers was 'no sleep, no rest'.[69]

Promoters of the 'people's police' ideal during the 1920s and 1930s held up Kawaji's nursemaid metaphor in support of their aim. They eulogised Kawaji's efforts to cultivate a spirit of frugality and courage, to enforce official discipline and to raise the sense of morality among police officers. They interpreted these endeavours as attempts to give respect to the people's rights and to teach police officers to keep vigilant against violations of the people's rights. They believed that Kawaji's exhortations to police officers to lead the people in a kindly way were aimed at making police officers real protectors of the people.[70]

There is no doubt that Kawaji encouraged these admirable virtues among police officers and intended police work to benefit the people. However, the ideals that he established for the modern Japanese police also fostered qualities that hampered achievement of a people's police. According to his nursemaid ideal, police officials stand in a hierarchical relationship between the emperor-parent and people-children. Their attitude towards the people is paternalistic. This involves concern for their education and welfare but at the same time implies feelings of superiority and authority, with the expectation of obedience and submission. A further implication is that compliance may be obtained by force, just as a nanny may discipline her charges for 'their own good'. Kawaji's emphasis on the police's importance for the nation's peace and prosperity also elevated the state above the people as the object of service. In both the 1873 petition and 'Hand and Eye of the Police' he spoke of the police as medicine for the internal state of the country. In his view the health of a state and health of a person followed the same principle: both would be found in the therapy of peace. The reason for imperial pride in the police was its care for the health of the Japanese empire.[71]

Several concrete examples from the Meiji period bear out these implications and have particular resonance for police-state and police-public relations during the 1930s. The high priority placed on police service and loyalty to the state is evident in the extensive political-control activities of the Meiji police. The government promulgated numerous laws aimed first against the people's rights movement, but these were later used against labour and leftist movements.[72]

The government adopted the German model of socialist repression along with other political forms and patterns. When the Far East Socialist Party was organised in 1882, the government deemed it harmful to public peace and prohibited its organisation and meetings, an action approved by contemporary newspapers and magazines.[73] It still knew little about socialism when the Social Democratic Party was formed in 1901, but Prime Minister Itô Hirobumi recommended banning the party, according to Bismarck's example, to a conference of the Superintendent-General of the Keishichô, the Director of the Keihokyoku and other officials.[74] His studies under the German scholars Rudolf von Gneist and Lorenz von Stein had included lectures on socialist parties, which they expected would inevitably appear in Japan, and on the need for their repression. News of socialist attempts to assassinate the German emperor reinforced feelings of animosity towards socialism among Japanese.[75] The police banned the new party within hours of its inauguration.

The infant labour movement met similar hostility. In 1897, for example, people hoping to raise worker consciousness and organise a society to promote establishment of labour unions decided to lead a march from Yurakucho in Tokyo to hold a meeting in Ueno Park.

The Keishichô prohibited this and all subsequent revised plans. The meeting eventually materialised some days later, but only because the leaders were able to use a festival celebrating the thirtieth anniversary of the capital's transfer to Tokyo as the reason for the meeting.[76] The government treated organised labour activity as a disturbance of the public peace and appeared to side with company owners in labour disputes. For example, it is said that the Fukushima police were responsible for propaganda against the Correction Society, a group including many Christians and temperance advocates who were seeking to improve treatment of Japan Railways engineers. The police also cooperated with the railway company to put the blame on the Society in a dispute over responsibility for train breakdowns. Later it ordered the Society to dissolve.[77]

Because of this determination to prevent and eliminate all forms of political opposition and disorders, political importance was attached to police positions from the beginning of the Meiji period, and the political police soon acquired a special status. The post of Home Minister became extremely important because it controlled police power. The same held true for the positions of Director of the Keihokyoku and Superintendent-General of the Keishichô. In 1898, for example, Yamagata Aritomo gave these appointments to Kenseitô members as a means of obtaining cooperation from the party in the Diet.[78] With only one or two exceptions these officials changed with each change in government. They remained 'free appointments' until 1914 and again during the era of party cabinets.

Until the 1906 Hara reforms the Superintendent-General of the Keishichô reported directly to the Prime Minister on national affairs and national police matters, and prefectural police chiefs bypassed the governors to report directly to the Home Minister. In 1906 the Superintendent-General of the Keishichô outwardly lost his special authority; but as politics moved into the age of party cabinets, government parties viewed the higher police as all the more important for controlling elections. Consequently, large-scale personnel changes in police positions down to police station chief throughout the whole country accompanied each cabinet change.[79]

The obverse of police loyalty and deference to the state was arrogance and condescension to the public. There existed a long tradition of antagonistic police-public relations, illustrated in the controversy over designating all names of local police officers *bannin* in 1873. The name aroused great opposition from all prefectural police departments because in Edo during the Tokugawa period there had been a mean occupation called *banken* or *bankenro* (watchdog retainers), autonomous police who were hated by the people. In 1875 '*bannin*' was changed to '*rasotsu*'.[80]

Meiji police leaders wanted harmonious police-public relations. This was the reason for initially arming patrolmen only with sticks.[81] Following Western examples police officers later came to wear swords. Because the privilege of wearing a sword was the traditional Japanese symbol of superior class status and power of life and death over subordinates, this part of the police officer's uniform enhanced his sense of authority over the people.

Police use of torture had been common in Tokugawa criminal investigation, particularly because of the necessity for a confession to obtain conviction. On the recommendation of the French advisor Emile Boissonade, torture was abolished in 1879 and the principle of trial based on evidence was introduced to facilitate treaty revision. However, use of torture and a preference for confessions continued.[82]

Certain violent encounters between police officers and citizens also exemplified the attitudes of Meiji police officers towards the people. For example, during the 1900 Ashio copper-poisoning dispute, farmers of Gumma and Tochigi prefectures clashed with police and Kenpeitai officers and were arrested for rioting on their way to petition the government in Tokyo. Diet member Tanaka Seizô criticised police actions in the assembly, describing how 300 police officers charged, sabres ready, shouting 'Peasants, peasants!' (*dobyakushô*, a vulgar term with scornful connotations).[83] Police actions during the Hibiya Park Incident of 1905 also drew criticism. The people gathering for the demonstration against the Portsmouth Treaty were already antagonised by the police blockade of entrances to the park, which they regarded as illegal. Consequently, they became enraged when some police officers drew their swords during clashes with members of the crowd. This provoked shouts of 'Running dogs of the *han* clique! Down with the police!' and attacks on police stations and substations.[84]

The police of the Taishô and Shôwa periods inherited this legacy of poor police-public relations, which made it all the more difficult to achieve a people's police. Despite sincere attempts by many police leaders, even they had to admit that a people's police did not yet exist in the 1930s. Part of the problem lay in the fact that, besides having to overcome a history of poor relations, they had to overcome the paternalistic implications of the nursemaid ideal that they themselves espoused. During the 1920s and 1930s even the most consistent advocates of a people's police also emphasised police authority to limit the people's freedom and the people's obligation to obey the police. Even they continued to describe the police as the emperor's police.[85]

Therefore, the police institution of the 1920s and 1930s cannot be

The police tradition 51

understood apart from its history. The adoption of the French and then the German models of government had served to establish a broad administrative role for the police. This conformed with Meiji leaders' concepts of an interventionist state resembling that of the *Polizeistaat*. Towards the end of the century it also led to the strengthening and expansion of the police's social and political functions, as Meiji leaders followed Bismarck's policies of socialist repression and state socialism.

The tradition inherited by the Taishô and early Shôwa police consisted of three main elements: a centralised organisation and structure, pervasive powers and functions (notably including political ones), and an ideology of service to the state and paternalism towards the people. The Tokkô epitomised these elements; but as is most evident in its ideological aspects, there were other somewhat contradictory strands in the tradition as well. The tradition had evolved during the course of 50-odd years; it was not inherited as a fixed or static legacy. It could not alone determine the development of the Tokkô or the actions of Tokkô officers. Historical traditions provided models for attitudes and conduct, and in a political culture like Japan's, where the political leaders consciously sought to preserve social traditions, these models probably were more compelling than in other cultures. However, the manner and degree of acceptance of these models were affected not by the mere existence of the tradition, but by its interaction with conditions and developments of the 1920s and 1930s. These included general ones, such as economic depression, the emergence of a mass society and international friction, but the developments most directly affecting the police's role in the suppression of the left occurred in the areas of law, internal institutional relationships and relationships with other institutions.

3

RULE BY LAW

'The police must be based on law ... a natural consequence of our country being a country governed by law.'
Police Training Book, 1932[1]

'Police law ... is free from formal restriction ... and must respond to needs of society and demands of the age.'
Police Reader, 1933[2]

No explanation of the police's role in the suppression of the left can overlook the body of laws, primarily peace preservation laws, that the police had responsibility for enforcing. Specific substantive statutes, such as the 1925 Peace Preservation Law, laid out the objects of police activities, while general procedural laws and regulations, such as the Administrative Enabling Law, stipulated the authorised means for carrying out their tasks. Police officials themselves always insisted that their exercise of authority must be based on law. At the same time the Tokkô's infamous reputation rests largely on its wide interpretation and abuse of the laws.

Police discretion exists in any society because laws provide only rough boundaries for police functions and powers. However, compared to Anglo-American laws, Japanese laws and regulations delegated relatively large areas of discretion to administrative officials. Consequently, an understanding of police actions towards leftists requires more than knowledge of the content or even thrust of specific laws. The legal order with which the police interacted also encompassed abstract and intangible concepts and attitudes towards law in general, its use and its purposes. These concepts and attitudes influenced the way in which police officials interpreted individual laws.

The key principle for understanding the legal environment within which the police of the 1920s and 1930s operated is the ideal of 'rule by law'. This term has been used by legal historians to distinguish the ideal pursued from the Meiji period until the end of the Second World War from the Anglo-American 'rule of law' ideal, which was first imposed by Occupation authorities but has since become generally accepted by Japanese jurists.[3] The former, which derived from the German principle of *Rechtsstaat*, is sometimes translated as 'rule of law'. 'Rule by law', however, more clearly indicates the existence of a distinction between the two conceptual ideals of the legal order. Under rule *by* law there is a formal commitment to administration under the law but a lack of legal limitation on policy formation. Under rule *of* law both official discretion and policy formulation are limited by law in favour of fundamental human rights and the electoral process.[4]

The fact that even rule by law was not completely established in prewar Japan largely accounts for the fact that administrative officials, such as the police, remained substantially outside the control of justiciable law. This left the individual citizen who became the victim of illegal police action with few channels of appeal for redress, which in turn put little restraint on police actions. Legal limitation on administration remained a formalistic commitment. The Meiji Constitution itself precluded complete establishment of rule by law because it left the executive wide legislative power, as in Article 9, which gave the executive power to issue administrative ordinances. Even the limitations that did exist were often disregarded in practice by administrative officials, as in Tokkô officers' use of detention and torture.

However, even if rule by law had been completely established in prewar Japan, this might not have prevented the stretching and breaking of the laws by the Tokkô, because the rule by law principle possesses inherent limitations for the growth of responsible administration. It derives from a view of law as an instrument for governing and social control. This is evident in the prescriptive nature of Japanese law and in the role of criminal law as auxiliary to administration. Appreciation of the rule by law ideal therefore permits an understanding of the Japanese police's insistence on both the necessity of a legal basis for its actions and the flexibility of the law.

The Tokugawa legacy

Despite the introduction during the Meiji period of many concepts and institutions without precedents in the Japanese past, such as a separate judiciary, the transition from the principle of rule by status to that of rule by law was not made suddenly or completely. Two characteristics of the Tokugawa legal order carried over not only into the Meiji period but also into the 1920s and 1930s and shed light on the police's attitudes and actions towards law.

The first and most important is the rule by status principle that unified Tokugawa law and administration. The Tokugawa system was a hierarchical power structure in which discretion in the form of duties was delegated downward. At each level in this hierarchy an official held responsibility only to his immediate superior, and against this superior's authority he possessed no rights of appeal either before a court or before the next higher official superior. All review and redress came from the top down. The lack of redress against abuses of authority was manifested in the lack of a judiciary separate from the administrative agencies. Moreover, shogunal law prohibited administrative officials from accepting a petition from a lower official against his superior unless the superior gave permission. Criminal law supported these prohibitions by stipulating heavy penalties for their violation.[5]

Rule by status administration and law were premised on the belief that, since the inequality of men was both natural and just, the law must treat men unequally. Laws were therefore expressions of natural laws, not means towards some ideal of justice. Politics and law constituted subdivisions of ethics; consequently, laws were viewed as rules of conduct for Confucian hierarchical relationships based on family and birth. There were elaborate rules for proper procedure and conduct for both superiors and inferiors in these relationships, for both interstatus and intrastatus relationships. In this sense Tokugawa society was highly legalistic, but it was not legalistic in the sense of individuals possessing justiciable rights.[6]

The second characteristic of the Tokugawa legal order that persisted in the interwar period, and persists even in the postwar period, is the tendency to avoid the formal justice apparatus and to settle disputes by informal conciliation.[7] During the 1920s and 1930s this appeared in the establishment of arbitration procedures for labour and tenant farmer disputes that directed most disputes away from the courts.[8] It also lies behind the small number of prosecutions relative to arrests and the frequent use of stays of prosecution not only for thought criminals but also for criminals in general.

Various explanations have been put forward for the preference for informal conciliation. One is the value placed on harmony by Confucianism. Another attributes the preference to a residue of the feudal sentiment that the lord should not be troubled with the private matters of his subjects.[9] However, the practice would probably not have continued unless non-legal sanctions continued to be available to enforce settlements. During the Tokugawa period villages exercised non-legal sanctions, such as ostracism and rumour, whose effectiveness depended on the existence of a close-knit community.[10] During the 1930s family and community pressure were also essential for keeping *tenkôsha* from backsliding. The low rate of recidivism among Peace Preservation Law violators suggests the continued efficacy of such pressures during the interwar period, although it was no doubt also due to official rehabilitation measures, which were institutionalised in a system of protection and supervision centres in 1936.[11] The Tokugawa legacy must therefore be kept in mind in order to understand the legal order of the 1920s and 1930s, although continuities should not be overemphasised.

The Meiji legacy

Introduction of the rule by law principle during the Meiji period brought great legal changes, for it resulted from a real desire to standardise and systematise the legal system as well as from recognition that the adoption of 'modern' Western legal practices and institutions was required for eliminating the unequal treaties and for achieving equivalence with the Western powers.[12] A major characteristic of the *Rechtsstaat* ideal is the existence of an orderly system of general rules and standards made known in advance to the public and applied equally by courts or officials to all who come within their competence.[13] Its establishment in Japan meant the end of rule by status law. The law thereafter would be applied equally to all Japanese. Correspondingly, modern police authority would also extend equally to all classes and geographical areas. Adoption of the rule by law principle in addition implied an end to rule by status administration. There was at least a formal acceptance of the idea that administration must be limited by law. This meant that the exercise of police authority and limitation of the people's freedoms required a legal basis.[14]

The introduction of equality in legal status for all individuals and of protection of the individual from the arbitrary use of authority certainly constituted giant steps away from the Tokugawa legal tradition. However, the Meiji leaders did not go as far as adoption of the Anglo-American rule of law ideal. Rule by law did not involve legal limitation of the lawmakers; Itô Hirobumi was emphatic on this point.[15] Consequently, legal limitation of administration possessed the quality of auto-limitation; administrative agencies were responsible only to themselves. Laws no longer represented declarations of natural laws but became instruments of the lawmaking power. A police textbook in the 1930s defined laws as 'expressions of the state's will'.[16] Laws continued to be regarded as rules of conduct, as the embodiment of morality imposed by the sovereign authority.[17] According to Ishihara Tsunejirô, Keihokyoku Peace Preservation Section chief during the mid 1920s and subsequently a professor at the Police Training Institute, 'laws are rules of conduct in social life which the nation thus recognises. They are the social order'.[18] Criminal law therefore remained a support for administration and a means of social control. The Justice Ministry in the 1930s declared maintenance of the social order 'the highest, the ultimate' purpose of the criminal law.[19] The rule by law ideal therefore carried authoritarian as well as democratising implications for the police.

The Meiji leaders had no intention of fostering the democratising implications when they went about establishing rule by law in Japan. For example, the 1889 Constitution retained relatively large legislative powers for the emperor. Particularly important for the limits of police authority was Article 9, stating that 'the emperor will issue or have issued ordinances necessary for the execution of statutes, for the preservation of the public peace and order, and for the promotion of the welfare of his subjects'.[20] The growth of such administrative law, as distinguished from law legislated by the Diet, provided the basis for the autonomy enjoyed by the executive and the police as its administrative agents. This development also characterised the Meiji government's French and German models.[21]

Chapter 2 of the Meiji Constitution represented a break with the past by guaranteeing certain rights of the people from the executive power. However, these were gifts from the emperor and could be limited by the legislative power.[22] Police textbooks of the 1920s and 1930s made it clear that the guarantee of the people's rights and freedoms by the Japanese Constitution differed completely from the French Revolution idea of natural rights.[23] They disagreed somewhat over whether limitation of these freedoms and rights required a written statute passed by the Diet,[24] but all agreed that freedoms could be restricted by an administrative ordinance so long as the ordinance did not go against a statute and when preservation of public peace and order necessitated it. Furthermore, textbooks pointed out that freedoms not enumerated in the Constitution could be limited on the basis of an ordinance.[25]

Establishment of rule by law involved a massive codification project during the 1880s and 1890s. Numerous police laws were enacted at the same time but not as part of the criminal code.[26] This illustrates the dichotomy between public and private law and highlights the position of the police as a section of the administrative system. It is important to outline this body of legislation because it largely defined and authorised the scope of police powers and functions during the 1920s and 1930s. The successive political police laws show the trend towards an increasingly powerful and centralised national police that was epitomised by the Tokkô and thus supported development of the police tradition and of the ideal of a regulatory and interventionist police state.

During the first decade after the Meiji Restoration the new government faced real threats to its continued existence from dissatisfied samurai groups, culminating in the Satsuma rebellion of 1877. To check dissidence and rebellion the government resorted to traditional means of repression, such as restrictions on publications and speech. In drawing up new censorship laws, however, Meiji leaders carefully used French laws as a guide, eschewing those aspects contributing to fundamental human rights and selecting those which would bolster state control over its opponents. In 1873 the Meiji government enacted a law prohibiting publications that violated the national laws, raised criticism of politics and law or made false charges about people's crimes. When a petition for opening a representative assembly was made the following year, the government felt that this necessitated stricter control of speech.

In 1875 the government promulgated a libel law and two important new regulations affecting newspapers and other publications. The Press Ordinance began a system of police approval for publications, instituted severe punishments for editors and writers found in violation of the regulations, and introduced 'suspension of publication' for certain procedural violations.[27] The Publication Ordinance also gave the Home Minister new powers, such as the power to prohibit sale as well as publication of any book considered harmful to the public peace or morals. Prior to this time book regulations had concentrated on controlling publication rather than circulation.[28] The Libel Law was designed primarily to protect government officials. It became a powerful weapon because of its broad and imprecise definition of 'libel', which could be applied even to statements of truth if they injured a person's honour or damaged his reputation.[29]

Samurai resistance and organisation of the people's rights movement also stimulated the government to move quickly to set up a modern police system along Western lines that would be capable of establishing peace and consolidating central authority. Consequently, the modern Japanese police put a heavy emphasis on preservation of the public peace and order from its beginnings. As in the case of censorship laws, these concerns shaped the choice of Western models for the police system, leading to the decision to adopt the centralised national administrative police system of France rather than the decentralised autonomous system of Britain. The 1875 Administrative Police Rules for this system reflected the government's concerns by stressing the peace preservation tasks of the police. They also showed the importance of the police's preventive role. For example, they established a system of household investigation to keep track of residents and such matters as their occupations and trends in thought, which the Tokkô later used for information gathering.[30]

Armed threats to the government ended with the victory over the Satsuma rebels, but the people's rights movement gained momentum and turned towards organisation of political parties in anticipation of the opening of a representative assembly. This provoked legal restrictions on public meetings as well as more control over publications. From 1878 until the Allied Occupation people intending to hold a meeting that involved political speeches or discussion were required to report this to the police, giving information about the site, time, and names and addresses of the chief participants.[31] Details of the requirements changed, but the basic requirement of reporting remained constant. Police officials gained authority to inspect meeting places and listen to speeches or discussions, although they were admonished against unreasonable restraint of legal meetings and associations. Failure to report a meeting or organisation and disturbance of the national peace constituted illegalities, and police officials were instructed to place the site under an immediate ban.[32]

The 1880 Public Meeting Ordinance demanded not only reporting of meetings but also police approval. This illustrates the preventive aspect of the police's role in Japanese society. Moreover, police officers could disperse a meeting as well as inspect it. These regulations applied to political organisations too. At the same time they instituted the principle of political neutrality for the police; police officials, along with military personnel and reserves and students, were prohibited from participating in political meetings and associations.[33]

Yamagata Aritomo's appointment as Home Minister in 1883 inaugurated a period of reforms that reorganised, modernised and strengthened the Home Ministry's peace preservation machinery, of which the police was the core. This was Yamagata's response to the expansion of the people's rights movement. Besides organisational police reforms, he pushed new laws to restrict and punish political opposition more harshly. For example, the 1887 Press Ordinance expanded the Home Minister's control over newspapers to include authority to prohibit their distribution as well as their sale and also to confiscate them, although he lost the authority to seize printing equipment. The Publication Ordinance of the same year also gave the Home Minister power to prohibit the sale and distribution of books, putting them in the same category as periodicals for the first time.[34] The Home Ministry's gains in power were not shared with other ministries. Courts did not receive authority to ban or suspend publication, and in the 1887 revisions local officials and the Foreign Ministry lost their powers to suspend publication.[35]

Yamagata's most drastic measure was the issuance of the Peace Preservation Ordinance in 1887. This not only prohibited secret organisations and meetings, but also gave the police great discretionary authority to prohibit even outdoor meetings that had received police approval, if it was deemed necessary. The Home Minister gained power to take necessary measures to prevent and halt contacts and communications among such organisations and meetings. With the Home Minister's approval the Superintendent-General of the Keishichô or prefectural governor could expel people residing within 3 *ri* (about 12 kilometres) of an imperial palace or residence, if he feared a plot or instigation of rebellion or a disturbance of the peace. He could prohibit their entry and exit and residence for a three-year period. Even Kiyoura Keigo, Yamagata's hand-picked Director of the Keihokyoku, and Mishima Michitsune, Superintendent-General of the Keishichô, who was popularly known as 'Chief of the Devils', opposed the law for its severity. Mishima hesitated to issue almost 600 orders for explusion until Yamagata threatened to carry them out himself.[36] The Peace Preservation Ordinance met so much resistance that it was finally repealed in 1898. However, the police retained power to control unapproved outdoor meetings and mass actions.

During the decade of the 1890s the treaty revision problem and movement to overthrow the Satsuma-Chôshû clique's domination of the government reached their height. The core of legislation during this period consisted of political police laws aimed at suppressing the opposition parties' movement. In 1890 a public meetings and political organisation law was enacted, which was similar to but more elaborate than the earlier regulations.[37] In 1897 the opposition won a victory by achieving abolition of the Home Minister's power to ban and suspend publication, but this was to prove only temporary.[38] Preparation for and achievement of treaty revision in conjunction with a budding labour movement accounted for a bulge in legislation in 1899 and 1900. This included laws that provided the legal basis for widening the sphere of political police tasks and limiting the activities of actual and potential opponents of the government. A severe critic of the Tokkô has singled out the Public Peace Police Law and Administrative Enabling Law passed at this time as repressive laws that, along with the 1925 Peace Preservation Law, 'wielded the most violence in the suppression of the people' and made police authority close to 'all mighty'.[39]

In its main points, such as the requirement of police approval and police authority to inspect, ban and disperse meetings and organisations, the Public Peace Police Law followed the earlier laws and regulations that it superseded. It differed in widening the scope of the regulatory system to non-political organisations and meetings and in extending police bans to street activities.[40] The law was intended to compensate for two deficiencies felt by the government when confronted by intensified labour organisation activities, strikes and socialist penetration of the labour movement after the Sino-Japanese War. One was lack of a law to control non-political organisations such as labour unions. The second was the inability to control secret societies as the result of the 1898 repeal of the Peace Preservation Ordinance. Article 17 filled the first gap by declaring organised action on the part of workers to be a disturbance of the public peace; this effectively made unions and strikes illegal. Article 14 made up for the second deficiency by prohibiting secret societies.[41]

The Administrative Enabling Law did not relate directly to political control but provided the legal basis for police authority to limit certain rights enumerated in the Constitution. While the 1925 Peace Preservation Law was the paramount substantive law relating to the Tokkô, the Administrative Enabling Law was the principal procedural law. Tokkô officials valued it as a powerful weapon for the control of social movements, with one textbook writer likening it to an 'heirloom sword'.[42] Authorisation of the powers of detention and entry of a private residence gave that sword its sharp edge. Article 1 provided that the police could take persons into custody in order to protect them or prevent a disturbance of the peace. This detention was not supposed to be used to make criminal investigations or to extend after sunset of the following day. Article 2 allowed the police to infringe on a person's privacy by empowering police officials to enter a residence against the will of the resident from sunrise to sunset in case of urgent danger to life or property or when they recognised the existence of gambling or unlicensed prostitution.[43] The law also authorised police officials to compel performance of a legally based police order with force if necessary.

Two other laws pertaining to general police powers but later utilised frequently by the Tokkô were the Regulations Governing Summary Decisions on Minor Offences and the Regulations for Punishment of Violations of Police Ordinances. Both gave police officials authority to carry out judicial functions in relation to certain offences.[44] For example, they authorised police station chiefs to prescribe punishments of up to 29 days' detention for such acts as loitering about without a fixed residence or job or interfering or tampering with another person's work.[45]

In 1908 Katsura Tarô formed his second cabinet, composed primarily of conservatives favouring destruction of the small but partially radicalised socialist movement. He placed an emphasis on more careful surveillance of meetings and publications. Consequently, when in 1909 a reform bill was introduced aimed at abolition of the power of courts to stop publication of newspapers, Katsura successfully transformed it into a repressive law giving the Home Minister significant new powers designed to destroy left wing publications. Under this new Press Law the Home Minister possessed the power to prohibit the sale and distribution of periodicals and to confiscate them if they disturbed the public peace or were injurious to public morals. This was a restoration of the power he had lost in 1897, but applied to a narrow category of offences. The new feature was the authority granted to the Home Minister to issue orders prohibiting sale and distribution of newspapers unilaterally, without making a simultaneous request for court action. He could renew these orders daily. Moreover, this administrative power was placed outside the jurisdiction of the administrative courts.[46]

After 1909 the political police did not enter new areas of jurisdiction or acquire new powers until passage of the 1925 Peace Preservation Law. By the end of the Meiji period, however, they could control both non-political and political meetings, organisations and publications by numerous methods in addition to arrest, such as bans, suspensions, inspections, seizures, dispersals and detentions. The trend in Meiji legislation had been to expand, not to limit, political police activities and power; and in view of the 1909 revival of the Home Minister's independent censorship powers, a tendency was also apparent to keep that increasingly powerful agency highly centralised.

The Peace Preservation Law

The passage of the Peace Preservation Law in 1925 reinforced the importance of the political police. It has been described as the spearhead of the Tokkô.[47] Article 1 contains its key phrases:

'Anyone who organises an association with the objective of changing the *kokutai* or denying the private property system, or who joins such an association with full knowledge of its objectives, shall be liable to imprisonment with or without hard labour for a term not exceeding ten years.

'Any attempt to commit the crime in the preceding clause will be punished.'

Articles 2 and 3 made discussion (*kyôgi*) and instigation (*sendô*) of the above crimes punishable by imprisonment for a term of up to seven years. Subsequent articles provided penalties for those who instigated violence or damage to life or property for the purpose of such crimes and for those who supported such crimes materially or financially. Those who surrendered themselves to the police would be exonerated or receive reduced punishment. The last article extended the sweep of the law even to those who committed the specified crimes in geographical areas outside the jurisdiction of this law.[48]

The term '*kokutai*', which came to excite so much controversy in the Tokkô's application of the law, drew relatively little criticism for its ambiguity during the debates over the bill. At the time of passage government sponsors of the bill and members of the Diet seem to have agreed that '*kokutai*' referred to the location of sovereignty and that the Japanese *kokutai* was a monarchical *kokutai* characterised by sovereignty residing in an eternal unbroken line of emperors.[49] It was distinguished from the *seitai*, which was defined as the methods and forms of exercising sovereignty.[50] The original proposal of the bill made alteration of the *seitai* a crime too, but there was so much opposition to this that the term '*seitai*' was eventually deleted.[51]

An *Asahi shinbun* editorial on 17 January 1925 summed up the major arguments against the law. It voiced the fear that the law could be used against the labour movement since the right to unionise and strike was still not recognised by law. The newspaper also warned that the law would result in 'the total violation of the people's rights and suppression of speech, the introduction of police control over the thought life of the people, and the disappearance of the freedoms of assembly and association'.[52]

In response to criticisms like this, government spokesmen made repeated assurances that the proposed law was intended to control anarchism and communism when they became manifest in acts. It was not directed against the labour movement, scholarly research or thought. It was also not directed against attempts to reform the House of Peers or abolish the Privy Council. Home Minister Wakatsuki Reijirô explained the conditions necessitating passage of the bill. In recent years, he declared, the influence of anarchism and communism had been rising, stimulated by news of the Russian and German revolutions and supported by assistance and money from foreign comrades. Wakatsuki agreed with certain interpellators, such as Andô Masayoshi, that foreign ideas had played an important role in Japanese history, but he did not believe that the ideas of anarchism and communism could be fused with the basic organisation of Japanese society as foreign ideas in the past had been.[53] Instead, he argued, these dangerous thoughts had led to a deterioration of newly organised social movements, and radical socialist movements were coming to the fore. The government feared that the restoration of relations with the Soviet Union would provide all kinds of opportunities for radicals to promote their ideas. Wakatsuki pointed out that there was already an ominous trend towards acts aimed at disturbance of the peace.

According to the Home Minister, the proposed law aimed to reduce the greatest dangers and evils resulting from present-day radical social movements by prohibiting organisations that sought to change the *kokutai*, change the constitutional government system established by the Meiji emperor, reject the Diet, fundamentally repudiate the private property system and institute communism, or destroy the fundamental principles of the state organisation. It also aimed to prohibit the receipt of money or goods for criminal conspiracy and agitation. While reducing these dangers the law would simultaneously guard society in general and prevent the occurrence of disturbing acts.

Wakatsuki denied that the cabinet was thinking of adopting a repressive policy towards thought or research. He assured Diet members that, as long as scholars did not discuss the practical realisation of the objectives specified in Article 1, their research would not be impeded.[54] He explained that it was precisely to prevent harm to the freedoms of speech and writing that the drafters of the bill had avoided 'abstract' terms, as had appeared in the 1922 bill, in favour of 'concrete' terms such as 'to change the *kokutai*', 'to change the *seitai*' and 'to deny the private property system', which 'by no means permit vague interpretation'.[55] Justice Ministry official Yamaoka Mannosuke expressed the same view about the clarity of the terminology used in the bill. According to him the terms 'anarchism' and 'communism' were not used because their meaning and scope were unclear and therefore presented more difficulties of application for the courts than the terms in the bill.[56] When passed, the phrase 'change the *kokutai*' therefore was meant to refer to anarchism and 'deny the private property system' to communism.[57]

When Honda Yoshinari expressed concern over the possibility of police officials' misusing the law,[58] Director of the Keihokyoku, Kawasaki Takukichi replied that police leaders would try as much as possible to make the intent of the law fully understood and that therefore he did not expect that such mistakes would be made. He added that the crimes stipulated in the Peace Preservation Law required establishment of a suspect's aim or motive. In his mind making police officers sufficiently aware of that requirement would prevent abuses.[59]

Despite professions such as these the Peace Preservation Law was bound to pose problems in application, because it possessed qualities unprecedented in Japanese peace preservation legislation. For the first time a law made acts based on a prescribed ideology the object of criminal punishment. The ideological motive rather than the methods utilised became the criterion for establishment of a crime.[60] Therefore, the police did in fact enter into a new area of control: thought.

Making the *kokutai* the object of legal protection differentiated the Peace Preservation Law from previous Japanese peace preservation legislation as well as from such legislation in other countries.[61] The term had actually been used in the 1873 articles on newspaper publication issued by the Dajôkan, but it was not strictly a statutory concept.[62] In any case this early Meiji usage was not generally known. Even Justice Ministry specialist Yamaoka stated that he thought this was the first time the term '*kokutai*' had been used in a statute, and this became the understanding of Diet members.[63] Its use in a law introduced the most problematic concept in interpretation. Most constitutional scholars of both the 'traditional' and 'liberal' schools of interpretation recognised its standing as a legal term defined in terms of the location of sovereignty. This included the three leading constitutional theorists of the Taishô and Shôwa periods, Uesugi Shinkichi of the traditional school and Minobe Tatsukichi and Sasaki Sôichi of the liberal school.[64] The Supreme Court decisions of 1929 and 1931 also supported the narrow legal definition that Home Minister Wakatsuki had made during the Diet debates over the bill. Nevertheless, in popular usage the term '*kokutai*' possessed vague and broad psychological and spiritual meanings connoting special national characteristics and customs.[65] This was also the sense in which it had been used in the 1890

Imperial Rescript on Education.⁶⁶ Consequently, there always existed the possibility of consciously or unconsciously confusing the *kokutai* of the Peace Preservation Law with these other meanings.

Rule by law during the 1930s

The practical consequences of these interpretive questions became visible during the 1930s when wide interpretation and abuse of laws in general, not only the Peace Preservation Law, became characteristic of the Tokkô's suppression of the left. The laws in any culture or political system do not constitute an abstract entity; they must be interpreted to be applied. No matter how carefully and tightly written, they cannot provide for all concrete situations. This is why police officers are important in shaping views of law and the legal process among the people. They are the government officials with whom ordinary citizens have the first and most frequent and direct contact in matters concerning the law. The manner in which they apply the laws therefore influences people's perceptions of law and the legal system.

In interwar Japan police actions were unlikely to have conveyed to ordinary citizens a perception of the system of legal justice as one working in their interest, particularly in matters related to the state. To begin with, Japanese laws gave police officers much discretion. The key Peace Preservation Law, for example, consisted of only seven short sections whose terms were neither defined nor explicated by exemplification. Despite the narrow definition made at the time of passage and supported by the Supreme Court, the official concept of *kokutai* did broaden during the 1930s. During discussions of the *kokutai* in the 65th Diet, the term was used to refer to ethical concepts such as the family state and familism and to historical concepts about the spiritual foundations of the state.⁶⁷ While most official Justice Ministry and police interpretations adhered to the narrow legal definition, many government authorities' explanations tended to construe it widely and to extend its meaning beyond the location of sovereignty to methods of exercising sovereignty as well.⁶⁸ In practical application of the law, people unrelated to communist organisations, even followers of certain religions, became objects of repression.

The various laws relating to censorship and to control of public meetings also illustrate the large discretion delegated to police officials. The Publication and Newspaper Laws included lists of 'relatively prohibited' in addition to 'absolutely prohibited' items, which meant that they could not be published without permission from the relevant authorities. Since there were no provisions concerning when authorities should permit publication of these items, the decision was left completely to the discretion of the administrative officials.[69] For example, Horikiri Zenjirô, who headed the Book Section of the Keihokyoku in 1917 and 1918, said that he and his assistants rarely sought guidance from higher officials.[70] The Home Minister's power to ban the sale or distribution of publications and to seize publications and printing presses was purely discretionary.[71] Again, an example from Horikiri's experience shows that in practice middle level officials such as he, rather than the Home Minister, made these decisions. During the 1918 rice riots Horikiri concluded that newspaper articles were instigating riots, so he banned the sale and distribution of all articles on the subject of the riots.[72] Similarly, the 1900 Public Peace Police Law empowered the police to determine when a meeting should be prohibited, inspected or dispersed.

Sometimes police agencies did establish guidelines for using discretion, but these were strictly for the use of police officials and were not made known to the public. For example, to guide censors there were lists of items considered harmful to the public peace and order. By such enumeration censors received general instructions about what matters to prohibit, but the phrasing of the items still left considerable room for interpretation by the individual official, such as items that 'confuse the financial world or markedly stimulate social unrest' or 'debase the dignity of the imperial house'.[73]

Even when laws provided express limitations, police officers flouted them with increasing frequency during the 1930s. The most serious contradiction of the laws was the Tokkô's use of torture. Other heavily criticised practices related to Tokkô abuse of detention powers. The laws prohibited use of detention for criminal investigation, but it became common for Tokkô officers to detain and examine persons when they lacked sufficient evidence for arrest. The Tokkô circumvented the time limit on protective and preventive detention by various techniques so frequently used that they received special names. At first Tokkô officers simply made out papers for release and re-detention simultaneously. There was such strong criticism of this *mushikaeshi* ('repetition') practice that they turned to other methods for extending detention, such as releasing the person at one door and detaining him again immediately at another (the *hikimodoshi* or 'pull-back' technique) or taking the person to another police station, releasing him there and having that station detain him (the *taraimawashi* or 'rotation' method). There were cases where detention was extended up to two years and perhaps more by these means.[74] Police textbooks did not condone use of detentions for criminal investigation but approved repetition of detention after sunset of the following day if the condition necessitating the detention continued to exist.[75] The Tokkô also became notorious for disregarding limits on police authority to enter a private residence against the resident's will without a warrant. Nighttime entries occurred, and the Tokkô used the provision 'when a police officer deems that there is a danger' to justify entry.[76]

In addition to widely interpreting and exceeding the limits of the laws, the police practised extra-legal methods of restriction and control. The police set up a system of issuing warning notices to newspaper publishers against publication of specific news. This system had no statutory basis, but it worked effectively because the Home Minister would almost automatically ban distribution of any newspaper that disregarded the warning. The Home Ministry issued three types of notices, differentiated according to whether violation would result necessarily, possibly or not at all in a ban: directions, warnings and advice (literally, 'friendly talk'). Notices remained in force until revoked. Between 1920 and 1935 the Home Ministry sent out a total of 241 notices, with a high of 68 (48 directions, 18 warnings, 2 advices) in 1932.[77] Censorship guidelines for the Yamagata prefecture Tokkô show that by 1939 the system had expanded to include three other types of notices.[78] Postwar defenders of the system argue that it emerged out of concern to try to prevent losses that publishers would suffer from bans on sale or distribution that came without a prior warning.[79] However, it also added a repressive prepublication dimension to the censorship system.

Police officials justified their wide interpretation of laws by emphasising that social conditions change and that therefore interpretation of the laws must also change with the times. They took the position that laws should change to fit new conditions but that, since changes in laws always lag behind changes in the times, interpretation of the laws must be flexible.[80] Matsui Shigeru, the outstanding leader in police education who constantly advocated a people's police, went so far as to say that 'police laws should be based on the life of the people and, in addition, should stand in a position free from formal restriction and respond to the needs of society and the demands of the age'.[81] After the Constitution was issued, he explained, respect for the people's rights rose and the police also came to place more weight on protecting individual rights. However, the demands of the present age required the police to shift its emphasis to the interests of society. Matsui's view was based on a feeling widespread among police leaders in the 1930s that liberalism and individualism were in decline and that Japan was entering a new age. They believed that the new era was not only bringing a new mission for the police, but also creating an exceptional lag between changes in laws and changes in social conditions.[82]

However, the Japanese police's position did not simply stress flexibility in interpretation, as might seem natural and characteristic of so-called fascist or terrorist police forces. At the same time it insisted on the necessity of a legal basis for exercise of police authority. This view contrasts with that of the Nazi German police's stance towards the law as expressed by Heinrich Himmler in 1937:

> 'The powers of the National Socialist police force are directed towards implementing the will of the leaders of the State and the protection of people and the State; they are therefore necessarily based not upon detailed laws but upon the realities of the National Socialist Führer State and upon the duties allotted to it by the leadership. The powers of the police force cannot therefore be restricted by formal regulations, since such limitations would impede fulfillment of the tasks given to it by the leadership.'[83]

The Japanese police's relatively legalistic attitude appeared in police textbooks and manuals.[84] Writers who on the one hand stressed the flexibility that the laws possessed on the other hand admonished police officers to study both the spirit and contents of the laws carefully and to interpret them in accordance with generally accepted ideas of society at the time.[85] Official interpreters of the Peace Preservation Law seemed particularly anxious to give these warnings because of the broad new aspects of the law.[86]

There is evidence indicating that these were not formalistic declarations. Legal study occupied a prominent position in police training and promotions in all regions and at all levels.[87] All programs included a course on police laws in their curricula, and a large proportion of the books published for the use of police officers were about the laws. Questions on the Constitution, specific laws and legal terminology appeared frequently in the qualifying examinations for promotions.[88] One writer explained that his book was an attempt to make up for the lack of studies about the police, except for police law.[89] The existence of legal handbooks for the proletariat, which gave what the authors considered the proper interpretation of various laws and the legal limitations of police action, suggests that the objects of police control also believed that the authorities retained respect for the laws.[90]

Although in practice there were numerous instances of disregard for proper legal procedures, there were other instances of adherence to proper procedures. Wilfrid Fleisher, former editor of the English language newspaper the *Japan Advertiser*, relates one example. When a Keishichô police officer paid a farewell visit before Fleisher left the country, Fleisher asked why the Japanese did not just serve notice on foreigners they did not like to leave immediately or revoke their residence permits, as the Germans, Italians and Russians did. Instead of jailing them, why not simply tell them to take the next boat out of the country? The police officer replied that the authorities must have a case in Japan. First, the police must arrest the person, then investigate him, and then the procurator decides whether to bring him to trial, deport him or free him. 'No other procedure is possible'.[91]

The apparent contradiction between police officials' legalism on the one hand, and bending or even breaking of laws on the other, dissolves with an understanding of the rule by law principle. Legalism comes from requiring a legal basis for police action, and the wide interpretation of the laws accords with the view of the role of law as self-limitation by the lawmakers. Under rule by law there are legal limitations on administration but not on the lawmaking power. These legal limitations protect the individual against the arbitrary use of power that was possible under rule by status administration, but they do not apply to legally delegated discretion. Laws serve as an instrument for administration. Rather than being absolute or immutable, they must change to fit new conditions in order to achieve effective governance.

The various revisions of the Peace Preservation Law illustrate these attitudes. The idea that police officials should have a legal basis for exercising their authority, that there should be legal boundaries to the scope of their discretion and that laws must change with the times and the needs of administration underlies the character of the revisions as ratifications of existing practice. The 1928 revision showed the shift in emphasis to suppressing those seeking to alter the *kokutai* more than those denying the private property system by creating separate sections for the two crimes and attaching much heavier penalties to attempts to change the *kokutai*. In their arguments for passage of the revised law, government spokesmen made clear that the communist movement was the chief target of both sections.[92] In addition to making the crime of changing the *kokutai* liable to the death penalty, the revised law introduced the crime of acts to accomplish the aims of organisations seeking to change the *kokutai* or to deny the private property system, in order to apply the law to communist sympathisers. This revision resulted from the experience of the March 15 Incident mass arrests, when the Tokkô and procurators found far more sympathisers than members of communist organisations. They had charged most of these people with the crime of conferring about achieving the aims of changing the *kokutai* or denying the private property system, but felt a certain unreasonableness in applying this and a dissatisfaction with the relative lightness of the penalty it carried.[93]

The 1934 and 1935 proposed revisions failed to obtain Diet approval, but they also show the attempts by police and Justice Ministry officials to gain legislative sanction for their actions. This time they were trying to institutionalise their *tenkô* practices, a shift in the use of the law from a criminal law to an administrative law, by establishing a system of observation and supervision for *tenkôsha* and a system of preventive detention for those who would not convert.[94] The former was accomplished in 1936, the latter in 1941 when a revised Peace Preservation Law did finally pass the Diet. The 1941 revisions also ratified the practice of applying the law to religious movements and individuals with no relation to any organisation.[95]

While the revisions of the Peace Preservation Law illustrate the rule by law principle operating at the specific concrete level of a practical law, the efforts to define the concept of the police show the working of the principle at the general abstract level. The concept of the police is comprised of the purpose, means and limits of authority of the police. The way in which it is defined by the police institution is therefore basic to how police officers view their role in society, which in turn influences their behaviour. The fact that it was defined primarily in reference to the law demonstrates the importance of law for the interwar Japanese police.[96] The additional fact that scholars and officials disagreed over the definition throughout the 1920s and 1930s shows again that laws do indeed leave room for interpretation and official discretion. The existence of a debate also draws attention to the crucial sphere in which the Meiji legacy was not fixed or uniform: ideology.

The two most eminent scholars of the 'liberal' school of constitutional interpretation during the Taishô and Shôwa periods, Sasaki Sôichi and Minobe Tatsukichi, represented the opposing sides of the debate.[97] Both the 'passivists', represented by Sasaki, and the 'activists', represented by Minobe, agreed that the police function is based on the general right of governance existing in the relation of rule between the state and the people that limits the natural freedom of action of individuals. They disagreed on the purpose of the police function. The passivists declared that the police limits the freedom of the people only for the passive purpose of removing obstacles to the social order, not for the active purpose of promoting social welfare. They argued that this passive purpose was clearly established by the 1875 Administrative Police Rules, Article 1.[98]

The activists argued that protection of the interests of society and the public constitutes the police's immediate aim. Protection of the interests of society and the public includes not only the passive prevention and removal of obstacles to the social order, but also the active promotion of public welfare. As a principle the police has only the passive purpose; but when there is a special provision in the law, the police should also work to achieve the active purpose. Activists agreed with the passivists that the Administrative Police Rules indicated this passive principle, but they interpreted Article 9 of the Constitution to mean that administrative ordinances could be issued for active welfare aims in addition to peace preservation aims.[99] Minobe's favourite example of laws recognising the police's authority to order and compel people by force for the active promotion of social welfare was the Urban Building Law, which restricted building, not only for the prevention and removal of obstacles to the social order, such as fire prevention or preservation of public health and sanitation but also for the sake of beauty.[100]

The debate over the concept of the police parallels the broader differences between Sasaki and Minobe over interpretation of the Constitution. It reflects a difference in methodology, not political values, for both supported constitutionalism. Sasaki adhered to the text in strict logical-positivist fashion when interpreting the Constitution and the laws, while Minobe departed from strict positivism to consider the history of the particular laws and the political factors affecting their origins and application.[101]

In Minobe's interpretive method, particularly applied to the concept of the police, the problematic aspects of rule by law for political democratisation become evident. It may not seem surprising that the prewar Japanese police leaned towards official acceptance of the activist definition of the police's purpose, since it fitted the expanding role of the police during the 1930s and seemed to be a suitable concept for what has been described as a 'fascist' or 'totalitarian' police.[102] But why did a prominent liberal and supporter of constitutional government like Minobe take an activist view of the police? The same question arises regarding the police textbook writers who adopted an activist position but at the same time displayed 'liberal' qualities by deploring Japan's shortcomings as a constitutional country compared with Western European countries.[103]

This is the kind of weakness or lack of commitment to liberalism for which prewar liberals have been condemned during the postwar period. However, it is a judgement resulting from a lack of precision in terminology and conceptualisation and from the use of inappropriate standards of comparison. To understand prewar liberalism it should be compared, not with twentieth-century Anglo-American liberalism under rule *of* law, but with nineteenth-century German liberalism under rule *by* law.[104] By recognising that Minobe and other activists were working according to the principle of rule by law, their support for a liberalism narrowly confined within the framework of the Meiji Constitution does not appear as a failure or betrayal. This is not to deny that Minobe's interpretive method based on rule by law assumptions possessed problematic aspects for achieving even this limited liberalism. His stand against a narrowly literal construction of the written law could have the opposite results of those he intended. His principle of 'no law, no penalty' could imply that, if a law exists, the penalty is justified. The latter comes close to the activist position that, if there is a legal provision, the police can restrict the people's freedom for the active promotion of social welfare. Once one active purpose is recognised, however, there emerges the possibility of other active purposes' being pursued as well.

The incomplete establishment of the rule by law principle, manifested in the lack of means for redress for misuses of official authority, contributed greatly to the lack of restraint on illegal action by police officers, for which the Tokkô became especially maligned. Administration remained outside the jurisdiction of the regular courts through the establishment of a separate administrative court. This had been common in European countries up to the end of the nineteenth century.[105] In addition, the nature of the administrative court hindered achievement of effective restraints on abuses of official authority. Only cases enumerated in the Administrative Court Law or special statutes came within its jurisdiction. Among Tokkô matters only organisational bans could be questioned in the court. On average the court received less than 300 cases annually between 1890 and 1930. The attitude of the judges tended to favour the executive rather than the individual, and the decisions of the court could not be appealed. The Privy Council was supposed to determine conflicts with regular courts under special rules; but since they were never issued, the Privy Council never functioned in this capacity.[106]

As for other channels of redress, victims of illegal police action could present a petition if the matter concerned the local police, or they could file a criminal complaint of official misconduct or a civil complaint for damages. However, criminal civil suits could be made only against an individual official, not against the state. Further, to constitute illegality it was not sufficient for the act to be illegal according to administrative law; illegality was limited to the abuse of official authority based on evil intent or desire.[107]

Especially in matters of security related to the state and the public peace, the courts supported the police and procurators' wide interpretation of the laws. They did not exhibit independence in Peace Preservation Law cases as they did in other areas.[108] The pattern of court sentencing paralleled developments in the application of the law. The courts tended to impose the harsher sentence of imprisonment with hard labour, rather than without hard labour. Between 1928 and 1933, for example, 2668 out of 2713 persons received sentences of imprisonment with hard labour for the crimes of organising an association with the aim of changing the *kokutai* or denying the private property system, or of acting to accomplish the aims of such an association.[109] Since this ran counter to the general tendency towards leniency shown in most other criminal cases,[110] it seems to indicate the seriousness with which authorities viewed Peace Preservation Law crimes. At the same time the rising number of stays of execution during the early 1930s reflected the increasing emphasis on *tenkô*. Among the 2713 persons sentenced to imprisonment for Peace Preservation Law crimes between 1928 and 1933, 956 received stays of execution.[111]

However, even if the rule by law ideal had been achieved, responsible administration might not have resulted, for the rule by law principle was based on a view of law that supported a constitutionalism premised on the existence of an absolute sovereign authority, not a parliamentary democracy. While the principle involved a commitment to administration under the law, that law consisted not only of statutes approved by a representative assembly, but also of ordinances issued by the absolute sovereign or his delegated officials, who included the administrators themselves. Like the nursemaid ideal of the police world, the ideal of the legal order within which the Tokkô operated therefore held elements potentially unconducive to the development of a police force with a narrow conception of its sphere of authority. These were the background factors to the growth of the Tokkô and the police state ideal during the 1930s. Immediate factors can be found in developments within the police institution and in developments impinging on the police, especially the Tokkô, from the outside. These interacted with the somewhat contradictory historical and legal legacy to expand the role of the police in general and the Tokkô in particular.

4

PROFESSIONALISM

'The police is police for the people, not police for the police.'
Matsui Shigeru, 1921[1]
'Work to achieve a crack police force.'
Home Minister Yamamoto Tatsuo, 1934[2]
'The most urgent need at this time is for police officials to ... become protectors of the *kokutai*.'
Matsui Shigeru, 1937[3]

Despite its elite status and despite its expansion and elevation during the 1930s, the Tokkô nevertheless remained part of the police. Moreover, despite its position as the key element in the police institution, the Tokkô did not acquire a monopoly over even political police functions. It continued to share some responsibility for political tasks with non-Tokkô police and therefore interacted with other kinds of police, sometimes harmoniously and sometimes not. Its personnel were recruited from regular patrolmen, so they underwent the same initial socialisation process as other police officers. Policies and developments applicable to the police institution as a whole therefore also affected the Tokkô and its individual members. Consequently, the Tokkô must be considered within this larger institutional context.

Attitudes towards law and consciousness of police traditions were cultivated in police training schools and reinforced by experience, by orders and instructions from superiors and by the accountability system. Recruitment, training, directives and the system of rewards and punishments were also means by which police leaders tried to instil their expectations of the role requirements of a police officer and thereby improve the performance of the police as a whole. Police socialisation and other internal institutional developments affected the behaviour of individual prewar police officers, including those in the Tokkô, since an individual's actions tend to conform to his self-image and role expectations.[4] More broadly, investigation of police socialisation sheds light on the social and political role envisioned by government leaders for the police as an institution.

If one asks what kind of police force interwar police leaders tried to shape through policies of selection, education and treatment of police officers, the answer in a word would be 'professional', although they did not use the term.[5] Police officers were seldom viewed as members of a profession like doctors or lawyers, yet the Japanese police did exhibit more and more the characteristics of a profession as time passed. A typology of the ideal profession would include expertise, social responsibility and corporateness.[6] A professional possesses specialised knowledge and skills acquired by prolonged education and experience, which become the basis for separating the professional from the layman. Because professional knowledge is intellectual, institutions of research and education are required for its extension and transmission. Ideally, a professional must also perform a service essential to the immediate existence and function of society, making both moral and technical decisions affecting its fate. Bureaucratic professions often possess a high degree of specialisation of labour and responsibility within the profession, but the profession as a whole renders a collective service to society. From the lengthy training, experience and the sharing of a unique social responsibility emerges a shared sense of organic unity and consciousness as a group apart from lay people. This manifests itself in a professional organisation that establishes and enforces standards of professional competence and responsibility.

In general, police groups do not develop the same professional codes of honour, certification and internal controls as the more recognised professions, such as medicine. In the police's case professionalisation refers to careful selection, training, skills and pride in work.[7] In addition, the police as a profession is neutral towards and independent of political and other local interests of the community.[8] These emphases have the effect of 'occupational reinforcement', the development of a sense of belonging to a particular occupation. This increases solidarity among police officers and desire for self-regulation.[9]

The adoption of the professional ideal by the Japanese police constituted part of a worldwide trend to which Japanese police leaders showed a keen sensitivity and awareness. They paid particular attention to August Vollmer's successful reforms in the Berkeley, California police force, which did much to mould the professional model and foster its acceptance by other American police departments.[10] While it became the universal ideal, a professional police was not easy to achieve in either prewar Japan or the United States outside Berkeley. Moreover, certain implications of professionalisation did not contribute to development of police responsibility to the public.

An important ingredient of professionalism and the crucial factor in the police's social and political role in interwar Japan was the purpose for which this professional police was to be used. The concept of the police's mission and role changed during the 1930s, largely in response to changes in the police's external environment. An 'emperor's police' concept of the police's mission and role gradually emerged out of the 'people's police' ideal of the 1920s. It was epitomised by the slogan *'tennô no keisatsu'* (the emperor's police) or *'heika no keisatsu'* (His Majesty's police). The shift reflected dissatisfaction with the existing political parties and the ascendance of nationalist and national socialist ideas over Western democratic ideas. It grew out of the overwhelming sense of both internal and external national crisis, created by a decade of economic stagnation and depression associated with the turmoil of social and thought movements and by rising international tension associated with domestic military terrorism and direct action—brought dramatically to national attention by the Manchurian Incident of 1931 and the assassination of Prime Minister Inukai in May 1932. The emperor's police ideology was not simply a defence of the status quo or an attempt to restore order, but also part of a larger movement to reform the political, social, economic and cultural system in preparation for future national advances and the possibility of war.

The ideology and organisational development of the Tokkô in particular illustrates the transformation of the interwar police ideal from that of a professional people's police to a professional emperor's police. As a result of the transformation the Tokkô's mission came to be seen as the most important mission of the prewar Japanese police as a whole. This represented an extension of the traditional interventionist administrative role of the police and an intensification of the police's traditional orientation towards the state and paternalistic attitude towards the people. It therefore contributed to the sense of superiority evident in the arrogance displayed by Tokkô officers and to a lesser extent by prewar police officers in general. It also represented an attempt to weld the police institution into a single entity. However, various internal divisions continued to exist within the police, and the expansion and elevation of the Tokkô and its social role exacerbated old points of friction and created new ones.

A professional people's police

The professional ideal was not newly adopted after the First World War, but the period saw greater efforts at professionalisation. This was the thrust of attempts to raise standards of recruitment and education of police officers and to improve their salaries and treatment, and of organisational changes showing increased specialisation of functions. Recruitment standards for patrolmen had risen gradually since the beginning of the Meiji period. The 1891 revisions raised the age minimum from 20 to 23, lowered the age maximum from 45 to 40 and increased the minimum height requirement from 5 *shaku* (152 centimetres) to 5 *shaku* 1 *sun* (155 centimetres). Successful applicants also had to present a certificate of diligence, pass a physical examination and pass a written examination on criminal and police laws, Japanese history and geography, writing and composition, and arithmetic.[11]

Police leaders became dissatisfied with these criteria during the early 1920s because they saw a decline in the quality of applicants. A former Tokkô official recalls that, when he entered the police as a patrolman in 1920, there were few other applicants. Typically, he says, they were failures or tramps, people who had nothing better to do or those who wanted to escape the army, for there was talk of war with the United States at that time.[12] Given this situation, police authorities advocated more stringent physical requirements and shifted the emphasis in the written test from legal knowledge to general studies.[13]

Police leaders also believed that improvement of the police as a whole depended on the recruitment of 'men of talent'.[14] In order to attract men of talent they worked to raise salaries and improve the spiritual as well as material compensation of police officers. In 1920 monthly pay scales for lower-level police officers were nearly doubled; for example, from a range of 15–45 yen to 30–70 yen for patrolmen.[15] However, police authorities felt that the postwar recession with rising commodity prices negated these gains.[16] During the second half of the 1920s the monthly salary of a patrolman averaged between 47 and 49 yen.[17] Police leaders did not regard this as low, but argued that salaries were inadequate considering the continual risks and worries of police work and the salaries of other government officials performing less dangerous tasks.[18] Because they worried about the high turnover of patrolmen, they pressed for changes in the systems of promotion and awarding of police prizes for meritorious service and even made recruits swear not to resign within five years. In 1927 they succeeded in obtaining a greater number of prizes to be conferred. These rewards included monetary prizes as well as medals and recognition from the Home Minister and other top-ranking officials.[19]

The ratio of applicants to recruits for patrolmen in the Keishichô remained about 3:1 during the first half of the 1920s, the years of an expansion in the police organisation. In the late 1920s police recruitment could be more selective; the ratio rose to almost 6:1 as the absolute number of applicants continued to increase while the number chosen declined.[20] However, this may have resulted more from the worsening economic conditions than from improvements in police remuneration. Occupational background statistics on recruits are not very revealing because the categories are broad, but recruits seem to have reflected the national average distribution of occupations. The large majority fell in the 20–30 age bracket. Until 1928 at least three-quarters of them joined the police with only a primary school education; but as the recruitment ratio rose in favour of the police, so also did the proportion of recruits with more than the minimum compulsory education.[21]

It is difficult to assess the influence of their educational backgrounds on police recruits, but studies of elementary school textbooks give some insights into the political ideas and values they were exposed to before joining the police. Recruits during the early and mid 1920s studied textbooks stressing nationalism and fears of social disintegration, whereas recruits during the late 1920s and 1930s used books attempting to strike a difficult balance between nationalism and internationalism. Internationalist elements included an appreciation of foreign countries' accomplishments and contributions to Japan and an association of international cooperation and peace with Japan's long-range national interests. At the same time all textbooks of the latter period, especially in moral education and history, emphasised clarification and protection of the *kokutai*, obligations and acts of heroic loyalty. They also focused more on emperors and presented creation myths as fact.[22]

Police leaders during the 1920s regarded improvements in police training as a fundamental means for professionalising the police. They thought that was necessary not only because of the generally low level of education of police recruits, but also because of the increasing number and complexity of police tasks. Moreover, they argued, a greater understanding of police spirit had to be instilled.

Professionalism 79

The history of national police schools since the first one founded under Home Minister Yamagata had been characterised by successive establishments and abolitions in accordance with the general state of government finances, but Home Ministry and police leaders had always considered them important.[23] After the abolition of the central training institute in 1904, for example, Director of the Keihokyoku Arimatsu Hideyoshi led a determined effort to have the Police Association,[24] a technically private though quasi-official organisation, establish a training institute until a state training institute could be re-established. That came in 1918 with the founding of the Police Training School due to the advocacy of Home Minister Gotô Shinpei. The re-establishment of this central institution for training middle-level prefectural leaders, mainly inspectors and assistant inspectors, represented a major triumph for police education advocates. The government's recurring financial difficulties later prompted calls for another abolition, but the school's director, Matsui Shigeru, saved it by shortening the education period and cutting expenses, and the school continued to operate until 1943.[25]

Although Japanese police authorities felt dissatisfied, Japan was actually ahead of many other countries in the establishment of police education organs and formal training programs. For example, the earliest police school in the United States was established by Vollmer in 1908, and police education in other countries was still in its infancy.[26] One of the main arguments in favour of Japanese police educational improvements was to prevent the police from lagging behind the times. Police authorities argued that police officers' knowledge and abilities had to keep up with recent advances in the educational and cultural level of ordinary people.[27] Their acceptance of the professional ideal is evident in their desire for unified and centralised national supervision of police education, including state-compiled textbooks, and in recommendations to lengthen the training period in schools and to involve more active-duty police officers in supplemental training programs.[28]

In 1919 the first national meeting of directors of prefectural training institutes for patrolmen passed resolutions supporting three months of school training and one month of practical training in a police station for new patrolmen, four or more months of special training within two years after appointment as patrolmen, and other special courses for appropriate time periods.[29] In 1923 the first of these resolutions was enacted by extension of the required training period for new patrolmen from two to three months. This represented the accepted minimum, for a large majority of prefectures already had three-month programs in 1919, and in 1924 twenty out of 47 operated four-month programs.[30] This compares with an average of two months for training programs in American police departments in 1965.[31] In the Keishichô a new patrolman's combined institute and in-service training lasted seven to nine months. For what was viewed as a transitional period, Matsui Shigeru considered this adequate, but his ideal was one year.[32]

These efforts to professionalise the police during the 1920s resulted from police leaders' perception of domestic and international changes and trends. They were conscious of tremendous changes in all aspects of Japanese society since the Meiji Restoration. They considered these changes a great advance but also observed that the advance was making Japanese society increasingly complex. Moreover, they argued that, with the dissemination of education among the people and spread of traffic and communications organs, the objects of police activity had multiplied and become nationwide. This became their explanation for the past proliferation and complication of police duties and tasks and increases in police personnel. It also became the basis of their advocacy of further reforms and improvements in recruitment and education to foster an efficient police.[33]

Discussions of desired police reforms show not only a knowledge of conditions in Western police systems, but also the use of foreign police forces as models to be emulated. They pay attention to foreign education systems (curricula, textbooks, length of training), transportation, communications and other technological facilities, use of scientific methods and equipment in criminal investigation, recruitment, salary and pension systems, and relations between police and political authorities. They also express the need for contacts and cooperation with foreign police for international policing.[34] In the eyes of Japanese police leaders, domestic and international trends were moving in the same direction. Of particular relevance for the political and social role of the police was their identification of the spread of people's rights ideas and of the establishment of a constitutional system in Japan as part of a world trend 'from despotism to emancipation'.[35]

Police leaders believed that Japan like Western countries had moved away from being a 'police state', which they defined as a government based on the power of a minority. They concluded that, because the government had come to rest on the power of the majority, the police must similarly be based on the people.[36] A 'people's police' (*minshû* or *kokumin keisatsu*) became the watchword of the police during the 1920s. Police textbooks, *The Police Association Magazine* and official speeches and instructions reiterated that the police existed for the people, not for the police, and exhorted police officers to become protectors of the people. Top officials felt that some progress had been made towards 'democratisation' of the police and mutual understanding between the police and the people, but they were aware that fear of the police was deeply rooted. They attributed this to the long tradition of police officials' viewing themselves and being viewed by the public as representatives of power rather than protectors of the people.

Police leaders even went so far as to take the British police as an ideal, which suggests the attractive force of British and American democratic ideas during the 1920s. As one writer declared, the London police were recognised by everyone as the most advanced in the world, and many countries were adopting aspects of the system. Matsui Shigeru pointed out that British police officers were regarded as 'a national treasure' because of their humanitarianism, which Japanese police officers in the past had unfortunately often lacked. Police leaders acknowledged the impossibility of direct transplantation of foreign systems and customs but argued that 'no one disagrees that the police are not representatives of power, but protectors of freedom'. Instead of brandishing power like the Paris police, they said, the Japanese police should emulate the London police. Although police leaders proudly considered the Japanese police system unsurpassed in its nationally unified organisation, they worried that, if police officers' attitudes towards the people did not change, a people's police would remain an unrealised ideal.[37]

It became the policy of police educators and leaders to arouse consciousness of being protectors of the people by encouraging kindness and politeness in police officers' dealings with ordinary people. They sought to foster a spirit of self-sacrifice for the state, society and humanity as a whole. While affirming the authority to use force to control criminals, they admonished against threatening good citizens with the sword. As an example they praised police restraint during the rice riots. They also appealed to Kawaji Toshiyoshi's emphasis on a display of benevolence and support towards the people and noted the necessity of patience, prudence and composure.[38]

Accompanying the stress on acting for the interests and welfare of the people as a whole was a desire to remove the police from partisan political struggles and end its use as a tool of politicians. Police reformers therefore concentrated their attack on appointment practices, such as the change of the Superintendent-General of the Keishichô and the Director of the Keihokyoku with each change in cabinet. They called attention to the fact that, although Paris had a police system like Tokyo's, its director did not change with each cabinet in spite of intense political struggles.[39]

While the London police became an ideal, the Japanese concept of a people's police retained distinct differences from the British one. Police leaders prodded police officers to act for the people but not to become 'public servants'. While police officers should be protectors of the people, they were not representatives of the people. Matsui Shigeru, one of the foremost advocates of a people's police and one of the leaders in police education during the interwar period, stands out as a striking example of this outlook.[40] Admonitions against intimacy or 'fawning on the people' therefore qualified injunctions to be kind and benevolent. This was considered important for maintaining the dignity and prestige of the police.[41]

The concern for dignity also appeared in discussions of the personal appearance and uniforms of police officers. Both were viewed as reflections of spirit and important for preserving the dignity and nobility of police officers. This was explicitly the main purpose of wearing a sword until the 1920s, when social disorders made it necessary for self-defence as well. The uniform changes of 1908 were described as having greatly simplified the showy uniforms of the previous decade and thus given police officers a very dignified appearance.[42]

A comparison of this discussion of uniforms with discussions over British police uniforms shows the significance of uniforms as reflections of the intended nature of the police. When the London police underwent a major reform in 1829, there arose the question of whether police officers should wear uniforms at all, because British leaders wanted to avoid any resemblance to the French gendarmerie with its military model and associations with an arbitrary regime. Home Secretary Robert Peel and his advisors finally decided that police officers should wear uniforms to make it easier for the public to identify them when in need of help, but that the uniforms should be as civil in style as possible.[43] The resulting uniform, consisting of top hat, blue tail-coat and wooden truncheon carried in the coat tail, contrasts sharply with the military-style uniform of the Japanese police, even in its less showy version. Moreover, the lack of concern for maintaining the 'dignity' of police officers evident in British discussions highlights the differences between the British and Japanese police in their views of their relationship to the state and the people.

The uniform manifested the fact that Japanese police officers were government officials and officials of His Majesty the Emperor. Police leaders saw their function of preventing and removing dangers to the people and society as a contribution to their ultimate purpose of aiding the prosperity of the state and the imperial house, which were viewed as one.[44] As His Majesty's police officials they were charged with the duties of protecting His Majesty's children, the people, and, by extension, of guiding and enlightening the people culturally and socially. Police leaders expected police officers to foster healthy thought in general and to provide inspiration for youth and moral reform of juvenile delinquents and other criminals. They believed that this would help to preserve social peace and order and further public interests without reliance on force.[45] As nursemaids of society police officers always were to be one step ahead of ordinary people, not only in their knowledge and abilities, but also in their 'common sense' about society and their moral and cultural attainments. This was the reason for instituting literary courses in police schools and establishing various societies as agencies of police self-cultivation.[46]

The view of the people as unenlightened children, which derived from Kawaji's nursemaid ideal, led police leaders to blame the people as much as the police for poor police–public relations. They considered that the lack of independence and experience in self-government of the Japanese people lay at the base of their lack of understanding of the police. By contrast, they thought, the British police's success derived largely from the 'fact' that, as the British people had long been trained in self-government, all considered themselves police officials. Resolution of problems in policing in Japan therefore required development of a sense of civic virtue and a concept of the people's obligation to obey police power, in addition to dissemination of an understanding of the duties and importance of police officials. Police leaders encouraged organisations for traffic safety and for fire and theft prevention and teaching about the police in elementary schools as methods of promoting these concepts.[47] They aimed at 'police-isation' of the people along with 'people-isation' of the police.[48]

Recognition of limitations in the Japanese people and police and attentiveness to foreign systems did not preclude national pride. Police authorities boasted that the Japanese police system's unity and centralisation exceeded that of even advanced countries. While encouraging police officials to look to foreign systems for the rationalisation and democratisation of the Japanese police, Matsui Shigeru insisted that they do this with a sense of self-esteem and warned against forgetting their Japaneseness. Japan must have a Japanese type of police, he declared, which meant a unique one. He traced Japan's uniqueness to its pure monarchical *kokutai*, characterised by sovereignty residing in a single unbroken line of imperial rule since the founding of the country. The Japanese police's uniqueness derived from this in being wholly under the command of the Home Minister in the service of His Majesty the Emperor. When Matsui declared that Japanese police officers were not servants of the people like some European ones, he strongly implied that they should not be.[49]

Promotion of a people's police devoted to leading the people gave added impetus to the development of police spirit. Police leaders put great stress on developing self-consciousness of being a police officer because they related the rise and fail of police spirit directly to the highest morality of the state.[50] The 1919 revision of rules of service for patrolmen showed the emphasis on police spirit and the concern for improving police relations with the people. Like the oath taken by police recruits, the rules demanded absolute obedience to orders from a superior, adherence to the law, loyalty, diligence, frugality, honour, irreproachable conduct, impartiality (specifically in political matters) and a readiness to die in the line of duty. They also enjoined police officers to study hard and practise military arts. Kindness and politeness, they noted, should be police officers' principles in dealing with the public, but police officers should maintain their dignity and avoid becoming too friendly or familiar. There were no recommendations, as for British police officers, to treat the people 'with good humour'.[51] The rules reminded police officers that they were the mainstay of the nation and must work for harmonious cooperation.[52]

Discussions of qualities of the ideal police officer repeated these commandments.[53] In addition, they stressed that police officers needed a self-sacrificing spirit because working conditions were hard, material compensation low and public criticism abundant, but their duty of preserving the public peace was extremely important and no one provided greater social service.[54] One writer in the late 1920s recommended that in recruiting patrolmen more attention should be paid to selecting people who understood the duties and spirit of the police and wanted to protect the people and work for society. He favoured recruiting reservists who had received a military education because of the similarity between the military spirit and the police spirit, although he cautioned that not all reservists would possess the good judgement, originality, resourcefulness and other personal qualifications necessary for police officers.[55]

Police authorities promoted the martial arts as a means of fostering the spirit of *bushidô* as well as physical health and strength. Official enthusiasm for the martial arts dated from the beginning of the modern police system. Martial arts instructors had been placed in the Keishichô in 1890. Thereafter competition among prefectures had gradually grown, and in 1919 martial arts training became a requirement for Keishichô officers. Pressure for a national tournament resulted in the first annual National Police Officers' Martial Arts Tournament in 1929, sponsored by the Police Association and supported by the Keihokyoku. Director of the Keihokyoku Ôtsuka Koreyoshi expected the annual tournament to raise morale and stir up martial spirit in the whole police community. That same year the Imperial Household Ministry supported the first imperial inspection tournament. There was also a large scale review of the Keishichô in the imperial palace plaza aimed at intensifying the self-consciousness of the police 'at the feet of the emperor', raising morale, strengthening a sense of public duty and giving training in group activities.[56] In addition to contributing to a definition of the police role, these stepped-up efforts to arouse police spirit during the late 1920s fostered a sense of corporateness, which is another essential element of professionalism.

A professional emperor's police

The 1930s witnessed continued attempts by Home Ministry and police leaders to professionalise the police.[57] All the elements of the professional police model appeared in Home Minister Yamamoto's instructions to the May 1934 prefectural police chiefs' meeting:

> 'The selection of talent is very important in the reform of police administration and the display of official discipline ... Along with working to select suitable talent, make special efforts in education and training. Rely on appropriate supervision, make clear the principle of "sure penalty and certain reward", create spirit and increase efficiency. In these ways work to achieve a crack police force.'[58]

Although hampered by tightened budgets in the midst of economic depression, the Japanese police displayed more and more the characteristics of a profession. The distinguishing traits of expertise, social mission, corporateness and neutrality in party politics became most developed in the Tokkô.

The 1930s thus emerges as a period when the Tokkô became more professional, but it is also the period when the Tokkô came to be more dreaded, not only by its victims but also throughout society at large. This suggests that professionalism in the police should not necessarily be equated with better police–public relations and police conduct. In the case of prewar Japan, the shift of emphasis in the police's social mission from a people's police to the emperor's police magnified the hierarchical aspects of the Tokkô's relationship to the people. At the same time greater emphasis on 'proper guidance of thought' expanded the scope of the Tokkô's mission and its interventionist role in Japanese society; moreover, pride in its expertise and a more highly developed sense of corporateness isolated it from external criticism.

The recruitment of men of talent continued to be viewed as the basis for improvements in the police. A revision of the regulations for recruiting patrolmen in 1930 again raised the criteria of recruitment. The maximum age of applicants was lowered to 30, although exceptions could be made for persons with special abilities or previous police experience. The height minimum rose from 5 *shaku* 1 *sun* to 5 *shaku* 2.1 *sun* (approximately 159 centimetres).[59]

Both the quantity and quality of applicants increased at this time. The ratio of applicants to recruits in the Keishichô leaped from 6:1 to about 10:1 and remained around that level until 1937, when it dropped back to 6:1. The number of applicants peaked in 1933 at 13 471. That year the Keishichô accepted 1829 persons, a relatively high number.[60] Applicants included a larger proportion of middle school graduates and others with more than the compulsory primary school education. Police authorities explained these developments as the result of poor economic conditions, just as good economic conditions had led to a decline in the number of applicants immediately after the First World War.[61] They were not completely happy with the recruitment situation, however. About half the recruits still entered the police with only a higher primary school education, and many joined the police only in order to make a living, not because they wanted to be police officers.[62] Police leaders' concern about the motivation of applicants helps to explain the emphasis on police spirit as much as knowledge and skills in police education.

The revised recruitment regulations also lengthened the minimum training period from three to four months. After this institute training, new patrolmen had to receive more than six months' training in practical duties while in a police station.[63] Despite the improvements police leaders still considered education facilities inadequate. Most police officers had to study independently to raise their knowledge because financially constrained training institutes, including the central Police Training School, could select only a few for additional training. While noting some improvements police leaders also expressed doubts about the competency of teachers and directors of local training schools and about the completeness of their curricula.[64] These conditions stimulated the publication of a substantial number of official and semi-official books about the police, intended as textbooks and reference books for ordinary police officers studying on their own.[65]

At the same time police leaders argued for more long-range improvements. Their recommendations indicate a higher level of expectations and refinement in their ideas about police education than do earlier discussions. For example, they differentiated between the types of education appropriate for patrolmen and for middle-level supervisors. Patrolmen, they argued, should receive a practical, commonsense education, particularly regarding laws, while future leaders should learn more legal theory and administrative skills and develop character and police spirit.[66] Police leaders hoped to expand the Police Training School and make it into a police university. They stressed the desirability of centralising police education to increase efficiency and unity. Matsui Shigeru proposed establishment of a central supervisory division for this purpose.[67]

To attract men of talent police leaders pushed for further improvements in salaries, promotion and treatment of police officers, but economic depression made budget expansion difficult. Working hours for ordinary police officers remained long, commonly 24 hour shifts or a schedule of 24 hours on duty, 8 hours off, then 8 hours on.[68] The average monthly salary of a patrolman ranged from just under 48 yen to somewhat over 51 yen between 1930 and 1937.[69] This was almost the same as that of a graduate of a teachers school. A patrolman spent about half of his salary on living expenses.[70] Police leaders like Matsui Shigeru deplored these conditions and argued for improvements in the pension system and fringe benefits as well as salaries and working conditions.[71] However, one writer recommended forbearance because so many other people, such as ordinary salarymen, also were suffering. In particular, he thought that a patrolman's uniform allowances and occasional bonuses made his situation bearable. Nevertheless he did argue for larger meal and travel allowances and increases in police sergeant (one rank above ordinary patrolman) salaries to encourage people to remain in police service.[72]

This concern reveals the continuing dissatisfaction among police leaders with the short average length of service of patrolmen, which was about six years in 1933. They blamed this on hard working conditions and the difficulty of obtaining promotions and salary raises.[73] The 1930 revision of regulations governing promotion to police sergeant gave more opportunities to active duty patrolmen to advance by requiring success on the qualifying exam and eliminating qualification by other means.[74] A patrolman could eventually become a superintendent[75] (*keishi*) by special appointment rather than by passing the higher civil service examination, but this remained rare. Promotion depended on order of seniority, career record and performance on examinations. There was a tendency for those with scholarly abilities to succeed because, if an officer did not pass the promotion examinations, he could not advance even if he showed skill and devotion in practical duties and possessed the appropriate amount of seniority.[76]

While trying to improve the quality of police personnel, police leaders urged the Tokkô, along with the police as a whole, to develop its scientific methods of investigation into the best in the world.[77] Their attraction to modern science and technology extended to its use in police communications and equipment. Direct telephone lines between the Home Ministry and prefectural police departments increased steadily, beginning with the line between Tokyo and Osaka in 1926.[78] In 1936 the Keishichô completed an 'epoch-making' communications system enabling a message to be sent from headquarters to all police stations simultaneously and among police stations as well as between stations and headquarters. Writers of the official Keishichô history proudly stated that almost all communication machinery had previously been imported but that the Telegraph Subsection chief himself had developed the new equipment, which had no parallel anywhere else in the world.[79] In 1939 the first ultra-high frequency wireless telephone was installed between Niigata and Sado.[80] Police leaders promoted these improvements in order to make police performance more efficient, unified and thorough. They felt a particular need for closer and faster communications among Tokkô police because of the revolutionary nationwide character of many social movements.[81]

Police leaders similarly developed police equipment to deal with large scale movements and the violent methods of communists during the early 1930s. For example, the police used tear gas for the first time in 1930 against a crowd of union workers besieging the Tokyo city electricity bureau. Keishichô Superintendent-General Maruyama Tsurukichi had ordered study and then production of tear gas bombs after reading in a magazine of their effective use against crowds in the United States.[82] That same year 30 000 yen were budgeted for making 50 bulletproof vests, steel helmets and steel shields. The 1932 Tokkô budget included funds for 200 more sets. Police officers used the equipment for the first time in the major arrest of communists in Atami in 1932.[83] Director of the Keihokyoku Matsumoto Manabu dramatised the achievement by taking a vest and helmet to the cabinet meeting where he reported on the arrests.[84]

Besides reforms in recruitment, education, compensation and equipment of police officers, the attempt to raise the level of expertise and talent of the police as a whole involved making branches of the police more specialised in certain tasks. The Tokkô stands out as a prime example of this. The requirement of special skills and knowledge to deal with social thought and movements was presented as the reason for establishing and expanding the Tokkô.[85] Police and Justice Ministry leaders regarded thought crimes as different from and more dangerous than ordinary crimes. Consequently, they put more stress on the preventive tasks of Tokkô officers. This is exemplified in the Tokkô's view of the arrest of primary school teachers in Nagano prefecture in 1933. Most of the teachers had no connection with either the Japanese Communist Party (JCP) or the Communist Youth League, but some of them who were trying to organise a branch of the National Council of Japanese Labour Unions did belong to those communist organisations. Tokkô authorities concluded from this that they had been right in making early arrests. Had they been slow, they were sure, more people would have joined the JCP or Youth League and the teachers' harmful influence on local youth and children would have been 'all the greater'.[86]

The importance placed on the Tokkô's preventive role and the underground activities of many social movements led the Tokkô to develop methods of secret investigation, information gathering, observation and use of informers and spies. Their aim was to 'hear what has no sound and see what has no shape'. Police leaders promoted special Tokkô courses to teach these techniques.[87] The class, hence national and international, nature of social movements and their organisational rather than individual basis became justifications for increased centralisation, expansion of personnel, extension of Tokkô agents abroad and recruitment of persons with foreign language abilities.[88]

Social movements by definition were attempts to put social theories into practice, and their participants included many university students and intellectuals. Consequently, Tokkô officers required greater scholarly and speaking abilities than police officers engaged in other duties, in order to understand the theories of these movements and be able to explain their defects to well-educated and socially respectable thought crime suspects. Persuasive interrogation skills were also emphasised, because *tenkô* rather than imprisonment became the preferred method of control and because police authorities found thought criminals more difficult to handle than ordinary criminals due to their strong convictions.[89] Besides special technical education Tokkô officers therefore had a particular need for general education in national and international social, political and intellectual matters. Most Tokkô officers possessed a middle school education.[90]

Despite the higher educational backgrounds and intellectual abilities of Tokkô officers compared to other police officers, these remained significantly lower than those of the suspects the Tokkô handled. The memoirs of former Tokkô officer Miyashita Hiroshi reveal the feelings of inferiority and resentment that Tokkô officers held towards these suspects. He says that many treated police officers 'like dogs' and were 'intoxicated with revolutionary heroism'. As Miyashita himself admits, Tokkô officers in turn resorted to coercion, long detention and other excessive methods to weaken suspects' spirits when logic failed to persuade them.[91] In addition, the crimes under investigation were crimes of belief, and both Tokkô interrogators and the objects of interrogation thought that they were in the moral right.[92] This moral element further increased the bitterness of the clash between Tokkô officers and suspects.

Studies of police violence and misconduct in other countries suggest that excessive use of force may result when citizens oppose police officers' invocation of authority, as Marxists challenged Tokkô officers. The police subculture's code in any society prohibits an officer from 'backing down', for all police officers are inculcated with a sense of self-importance as personifications of bureaucratic authority. However, possessing discretion over their behaviour and lacking clear standards for behaviour in a myriad of practical situations, they may not always be able to distinguish attacks on their position of authority from attacks on themselves personally. When challenged they may therefore react in a manner that is more a fulfilment of personal needs than a disinterested enforcement of law.[93] These general factors in police behaviour appear clearly in Miyashita's recollections of Tokkô officers' reactions towards suspects displaying arrogance derived from both strong revolutionary convictions and elite status.

Besides raising police expertise the specialisation of functions within the police helped to create a police aristocracy in the Tokkô. Police leaders believed that police tasks in general had become too complicated for ordinary people to perform but felt this to be particularly true for thought police work, which required special knowledge and skills.[94] Their attempts to develop the professional qualities of social responsibility and corporateness bolstered Tokkô elitism even further. Adoption of the activist interpretation of the police purpose characterised these efforts. The activists did not monopolise official views; the debate continued to be presented as an ongoing controversy.[95] However, with the growth of social movements and the government's fear of them, officials tended to espouse an expanded social and cultural role for the police. They put greater stress on police officers as leaders, not just protectors of the people. Since the Tokkô was the branch most directly responsible for controlling social movements, it benefited most from these developments.

Books and instructions for police officers concerning the Tokkô and social movements insisted that guidance of thought and social movements into the proper channels was as important as suppression of 'radical and illegal' movements and thought. It was to be pursued if the degree of commitment of the person involved left open the possiblity of guidance or conversion. The expansion of a guiding role for the police into intellectual and cultural areas conformed with police leaders' explanations of the origins of social movements. They traced the emergence of social problems in Japan and other countries to economic and social evils accompanying the development of capitalism, industrialisation and cultural development, especially the rise of individualism and liberalism. The police defined social movements as movements seeking emancipation of a class deprived of a decent life in the existing society, which pointed out the undesirable features of present society and proposed a new ideal society. Police leaders regarded them as inevitable products of social development, indicative of national progress and desirable for future social advances. Not all such movements were considered intrinsically dangerous. Therefore, the Tokkô's appointed task lay in guiding the direction of social movements so that society would advance without disturbances of social peace and order.[96]

In the eyes of police leaders, the nature of thought crimes differed from that of ordinary crimes. Society bore a greater share of the blame for thought crimes than ordinary crimes. Consequently, thought criminals had to receive special treatment. Through a policy of guidance police leaders hoped in particular to win the trust of youth and students. Moreover, they believed that thought must be controlled by thought. Suppression by police power, while necessary to prevent disturbances of social peace and order, could not alone effectively control thought. Tokkô officers were instructed to aim at prevention, not suppression. Thought was something to be guided or redirected into the proper channels without using force, while the government took measures to remove the sources of thought problems by rectifying the capitalist system.[97] Conciliation, cooperation and harmony were simultaneously supposed to be the Tokkô's methods and aims.[98]

During the 1930s the Tokkô therefore moved into more areas of ordinary administrative functions touching daily social life. Its new role in arbitrating tenant farmer disputes with landlords exemplifies this. The Tokkô had been involved with surveillance and control of the tenant farmers' movement since the early 1920s, but during the

1930s it emphasised prevention of disputes rather than forcible control alone. The 1934 Tenant Farmers Arbitration Law set up arbitration committees, but these functioned only after a dispute had arisen. The Tokkô tried to remove causes of disputes and to mediate disagreements before a dispute erupted. Beginning in 1935 in Aomori prefecture, for example, a Tokkô officer was assigned in each police station to act as a consultant for rural social problems. In Niigata a prefectural consultative committee for policies regarding rural problems was established, headed by the prefectural police division chief and located in the prefectural Tokkô section's office. Within the committee was a dispute arbitration subcommittee with the Tokkô section chief as its chairman. The organisational relationships set up in these two prefectures were extended by the Home Ministry to fifteen prefectures during the course of 1935.[99]

Similarly, in the area of controlling the labor movement, Home Ministry leaders during the mid 1930s increased emphasis on an active preventive role for the Tokkô. This was reflected in practice by a decline in the per cent of mediated disputes where professional conciliation officers played the role of mediator, paralleled by a striking increase in the percentage mediated by the police from 24 per cent in 1929 to 62 per cent in 1936. The largest increase in police mediated disputes occurred between 1934 and 1935 when the Social Bureau of the Home Ministry instructed the Tokkô to intervene in disputes as soon as possible instead of waiting until a strike broke out. The bureau also encouraged the Tokkô to organise 'labour-management discussion councils' to help prevent disputes. Consequently, the Tokkô did not wait for any formal request for mediation from either labour or management.[100]

Stressing prevention through a spirit of guidance also followed from the belief that the police's use of force differed from the military's in that it should be exceptional and in the minimal degree necessary to secure obedience to the law or to suppress resistance. Police leaders expected that any mistaken use of force would 'naturally' receive criticism. Moreover, they believed that ignoring individual freedoms and employing coercive measures would in themselves destroy the social order that police were charged with protecting.[101] Police actions lacking a spirit of guidance, legality, understanding or rationality would contribute to radicalism and push people towards criminal behaviour. Police therefore showed an awareness that the manner in which the Tokkô sought to control social movements could either aggravate or ameliorate the movements.[102]

Recommendations on the attitude and manner for police officers to adopt aimed to acquire the people's trust and cooperation. This in turn would enable achievement of police goals. A former Tokkô offical noted that the number of police officials in proportion to the population was so small that they could maintain peace only if given the people's cooperation.[103] Police leaders repeated over and over again that police officers must be kind and polite to the people. This was appropriate given that the people were His Majesty's children. Textbooks rebuked police officers who arrogantly and insolently treated good citizens as if they were criminal suspects and used impolite and scornful language. At the same time they warned against becoming intimate with the people or compromising justice.[104] The similarity of these recommendations with those of the 1920s suggests that police practices still fell far short of the ideal.

Stepped-up efforts to develop police spirit and an *esprit de corps* accompanied the expansion of the police's social and cultural role during the 1930s. 'Promotion of police spirit' became the central slogan in police circles, explicitly in response to the national crisis made manifest by the Manchurian Incident and the May 15 Incident. The campaign was repeatedly the chief topic of discussion in police conferences and writings by police leaders.[105] 'Promotion of police spirit' aimed at heightening the sense of importance of the police's mission, often equating its importance for the nation with that of the military and emphasising the risks and self-sacrifice of police service.[106] Police leaders used various triads to sum up the traditional elements of the police spirit, such as '*akaruku, shitashiku, tsuyoku*' (bright, benevolent, strong) and '*kôsei, kiritsu, shinsetsu*' (impartiality, discipline, kindness).[107] A police with all these qualities would be the ideal *tadashii* (correct) police.[108]

At the same time certain high-ranking Home Ministry and police officials, called 'new bureaucrats' by journalists, began to raise the slogan of '*tennô no keisatsu*' (the emperor's police). They added new elements and emphases to the traditional elements of police spirit, for they felt that the current 'time of crisis' necessitated police reforms. They believed that new political conditions, such as the declining popularity of the political parties and rising patriotic fervour since the Manchurian Incident, required changes in the police's role. Blaming liberal individualism and capitalism for poverty and other social problems, they foresaw the coming of a 'new age' when the liberalism of the past would be liquidated and superseded by social control in the interest of all the people rather than isolated individuals. In the past, they observed, the police had been prone to favour the political parties and the propertied over the poor and unpropertied, but now it must reform itself to take on the new social and national tasks of the new age.[109]

The focus on promoting the welfare of the state and people as a whole brought greater emphasis than in the past on the position of police officials as officials of the state and especially of the emperor, as opposed to officials of a locality serving individual, party or other private interests. 'New bureaucrat' police leaders also proclaimed a new role for the police as defender of the *kokutai*, standing in the vanguard of the state, society and the people and exalting and displaying the essence of the *kokutai*. They insisted that a 'deep awareness and self-consciousness of our *kokutai* and nothing else' must become the foundation of police spirit. In contrast to the narrow definition employed by Home Ministry officials at the time of passage of the Peace Preservation Law, they defined the essence of the Japanese *kokutai* broadly as the sum total of the special spiritual and physical characteristics of the Japanese state that had been formed through Japanese history. Among these characteristics they included not only the moral and ethical principles of loyalty and filial piety, but also the special organisational principles and purposes of the state, centred on the eternal unbroken line of imperial rule and the familial relationship between the monarch and the people.[110]

Tokkô officers, even more than other police officers, were required to have both the traditional qualities of the ideal police officer and the new qualities of *tennô no keisatsukan* (the emperor's police officials). Tokkô recruiters sought police officers who showed especially strong national consciousness, zeal for their work and desire to serve the state.[111] The regulations governing the performance of Tokkô duties specifically demanded a hard and unswerving belief in the basic principles of the *kokutai*, and the Home Ministry published an outline of the Tokkô that identified protection of the nation-*kokutai* as its absolutely highest mission.[112] Because Tokkô officers performed special tasks in addition to the routine work of ordinary police officers, police leaders looked for those with strong independent characters and decision-making powers. They also emphasised impartiality, first because the Tokkô's national mission should raise it above political party or class interests, and second because Tokkô officers came into contact with people of all classes and ideological persuasions.[113] Police leaders anticipated criticism of Tokkô officers from all sides no matter what their actions, so they stressed the necessity of indifference to fame and wealth and insensitivity to criticism.[114]

Interviews with former Tokkô officers indicate the successful inculcation of pride in their work and of identification with the nation and the imperial institution. Miyashita Hiroshi, for example, explained that Tokkô officers endured poverty because of satisfaction received from the recognition of and respect for the work they did. He also expressed happiness in carrying out work to protect the nation from violent revolution.[115] The combination of moral righteousness and explicit rejection of criticisms from outsiders would have contributed to the insulation of the Tokkô from external control.

During the 1930s police leaders elevated Tokkô duties to the most important among all police duties. They explained that the current period of national crisis necessitated the promotion of Tokkô knowledge and tasks among all police officers, the 'Tokkô-isation' of the police. The rise of nationalist movements and right wing violence since the Manchurian Incident and London Naval Disarmament Treaty had increased and complicated the Tokkô's duties. Besides expansion of the Tokkô specialist network itself, police leaders therefore urged cooperation of all police officers in Tokkô cases.[116] This response to the national crisis and the emergence of the emperor's police ideology, in addition to the special centralised structure of the Tokkô, its requirements of secrecy and special expertise, and its already well-established national orientation, contributed to the growth of the Tokkô as the 'aristocracy' and 'favourite child' of the police world.[117]

The ideal of the emperor's police gradually replaced that of the people's police in official police rhetoric and became accepted by the police institution as a whole by the late 1930s. However, the shift should not be viewed as the complete rejection of the people's police in favour of an antithetical concept. 'People's police' did not mean that police officials were servants of the people; they emphatically remained state officials. Consequently, there was no fundamental contradiction when people's police proponent, Matsui Shigeru, in 1937 advocated the need for police officials to become protectors of the *kokutai*. Significantly, he reminded police officials that, at the same time that they were His Majesty's police officials, they were also police officials for 90 million people. He also continued to call for a 'bright, benevolent and strong' police.[118]

The acceptance of the emperor's police ideal does, however, represent a shift in emphasis, which is illustrated by the reinterpretation of 'people's police' when the phrase was still used during the 1930s. Instead of indicating police reforms to make police officials conscious of being protectors of the people, it came to mean making the people conscious of themselves as all being police officials in the same sense that all the people were soldiers.[119] These elements of self-vigilance and the importance of duties over rights were present in the 1920s concept of the people's police, but they received much more attention during the 1930s.

Internal divisions

The adoption of the emperor's police ideal raised the sense of high social purpose and status among police officials and contributed to the development of corporateness. However, despite police leaders' efforts to make the police into an organisation that moved as a single body, the police institution did not become completely unified. In part this was because specialisation and the systems of recruitment and promotion encouraged factionalism and sectionalism. These conflicts resulted in considerable inefficiency and undermined reform efforts. The systems of recruitment and promotion also precluded formation of a police profession whose members were recruited according to uniform standards. These internal divisions may help to explain the prewar police's record of legal abuses and generally harsh treatment of the people despite police leaders' efforts to the contrary.

Vertical cleavages followed the structural and organisational divisions of the police represented by branches performing specialised police tasks. The Tokkô especially became separate from other branches of the police. A horizontal cleavage cut across branches, dividing the top leadership group of higher civil servants from the lower level group of patrolmen and middle grade leaders who had worked their way up from patrolman. The division was based on a generalist philosophy of administrative leadership requiring a certain social and educational background for individual success. It became problematic as requirements of technical expertise grew along with the complexity of police tasks.

The development of professionalism fostered an elitist attitude within the Tokkô. Tokkô officers felt a sense of superiority towards other police officers because of their specialised knowledge and skills and highly vaunted national mission. A spiritual sense of corporateness was given concreteness by a special organisation and structure. It was easy for Tokkô officers to feel separate because they were separate from other police branches in their command structure, appointments procedures and distribution of funds. Their particularly centralised and secret manner of operations further reinforced independence and isolation from other police as well as from other Home Ministry officials.

Creation of a specialised Tokkô elite was intended to increase efficiency in thought control, but it sometimes produced the opposite effect. Textbooks and instructions calling for all police officers, not only Tokkô officers, to carry out Tokkô duties represent an attempt to counter the negative effects of overspecialisation and secrecy as well as an expression of police leaders' belief in the top priority of thought control. They reveal that Tokkô officers often did not receive cooperation and assistance from 'ordinary' police officers and that they themselves often failed to offer cooperation by notifying related police stations about their activities. Textbooks also show that intense competition for honours among individual police officers and among police agencies contributed to breakdowns in communications and cooperation.[120] The extent of mistrust of people outside one's section is illustrated by a statement of the first Keishichô Tokkô Division Chief, Abe Genki, when asked whom he consulted in making decisions about the timing and form of arrests, as in the Shinpeitai (Heavenly Soldiers) Incident of 1933.[121] Abe replied that he did not talk with people such as the Home Minister or Director of the Keihokyoku because he feared that they would leak Tokkô secrets. When a problem required discussion with other Home Ministry officials, Abe said, he spoke with the Peace Preservation Section chief because this person was the head of all Tokkô sections in the country, but if he considered the person 'talkative' he refrained in order to prevent leaks.[122]

Competition over spheres of authority within the police was very severe between the Tokkô and criminal affairs police. It began with the outbreak of right wing violence, especially the 1932 assassinations of Prime Minister Inukai Tsuyoshi and two other prominent political and economic figures. The Criminal Affairs Division handled the arrests in the Blood Brotherhood (Ketsumeidan) and May 15 Incidents, for the Tokkô had specialised in control of left wing movements. However, these incidents prompted expansion of the Tokkô to include a subsection in the Keishichô with jurisdiction over right wing movements. Conflicts arose, as the Tokkô began carrying out initial investigative and spying activities while the criminal police insisted on carrying out arrests and interrogation of right wing suspects. The struggle was finally resolved in favour of the Tokkô when the Shinpeitai Incident occurred. After the Tokkô had arrested the coup planners, Tokkô Division Chief Abe obtained Keishichô Superintendent-General Fujinuma Shôhei's approval for the Tokkô to handle the case in its entirety and without any participation of the criminal police in the investigation.[123]

Friction between police agencies sometimes reflected strains that characterised the Japanese bureaucracy as a whole. This was evident in the gap between Tokyo and other prefectural police agencies or between central police headquarters and prefectural departments. It also may be seen in the tendency of the large Tokyo Tokkô to look down on the Tokkô of rural areas. For example, in the arrests of the JCP in 1923, the Keishichô carried out its arrest plans without consultations with other prefectures or the Keihokyoku.[124] In this instance the Keishichô soon realised its mistake, but friction between the Keishichô and Keihokyoku resulting from insufficient communications was never completely eliminated.[125]

Cutting across these vertical lines of agency loyalties and rivalries ran a horizontal divison between top and middle-level police leaders, which corresponded to the overall system of two career ladders for higher (*sônin* rank and above) and lower (*hannin* rank) civil servants. Although some steps were taken during the interwar period towards opening the way to advancement to those who entered the police as patrolmen, the top positions in the police remained closed to those who did not pass the higher civil service examinations, which in practice also meant those who did not possess a university education.

The establishment of an upper civil service with the 'specialised technique' of administration acquired by uniform generalist legal training and verified uniformly by the higher civil service examinations had met the needs of government in the generation after 1885, but it contributed to resentment and inefficiency in the police during the 1920s and 1930s. Meiji leaders were primarily concerned with administrative stability and uniformity to avoid chaos in the execution of the massive legal reforms of the early Meiji period. Consequently, generalist legal training rather than technical expertise became the criterion for recruitment of higher civil servants. Once they entered the civil service they specialised in one administrative area (one ministry); but as in the case of the Home Ministry, this area might encompass a wide range of functions. Yet their advancement did not require acquisition of technical skills or knowledge of a particular locality. The barrier between generalist superiors and technical subordinates became problematic when the multiplication and complication of government tasks in an urban and industrialised Japan made the need for technical expertise greater than the need for uniformity.[126] The lack of trust and inefficiencies resulting from this administrative leadership principle can be seen in the attitudes of top and middle-grade police leaders towards each other.

High-ranking police leaders during the interwar period belonged to the higher civil service elite. Possession of a university education (almost without exception from Tokyo Imperial University) and success on the higher civil service examinations practically guaranteed their futures.[127] Their acceptance into the Home Ministry, which along with the Finance Ministry was the most prestigious and politically powerful civil ministry, attested to their ambition as well as their high performance in school and the examinations.[128] They were often advised and aided by a top bureaucrat whose patronage can usually be traced to some family, hometown or home prefecture connection.[129] A university graduate often entered the Home Ministry as a trainee and, if assigned to a police post, usually began at the rank of inspector or assistant inspector. After about a year he became a police station chief or section chief. Thereafter he was transferred among the various agencies of the Home Ministry so that he received brief experience in its many functions. After five years he generally became a prefectural police chief and around age 40 a governor.[130] Until this time seniority and experience primarily determined his advancement. However, for advancement beyond governor to the highest positions in the ministry, which included bureau chiefs, Home Vice-Minister and Superintendent-General of the Keishichô, personal relationships with superiors and (until the mid 1930s) party affiliation became extremely important.[131] The top police posts of Director of the Keihokyoku and Superintendent-General of the Keishichô, along with Vice-Minister, were the most desirable and politically powerful in the ministry. From 1919 to 1934 and again after 1941, they were 'free appointments', that is, political appointments that changed with each cabinet. Nevertheless, during the period of party cabinets this did not mean that party politicians filled the two posts; rather, party affiliation became more important in the choice among career Home Ministry bureaucrats.[132]

Those who joined the police as patrolmen climbed a separate career ladder, which could reach the rank of superintendent (generally that of police station chiefs and section chiefs) by special appointment instead of by passing the higher civil service examination. However, although the way was open, it was and remained narrow. According to one police leader, it was harder than a primary school student passing through 'examination hell' to enter middle school.[133] Promotion depended on seniority, performance record and success in a series of examinations. Because the last was required no matter how much skill or zeal one displayed in practical duties, the few who advanced beyond patrolman tended to be the most diligent and talented in scholarly studies.[134] Comparison of the average age and average length of service of police officials in the different ranks from patrolman to police division chief indicates that, after initial promotion to police sergeant, the stages of advancement from police sergeant to assistant inspector and from inspector to superintendent were the main weeding-out points. In both cases the average age of holders of the lower rank was higher and their length of service longer than those of the higher rank.[135]

Although a number of top-ranking police leaders recognised the energy and abilities of the few who worked their way up from patrolman to superintendent, they still tended to defend the system of generalist supervisors. Abe, for example, presumed that specially appointed superintendents would have become important people if they had gone to university. Two exceptional ones whom Abe knew while he was Tokkô division chief even became prefectural police chiefs, an assignment normally filled only by successful higher civil service examinees. They were Tokkô Section Chief Môri Moto and Mikame of the Police Affairs Division. However, Abe pointed out that both quit soon after being promoted and theorised that this lack of further success may have been due to a narrow field of vision traceable to their experience being limited to police work. He linked these examples with criticism of the postwar police system in which police leaders specialise in police work throughout their careers.[136] However, this postulation of a narrow field of vision contradicts Abe's previous attribution of a wide field of vision to Môri because Tokkô work required it. The contradiction reveals the extent to which prewar higher civil servants absorbed the generalist ethic and felt suspicious of technical expertise. Rather than a narrow field of vision, it was perhaps the difficulties of coping with the condescension and lack of cooperation of university-educated subordinates in a different agency and different locale that prompted the early retirement of Môri and Mikame. One admirer of police officials like them notes that 'conceited' higher civil servants did not admit their extraordinary accomplishments but rather looked down on them for their lack of education.[137]

Suspicion and lack of trust were not one-sided. Numerous institutionalised manifestations of differences in ranks and status reinforced the arrogance of higher civil servants and aroused the resentment of lower civil servants. For example, there were separate dining rooms and toilets, and a higher civil service trainee would have a larger desk than that of a lower civil service section chief.[138] When Nagaoka Ryûichirô received his first prefectural police chief appointment, his senior patron warned him against telling anyone except the governor any criticisms of his subordinates and against playing *go*, *shogi*, or other amusements with subordinates.[139] Former Tokkô officers who attained superintendent rank only after many years of police experience have criticised the prewar system of generalist administrators. They resented young university graduates entering the Home Ministry and immediately being appointed assistant inspectors or inspectors. They have pointed out that, since these young higher civil servants were transferred every one or two years, they regarded their posts as mere stepping stones to prefectural police chief or governor and therefore did not take their work seriously or develop any practical knowledge.[140]

Because these lower-ranking officials felt that they possessed experience and expertise and bore the real burden of responsibility for policing, they often gave their young and apparently incompetent superiors a difficult time. Abe reports that this was particularly the case in the Keishichô, where there were a number of these older, intelligent and confident officials who had worked their way up to section and subsection chief. It became so notorious as an agency where young higher civil servants encountered difficulties that they felt blessed if they escaped early assignment to the Keishichô. Failure in the Keishichô virtually doomed one's career, especially because the Keishichô attracted the attention of the mass media.[141]

Like the friction between top and middle-level police officials, factional conflicts among top officials stemmed partially from the promotion system, but they also derived from political party preferences and policy differences. The lack of objective criteria for promotion of higher civil servants, other than experience and seniority, encouraged the development of personal ties with superiors and hence personal cliques that would support one's promotion.[142] Such personal associations and loyalties lay behind the formation of the dominant faction in the Keihokyoku during most of the 1920s and 1930s. The faction centred on Izawa Takio, who served as Superintendent-General of the Keishichô from 1914 to 1915 and later, as a member of the House of Peers, was known as the 'wirepuller' of the Minseitô and 'president outside the party'.[143] The faction's members included people who occupied the top police positions and influenced police policy, such as Gotô Fumio, Kawasaki Takukichi, Ishihara Tsunejirô, Maruyama Tsurukichi and Matsumoto Manabu.[144] Gotô attracted Izawa's attention when he served under Izawa in Taiwan.[145] Maruyama similarly came under Izawa's wing by his performance as Tokkô section chief when Izawa was Superintendent-General of the Keishichô. Maruyama, however, originally received the appointment because Kawasaki, an old friend of Izawa's, was Maruyama's senior patron by virtue of their both originating from Hiroshima.[146]

Besides personal ties, this group of officials shared a party preference for the Kenseikai and its expanded successor, the Minseitô, which corresponded to their relatively flexible attitude towards social movements and strong support for universal manhood suffrage and state social policies.[147] During the first half of the 1920s these officials shaped the Home Ministry's position of opposition to the strong suppression policies advocated by the Justice Ministry. They were also opposed from within by a few police officials, such as Kawamura Teishirô. Kawamura's memoirs attest to their predominance in the police at that time. He states that he suffered the ridicule, insults and contempt of these so-called 'men of advanced ideas' for his strong support of the 1922 bill and an increase in Tokkô expenditures.[148] Kawamura's bitterness indicates that, even though it dominated the Keihokyoku during the first half of the 1920s, this faction did not create a sense of cohesion and solidarity in the bureau.

During the 1930s many members of this faction became 'new bureaucrats' and promoters of the emperor's police ideal. Although their core was in the Keihokyoku,[149] the new bureaucrats differed from other bureaucratic groups in their willingness to break down the usual barriers between ministries and between civilian and military agencies by seeking non-Home Ministry cooperation to achieve desired reforms. In particular, Home Ministry new bureaucrats collaborated with Nagata Tetsuzan, the leader of the Control Faction (Tôseiha) in the army, who was assassinated in 1935 while carrying out a purge of the Imperial Way Faction (Kôdôha).[150] According to two former Home Ministry police leaders, as new bureaucrats this group did not arouse the kind of hostility and enmity among the other Home Ministry officials that it had during the early 1920s.[151] However, an official from the Local Affairs Bureau recalls a different picture. According to him the new bureaucrats, centred on the Tokkô, clashed with his department as they vigorously promoted changes.[152] Consequently, during the 1930s there remained differences within the ministry, even though as a whole the Home Ministry, like its subagency the Tokkô, extended its influence into local affairs to an unprecedented degree.[153]

Problems of professionalism

Despite police leaders' constant efforts during the 1920s and 1930s to improve the quality of police officers through better recruitment, training and compensation, they were able to make only limited gains in these areas because the economic depression made budget expansion very difficult. Police leaders remained dissatisfied with police education and were unable to make the police occupation attractive enough to attract men of talent. The high turnover of patrolmen hindered adequate socialisation, which was particularly important in an organisation like the police where rank-and-file members possessed so much discretion.[154] Factionalism and sectionalism also contributed to the failure to realise the professional ideal.

The difficulties encountered by the Japanese police in combining crime-fighting, peace-keeping and social service roles are faced by police forces in all countries, because it is difficult for a single police officer to exhibit the different attitudes and behaviour required for the three roles. Police officers were told to be kind and polite but warned against intimacy, fawning on the public and humouring the people. Finding the proper balance in actual behaviour was difficult.[155] Given the traditional emphasis on a guiding role, it is not surprising that police officers acted arrogantly.

The official definition of the police as an agency of state power (*kenryoku sayô*) that restricted the freedom of the people may also have encouraged ordinary police officers to feel justified in the use of force. This was the very argument made by a police educator in a series of articles in the official journal *Police Studies* in 1936. He argued that use of this definition in all textbooks had led to a misunderstanding of the police mission and spirit and to a gap between the police and the people. New patrolmen came to think that work not requiring use of force was not police work and that their authority to use force made them part of a special class. He warned that, if the narrow legal conception of a *kenryoku* police remained unchanged, police officers' pride in their power would prevent the realisation of good relations with the people even if police leaders emphasised kindness and courtesy.[156]

However, the achievement of professionalism would not necessarily have prevented abuses of authority. Under unstable political conditions certain aspects of professionalisation and the nature of the police role in general, as well as the specific nature of professionalisation and the definition of the police role in prewar Japan, could work against the development of a police that was responsive, if not responsible, to the public. Under stable political conditions, professionalisation may result in better police conduct and efficiency and greater public respect. However, when the police has violent confrontations with the public, as the Tokkô did with leftists, certain aspects of professionalism, specifically expertise and corporateness, may cause it to draw away from the public and resist public control and accountability.[157]

Professionalism in the police means possession of specialised knowledge and skills and detachment from local interests and partisan politics, both of which contribute to corporateness. However, these features can lead to isolation of the police from society.[158] Pride in specialised expertise can lead to immunity from outside criticism. Japanese police leaders did show sensitivity to public criticism, but they also expressed the feeling that police officials would never be appreciated or rewarded no matter what they did.

The hard lot of the police officer was the reason why he must be self-sacrificing and indifferent to wealth and fame.[159] These problems of professionalism were most apparent in the case of the Tokkô, where expertise, sense of high social mission and corporateness were best developed. In particular, the self-image of Tokkô officers as an elite group among His Majesty's police officials and as defenders of the *kokutai* helped to widen the gap between the police and the public. This definition of the Tokkô's role was shaped by the sense of crisis in the late 1920s and 1930s and by conflicts between the police and other institutions.

5

THE EMPEROR'S POLICE IDEOLOGY

'The thought police ... must not be the police of political parties. It must not be the police of local officials or the police leadership. It must have the spirit of His Majesty's police officials even though they are of different ranks and classes, the same spirit as army and navy men have as His Majesty's soldiers.'

Nakagawa Norikata, 1934[1]

The emergence of the emperor's police ideology suggests the importance of relations between the police institution and its external environment. The specific form and timing of the ideology were influenced by conflicts with other institutions, particularly the Justice Ministry and Kenpeitai. At the same time that professionalisation of the police brought about increased specialisation of functions, specifically the growth of the Tokkô, competition increased among institutions over the Tokkô's expanding specialised function. The emperor's police ideology was in part occasioned by these external challenges to police control over Tokkô functions. The conflicts involved policy content as well as limits of authority and therefore show that the 'ruling class' was more complex than the united monolith depicted by postwar critics of the Tokkô and government repression.

While disputes with other institutions provided the stimulus for expressed formulation of the emperor's police ideology, general social and cultural changes lay behind its emergence. As anthropologist Clifford Geertz suggests, ideologies are 'most distinctively, maps of problematic social reality and matrices for the creation of collective conscience'.[2] Ideologies reflect and interpret the social realities of a given historical period. Conflicts over such issues as the proper policy for dealing with social movements and who was to execute that policy showed the penetration of broad intellectual and social trends and developments among the police leadership and other government institutions responsible for police policy making. The contention among these leaders demonstrated the variety of responses generated by the problems of social change during the interwar period. The *tennôsei* ideology of the prewar period therefore emerged neither as a direct linear descendant of Meiji ideology nor as an aberration from Taishô democratic developments.

In addition, ideologies do not only reflect social realities; they, in turn, also shape those realities in a constant dialectical relationship. The emperor's police ideology represented the particular response of the police leadership during the 1930s to social and cultural strain. The shift from a people's police to the emperor's police ideal involved a reorientation towards the state in an attempt to restore social harmony and cultural identity. It also involved an expansion of the role of the Tokkô and the police as a whole in mobilising popular support for both present and future national tasks, including war. This took the interventionist view of the police beyond the ideals and techniques of the seventeenth and eighteenth-century European police state. The enlargement of the police's role in society, particularly the Tokkô's role, therefore contributed to changes in the political realities of prewar Japanese society at the same time as it was a reflection of those realities. The Tokkô's particular relationship with the targets of its control as well as its expanded social and political role also help to explain the breadth and depth of police repression in prewar Japan.

Conflict with the Justice Ministry

There is a close relationship between the police and judiciary in any political system. The courts in a sense approve or disapprove the actions of police in making arrests. However, while standing in a position where they make judgements on the propriety of police behaviour, they at the same time make those judgements largely on information provided by the police. In interwar Japan the courts showed a tendency to support the police by a high rate of convictions, especially in thought crime cases.[3] This was related partly to the traditional aversion to formal court proceedings, and hence a resort to the courts only when guilt appeared quite certain, and partly to the seriousness with which thought crimes were viewed.

Justice Ministry officials' concern with thought crimes led them to challenge the police's traditional monopoly over control of political crimes. During the 1920s conflicts between police and Justice Ministry officials centred first on the necessity, then on the form of more severe peace preservation legislation and later on the application of the Peace Preservation Law. During the 1930s the source of disputes shifted to jurisdictional questions and to who was to control the expanded peace preservation tasks. Such disputes derived from the fact that the spheres of authority between police and Justice Ministry officials were not easily separated in practice. In particular, so-called judicial police officials (as opposed to administrative police officials), who performed primarily post-arrest functions of interrogating and investigating criminal suspects, were placed in the awkward position of having two superiors, who might disagree. The Justice Ministry theoretically gave them operational commands; but because the Home Ministry controlled all matters concerning their appointments, transfers, salaries and promotions, they tended to maintain Home Ministry loyalties.[4]

After the eruption of the rice riots of 1918 and the emergence of numerous social and thought movements, the Home Ministry and Justice Ministry clashed bitterly over the appropriate policy for controlling the new movements, particularly over the necessity of new peace preservation legislation. Examination of the differences between Home and Justice Ministry leaders reveals that the debate centred on means rather than ends. Although they disagreed significantly over methods of control, they shared a fundamental assumption that the new movements must be controlled and that anarchism and communism in particular must be suppressed.

The differing views of Home and Justice Ministry officials on the best methods of controlling social movements derived from their differing views of the origins and nature of those movements. Home Ministry and police leaders were not completely united, but the majority adopted an attitude of relative flexibility towards social movements, more flexible in fact than either the Justice Ministry's attitude or past government positions. Even after passage of the Peace Preservation Law, police leaders differentiated among social movements as to their degree of danger, because they regarded the movements as the 'natural consequence' of 'many contradictions, defects and evils in present society' and as necessary and desirable for the healthy progress of society.[5] In their view the growth of capitalism had created a gap between two classes: the rich and the poor. Workers and farmers had become self-conscious of their poverty and 'inevitably' organised movements to promote their common interests and to try to improve their economic and social positions themselves. These essentially economic movements then became influenced by 'thought movements' advocating class resistance to landlords and capitalists and thus became imbued with a political and class coloration. Police leaders therefore did not blame Marxist theory for creating social movements. Rather, they blamed the evils of the capitalist system and saw socialism as one means of solving social problems, which had come to be adopted by these spontaneous, self-generated movements of workers, tenant farmers and other deprived groups.[6]

In contrast, the Justice Ministry, dominated by the faction headed by Hiranuma Kiichirô[7] and Suzuki Kisaburô,[8] traced the emergence of social movements to the influence of modern ideological currents and the skilful propaganda of radicals aided from abroad. To Justice Ministry officials the widespread acceptance of 'evil thought', by which they meant Anglo-American democratic ideas as well as socialism and communism, revealed a deplorable decline in national spirit.[9] These views grew out of traditional conservative predispositions in response to the left's challenge to the status quo. During the 1930s contemporaries accused Hiranuma and his group of high-ranking bureaucrats of being fascists, but his moral political ideas are more appropriately labelled 'Japanist' or 'idealist right wing', rather than radical nationalist.[10] In fact, Hiranuma criticised the 'new bureaucrats', centred in the Keihokyoku, as European fascist-inspired. In calling for a Shôwa Restoration he meant the revival of the traditional spirit of unity and national service rather than a revolutionary reorganisation of society and national institutions. This opposition to institutional reform and political reorganisation was consistent with his position during the 1920s.[11]

The difference between Justice Ministry and Home Ministry police leaders was not one between conservative absolutists and reform democrats. The liberalism of police leaders showed the influence of the German Younger Historical School and Association for Social Policy among interwar bureaucrats, spread through the teachings of Kanai Noburu and Kuwata Kumazo at Tokyo Imperial University. In particular, the founding of the Conciliation Society in 1919 by the Home Ministry, with Kuwata as a director, demonstrates the penetration of the German social policy approach among Home Ministry bureaucrats.[12] This approach was rooted in the 'ideal of a monarch and a neutral bureaucracy standing above narrow class interests, regulating economic conditions, reconciling opposing social forces, seeking to advance the interersts of the whole by intervening in the economy to protect and integrate the lower classes into the nation'.[13]

In the Japanese context state social policies were regarded as preventive action intended to avoid labour problems, so that Japan could forestall development of an alienated working class bent on pursuing its own narrow interests. Kanai and his students also emphasised thought guidance based on nationalism to prevent the growth of class consciousness.[14] This attitude underlies the expansion of the Tokkô's social and political role during the 1930s as well as the mobilisation of the schools and semi-official popular groups. Social policy linked with thought guidance constituted the means to reintegrate the various social classes, which were becoming increasingly separate. The ultimate end, however, was the welfare of the nation as a whole.[15]

Given these guiding principles, police leaders did not favour severe suppression of all social movements, only those that threatened public peace and order, endangered the *kokutai*, or were conducive to illegal acts. Their fears and repressive actions centred primarily on communism and anarchism during the early 1920s, although they kept vigilant towards all social movements. Moreover, because they held defects in the existing social system responsible for social movements, they believed that police repression alone would not eliminate dangerous thought. They therefore also recommended social policies as the alternative to socialism in order to remove the sources of social problems. They advocated taxation and social projects aimed at protecting the poor and mitigating the acquisition of wealth by a minority.[16]

At the same time they argued that thought must be used to redirect undesirable thought into proper channels, foreseeing terrible consequences if severe repression alone was used to combat radical thought.[17] They went even further to consider reforms in the traditional system of prohibitions on political organisation and expression and on expansion of popular participation in the political processes. For example, they supported changes in the 1900 Public Peace Police Law and Newspaper Law to eliminate ambiguous terms, such as 'subvert the Constitution and laws of the state', that had been used in the past to hinder freedom of speech and publication. They also favoured universal manhood suffrage.[18] While opposing new repressive laws, they did not, however, favour any fundamental changes in police powers, such as the Home Minister's authority to prohibit sale and distribution of publications and to ban organisations.[19] This opposition to a reduction of police powers underlines the fact that repressive police measures against radical movements were still considered necessary as the short term solution to the leftist problem. The social and political reforms that police and other Home Ministry leaders advocated comprised the long term solution.

These attitudes of police and other Home Ministry leaders were evident in their handling of the 1918 rice riots. The Home Minister imposed an absolute ban on newspaper articles about the riots, and the police made many arrests and administrative detentions. However, Home Ministry instructions to local officials adopted the opinion that ideologues and other agitators were not the main source of the violence. Rather, they blamed the sudden rise in the price of rice and hoarding by rice shops for precipitating disturbances involving many 'good' people who simply felt insecure about their lives. They encouraged local officials to show sympathy for these people.[20] Harsh pacification of riots, such as Police Division Chief Fujinuma Shôhei's early request for soldiers to put down the first riots in Kyoto, received vociferous criticism from Home Ministry headquarters.[21] Police leaders later pointed to the generally restrained police handling of the rice riots as a model for behaviour.[22]

The Justice Ministry criticised the police's handling of the rice riots as too passive and advocated strong suppression. Procurators ordered the police to make arrests and stretched interpretation of laws to punish rioters severely with long prison terms.[23] Justice Ministry officials considered the Home Ministry's peace preservation policies vacillating and ineffective, as demonstrated by the outbreak of the rice riots themselves. In order to counter what they perceived as a deterioration in the people's thought, they instituted a policy of harsh punishment, beginning with active application of criminal laws against manifestations of anti-*kokutai* thought.[24] For example, in 1920 Hiranuma visited Prime Minister Hara Kei twice in order to obtain approval for prosecuting an economics professor at Tokyo Imperial University, Morito Tatsuo. The Home and Education Ministers were recommending a lighter punishment. Morito was subsequently found guilty of 'subverting the Constitution and laws of the state' under the Newspaper Law because of his article on Kropotkin's social thought.[25] During the same year procurators prosecuted several other publications that police censors had passed over.[26]

Justice Ministry officials, led by Hiranuma and Suzuki, believed that ideas that might disturb the law and order of the state or destroy the basic social structure could not wait for administrative measures; they must be denounced and immediately cut away. Suzuki's speeches to police and Justice Ministry officials emphasised eradication of evil thought and protection of Japan's unique customs.[27] He and Hiranuma began to discuss the need for new repressive legislation while forming contacts and semi-official organisations with other bureaucrats to discuss ways of eliminating radical thought.[28]

The resulting proposal for the Law to Control Radical Social Movements and its failure in the Diet show the difference between the Justice and Home Ministries over peace preservation policy. In 1920 the Keihokyoku had also begun to investigate foreign laws related to control of radicalism, but it was the Justice Ministry's proposal of an emergency imperial decree that precipitated drafting of the 1922 bill. In 1921 officials had learned that the Comintern had provided Kondô Eizô with funds to establish a communist party in Japan. Worried over these international connections, the Justice Ministry proposed an emergency imperial decree to control radicalism. The Home Minister, however, did not believe that the situation required such urgency and instead recommended proposal of a law.[29] However, it was only after numerous heated debates and negotiations that the two ministries settled on the 1922 bill. Home Ministry officials objected to use of the vague phrase 'subvert the Constitution and laws of the state', as they were opposing its use in the existing Newspaper Law. Nevertheless, this phrase was kept, along with other Justice Ministry proposals. For this reason the Home Ministry showed little enthusiasm for the bill although co-sponsoring it in the Diet.

Justice Ministry officials dominated government responses to questions about the bill and revealed the extent to which the bill embodied their views. In addition to the phrasing, the structure of the bill reflected Justice Ministry opinions. Propagandising subversion as a crime was placed in Article 1 ahead of the provision making organisation of a society, meeting or mass action for that purpose a crime. This resulted from Justice Ministry officials' desire to carry out broad overall control of anti-*kokutai* thought, in contrast to Home Ministry bureaucrats' preference for narrow control of only revolutionary movements.[30] In addition to Home Ministry representatives' silent lack of support for the bill, certain members of the House of Peers, who were former Home Ministry bureaucrats but still very influential in the ministry, openly opposed the bill. In particular, Izawa Takio and Yuasa Kurahei questioned the Justice Ministry's assertion that existing laws were inadequate, criticised the inclusion of vague terms in the draft, and predicted that the law would not stop at controlling anarchism and communism but would hinder freedom of expression as well.[31]

While revealing greater tolerance towards recent thought currents than Justice Ministry officials, Home Ministry opponents of the 1922 bill nevertheless did not disagree fundamentally with the goals of Justice Ministry bureaucrats. In questioning the necessity of a new anti-radical bill with heavy penalties, they were doubting its probable efficacy in preventing and removing the dangers of anarchism, communism and other movements dangerous to the state and society. They were not rejecting the goals of the law. Both Yuasa and Izawa argued that thought rather than repression must be relied on to control thought.[32] 'Controlling thought with thought' became an adage of police leaders in the 1930s and was closely related to the emphasis on a guiding role for the police.

This unity of goals helps to account for the passage of the Peace Preservation Law in 1925, just three years after rejection of the Law to Control Radical Social Movements. Moreover, during those three years several startling events not only intensified Justice Ministry officials' belief in the necessity of a new anti-radical law, but also swung certain Home Ministry and police leaders to this view.[33] The exposure of the Japanese Communist Party (JCP) and arrest of its members in mid 1923, the disorders surrounding the September earthquake, followed rapidly by the Pak Yol treason trial, and especially Nanba Daisuke's attempt to assassinate the prince regent prompted Home Ministry opponents of the 1922 bill and expansion of the Tokkô budget to condemn themselves for lack of police preparedness and to reconsider new legislation.[34] Yet although both the Home and Justice Ministries began to deliberate on drafting a new peace preservation law in the beginning of 1924, many Home Ministry officials, including Vice-Minister Yuasa Kurahei, remained strongly opposed to it until the end of January 1925. Because of this opposition Director of the Keihokyoku Kawasaki Takukichi tried to get the Justice Ministry to sponsor the bill alone.[35] When this proved unsatisfactory, he then worked to draft a proposal eliminating the objectionable phrases of the 1922 bill.

After Home Ministry opinion, except for Yuasa,[36] finally became unified behind a proposal, it then clashed with the still tougher policy embodied in the Justice Ministry's proposal. The two ministries reached agreement only after the Justice Ministry made concessions. Consequently, the bill presented to the Diet in February 1925 was based primarily on the Home Ministry's proposal. The phrases 'attempt to change the *kokutai*' and 'denial of the private property system' represented Home Ministry officials' attempts to limit and clarify the scope of the law, for they replaced traditionally used but vague phrases, such as 'subvert the Constitution and laws of the state' and 'public peace and order'. The bill also represented the narrower Home Ministry, as compared with Justice Ministry, aim of suppressing revolutionary movements centring on the Communist

Party, for it did not make propagandising a crime but focused on acts related to organisation and motives.[38]

The wide application of the Peace Preservation Law in later years shows that the term '*kokutai*' was no more narrow and precise than the objectionable terms of the 1922 bill, but opinions on the law during drafting and Diet debates were largely formed with reference to the previous 1922 bill. Objections to that earlier bill had centred on terminology and methods of control rather than its goals. Consequently, when these were revised in the 1925 bill through Justice Ministry compromises, Home Ministry officials' opposition declined, and the Home and Justice Ministries presented more united support for the bill in the Diet than they had in 1922. Initial Diet opposition seems to have been overcome for the same reason. The House of Representatives committee was receptive to the idea of a new law although questioning its terminology and possible application.

The basic agreement on goals among politicians and bureaucrats becomes apparent in the relatively few objections to use of the term '*kokutai*' in the proposed law. The term '*seitai*' (form of government) aroused far greater controversy and eventually had to be dropped from the bill before presentation to the whole Diet. Opponents showed more concern about the *seitai* clause's being used against movements other than anarchism and communism than about misuse of the *kokutai* clause. They feared its wide interpretation for use against movements to reform the House of Peers and to abolish the Privy Council. They did not express the same fear of wide interpretation regarding the *kokutai* clause, for they did not believe that any Japanese would want to alter the *kokutai*.[39] Since the bill presented the first statutory use of the term '*kokutai*', they asked for clarification of its meaning. However, perhaps because of its newness, Diet members then accepted the narrow legal definition provided by Home and Justice Ministry officials of *kokutai* as the location of sovereignty, which in Japan's case meant the 'eternal unbroken line of emperors'. Home and Justice Ministry officials even claimed that the term had been chosen for its clarity. At the time of passage 'attempting to change the *kokutai*' seemed to be clearer than 'subvert the Constitution and laws of the state'.[40]

This consensus on the need to protect the *kokutai* again becomes visible in the 1928 revision of the Peace Preservation Law. Objections centred on the Tanaka cabinet's use of an emergency imperial decree to carry out the revision and on the death penalty as excessively severe as well as a doubtful deterrent. The Tokyo *Asahi shinbun* also expressed these arguments, but it prefaced its opposition by disclaiming any disagreement with the idea of punishing people who tried to change the *kokutai*.[41] Moreover, criticism was not strong enough to prevent the Diet from accepting the decree as law during its next session.

Therefore, throughout the process of passage and initial revision of the Peace Preservation Law, participants shared a fundamental agreement on goals and a strong identification with the political system revolving around the emperor despite certain serious differences over methods to achieve those goals. Partly because of their greater knowledge of current social and political movements and ideas and partly because of personal beliefs and inclinations favouring increased popular participation in the political processes, the majority of police and other Home Ministry leaders supported a more tolerant policy towards social movements than Justice Ministry leaders. However, this tolerance did not extend to communists, anarchists and other who sought to destroy the imperial system or to upset the social order. Consequently, although police and other Home Ministry leaders succeeded in gaining Justice Ministry support for a more narrowly conceived policy of controlling social movements, the scope of police functions expanded as a result of the Peace Preservation Law's passage and revision. The authority and importance of the Tokkô especially grew.

Ironically, at the same time that the Tokkô's role widened, the police lost its previous monopoly on political control functions as a result of the Justice Ministry's move into thought control. Continuing policy differences over methods of control and jurisdictional clashes emerged during the late 1920s with the first applications of the Peace Preservation Law. Even though they finally supported the Peace Preservation Law after Justice Ministry concessions, police officials showed their preference for small scale arrests and administrative measures rather than large scale arrests and imprisonment and for controlling thought with thought instead of police repression alone.

This difference was evident in the Kyoto Gakuren case, the first application of the Peace Preservation Law. Although Kawasaki Takukichi had actively worked for Home Ministry support of the Peace Preservation Law, as Director of the Keihokyoku and then Home Vice-Minister, his general policy towards social movements emphasised tight secret surveillance, and arrest if necessary, of their key figures but not of ordinary members. Therefore, when in late 1925 the Kyoto and Osaka Tokkô sections obtained what they thought were Communist Party-instigated pamphlets at Doshisha University and asked the Keihokyoku for instructions, the Keihokyoku directed them to delay arresting the students. Kawasaki's biographers explain that he and Director of the Keihokyoku Matsumura Giichi preferred attempts to convert the students from revolutionary thought in order not to ruin their futures by arrest and imprisonment nor to radicalise the yet unfirmly committed. Kawasaki, Matsumura and Peace Preservation Section Chief Ishihara Tsunejirô decided to make arrests only because the Kyoto District Court procurator insisted it. Then Ishihara was sent to the Justice Ministry to explain that what eradication of the communist movement really required was arrest of its leaders. Ishihara found the procurator extremely uncompromising, although he finally agreed to release the majority of the students from the initial roundup as a public service.[42]

The appointment of Suzuki Kisaburô as Home Minister in the Tanaka Giichi cabinet represented a blow to Home Ministry officials and a victory for the Justice Ministry faction. The appointment of the career Justice Ministry bureaucrat, especially because he was considered a reactionary, provoked shock and resentment among Home Ministry officials.[43] It was highly unusual to appoint someone from outside a ministry to head it. Upper civil servants in general rarely served in more than one ministry.[44] Home Ministry bureaucrats felt even more resentful when Seiyûkai-affiliated Justice Ministry officials were also appointed to the top positions of Home Vice-minister, Director of the Keihokyoku and Peace Preservation Section chief.

These appointments provided Suzuki's faction with the opportunity to end what it considered vacillating policies of Home Ministry bureaucrats. The mass arrests of 15 March 1928 (the March 15 Incident) therefore represent the Justice Ministry's preferred style of suppression. Unlike later arrests of the 1930s, the Chief Procurator of the Tokyo District Court, Shiono Suehiko, commanded planning, execution of arrests and investigation. Only two other procurators and a few police leaders, such as the Tokkô section and subsection chiefs, assisted in the planning, and all police officers who participated in the arrests acted under procuratorial orders. The maintenance of absolute secrecy was also exceptional and appeared strange to Justice Ministry officials of the late 1930s.[45] Suzuki's group probably felt that such secrecy and centralisation were necessary because this was the first large scale organised application of the Peace Preservation Law, but it also could not trust the majority of Home Ministry and police leaders to agree to this departure from past arrest policies. The fact that the pattern of procuratorial command and united procuratorial and police action was not repeated in later thought crime arrests shows that it had been possible only because Justice Ministry bureaucrats occupied the top Home Ministry and police positions.

After the March 15 Incident the Suzuki faction was similarly able to push through the revised Peace Preservation Law with harsher penalities and expansion of the Tokkô. These two measures of intensified suppression issued from high-level political decisions of the Tanaka cabinet. They did not derive from any strong demand from the police officials at the administrative levels of the Home Ministry.[46] Hiranuma and Suzuki also attempted at this time to establish within the Justice Ministry a new police organisation that would be independent of the Home Ministry. Although this was rejected, the nationwide system of thought procurators was established.[47]

The Tanaka cabinet's hard line policy is generally viewed as the irreversible step towards welding a united government policy of thorough suppression.[48] Even though the 'moderates' returned in the succeeding Hamaguchi cabinet, the suppression did not let up for the communists, and it expanded to others as interpretation of the Peace Preservation Law widened during the 1930s. This may be seen as the partial result of further expansion of Justice Ministry officials' power in thought control. Procuratorial control rested on its authority to direct police officers carrying out judicial functions such as post-arrest interrogation and disposition of suspects. Unlike most police officers Tokkô officers performed both judicial and administrative functions. When performing judicial tasks they technically fell under Justice Ministry jurisdiction, although appointed and funded by the Home Ministry. During the 1930s the procuracy expanded its role in thought control and its operational control over the Tokkô. In 1936 the Justice Ministry successfully won Diet approval for establishment of the system for supervision of *tenkôsha*. Procurators as well as police officials, judges and prison officials staffed the Protection and Supervision Examination Commissions attached to each district court.[49] In that same year the Justice Ministry also succeeded in establishing a system of training Tokkô and other judicial police officers in the Procurator's Bureau, and in 1937 procurators began to make rounds of inspection of police stations in their jurisdiction in Ibaraki prefecture.[50]

Nevertheless, continual friction and lack of cooperation is evident in Home and Justice Ministry instructions to police officers regarding their reports and contacts with procurators. Directives frequently called for close contacts and cooperation between the police and procurators and reminded Tokkô officers to inform procurators about thought conditions and arrests.[51] In the May 1934 prefectural governors and police chiefs meeting, the Procurator-General lamented the tendency for police officers to regard judicial police work as less important and prestigious than administrative police work. This had resulted in a dearth of experienced people in the judicial police and the transfer of people out of the judicial police when they were promoted. He also admitted the existence of a barrier between police authorities and procurators in both the execution of duties and their sense of purpose.[52] As late as 1941 a Justice Ministry official complained that police officers were sending only 10 or 20 per cent of their reports to thought procurators.[53] The Home Ministry also refused to share copies of the *Tokkô Monthly Report* with the Justice Ministry.[54]

Procurators' dependence on the Tokkô was necessitated by their relatively small numbers. In September 1938 there were still only nineteen thought bureaus throughout the country, and in late 1941 some remote areas did not have thought procurators. Thought procurators were concentrated in the major cities where communists were most active. Even in Tokyo, however, they numbered only twenty in the district court in 1941.[55] Consequently, they relied on the Tokkô for collecting information. In the small scale arrests that came to typify the suppression of the 1930s, the Tokkô often acted without consultation with thought procurators. This also happened in the smaller cities. For example, in Fukuoka after the arrest of members of the legal Japan Proletarian Party in 1938, Tokkô officers had to explain to the district thought procurators the reason why the suspects were considered violators of the Peace Preservation Law.[56]

Police regulations and textbooks sometimes encouraged bureaucratic sectionalism by emphasising secrecy in police work and the independence of judicial police officers from procurators. In addition to general admonitions about the necessity of secrecy in all police work,[57] Tokkô internal regulations included a specific provision for maintaining extreme secrecy when requested by a chief district procurator to show a name list of persons under surveillance.[58] Police textbooks noted that the judicial police was established as an auxiliary agency to the procurator and that therefore the procurator could theoretically issue orders to judicial police officers and certain actions must formally be made on his authority. However, in practice, they declared, judicial police officers were independent of the procurator. They did not require the command of a procurator to engage in investigation and in principle were the same as administrative police officers.[59] While acting as assistants to the procurator, judicial police officers were instructed to carry out their duties actively, not passively, and to act authoritatively. This meant that they should express their opinions to judicial authorities about past incidents, timing, methods and action in arrests, and future measures and policies.[60] Consequently, the Tokkô was forced to share more and more of its role in thought control with Justice Ministry officials, but it resisted loss of its autonomy.

The emphasis on *tenkô* and the administrative use of the Peace

Preservation Law during the 1930s also gave the Tokkô much discretionary power. The policy of making *tenkô* the objective in application of the Peace Preservation Law originated in the Justice Ministry, beginning around 1930. Although cultural legal traditions supported it, the immediate factor behind the policy was procurators' desire to show more leniency towards members of the student movement. This constitutes a shift from their position during the 1926 Kyoto Gakuren incident.

According to former Tokkô official Miyashita Hiroshi, the first use of the 'prosecution withheld' measure came after a procurator received pressure from the family of Kurokawa Nobuo, grandson of the president of the Japan Mail Steamer, who had been arrested for distributing communist pamphlets. Miyashita recalls sympathy for the many 'innocent, intelligent youths who studied hard' and 'many women from good families' among Peace Preservation Law suspects.[61] So there were many appeals from influential parents and relatives for such leniency.

According to Miyashita, as use of the measure increased, instructions on standards of its use came to Keishichô Tokkô Subsection Chief Môri Moto from the thought procurators' bureau. 'Prosecution withheld' was to be used for university students showing signs of repentance, whether JCP or Youth League members, but not for workers. However, Miyashita says, Tokkô officials sympathised with the workers, who had joined communist organisations with a lower degree of ideological commitment and knowledge than students. Consequently, Môri on his own authority decided to release repentant workers as well.[62]

The January 1933 issue of the *Tokkô Monthly Report* also shows how status and social influence played a key role in bringing about more lenient treatment for thought offenders. These were the reasons given to explain the relatively small number of teachers prosecuted: 29 out of 595 arrested throughout the country.[63] It also shows that Tokkô officers exercised considerable discretionary power in the disposition of cases. Since the number of thought procurators remained relatively small compared to Tokkô officers and since most cases never went on to prosecution, the Tokkô remained in the front line of application of the Peace Preservation Law.

The large discretionary power of individual Tokkô officers helps to explain a somewhat contradictory picture of Tokkô policy and methods during the first half of the 1930s. The Justice Ministry's shift to *tenkô* should have dovetailed with police and other Home Ministry leaders' advocacy of 'controlling thought by thought'. Yet Tokkô historian Ogino Fujio argues that the Tokkô did not wholeheartedly adopted a *tenkô* policy until the latter half of

1934.[64] Justice Ministry officials also complained about Tokkô actions' hindering reintegration of *tenkôsha* into society and wanted greater cooperation from the Tokkô to lower the rate of recidivism among Peace Preservation Law offenders.[65] Directives from the Home Ministry ordering police to 'avoid causing the suspect to be discharged from his position' and not to mistreat suspects during questioning[66] indicate a gap between official policy and daily practice during this period.

An improvement in Tokkô handling of thought offenders during 1934 is suggested by a Home Ministry investigation of *tenkôsha*. First, it revealed a smaller proportion of people refusing to convert compared to 1933. Second, among motives for conversion, family-related ones had increased while those related to 'introspection during confinement' had declined.[67] The latter presumably included physical duress and the threat, if not actuality, of torture. By 1937 a Justice Ministry specialist on thought offenders felt that police treatment had improved.[68] Incidences of Tokkô brutality still occurred, but it appears that a consensus was eventually reached at both lower and higher levels on the undesirability of relying on forcible repression alone.

For the Tokkô this working out of a consensus on methods meant that thought guidance became as important a method of control as arrests.[69] It led to the strong emphasis on preventive tasks and techniques. It did not eliminate friction with the Justice Ministry over jurisdictional matters, such as Tokkô reports and surveillance of *tenkôsha*,[70] but it gave the Tokkô a larger social role than it had played in the early and mid 1920s.

Conflict with the Kenpeitai

At the same time that the police–Justice Ministry consensus on thought control was expanding concepts of the police's social and cultural role, the Kenpeitai was challenging the police's main sphere of authority: its peace preservation role. Until communists began agitating among military personnel, the Kenpeitai did not go beyond its designated auxiliary role in domestic peace preservation; and until the Manchurian Incident, incidents between individual police officers and soldiers did not erupt into major confrontations between civilian and military authorities. During the 1930s, however, numerous conflicts over jurisdiction and institutional autonomy occurred. Although they had the overall result of a contraction of the police's sphere of authority, they also served to strengthen the identification of the police with the nation-state and especially with its symbol the emperor. Specifically, the rivalry with the Kenpeitai precipitated proclamation of the emperor's police ideology.

According to a former Kenpeitai officer, Ôtani Keijirô, the Kenpeitai did not intervene in civilian matters until the 1930s except when requested by a governor to supplement ordinary police power. Then, alarmed by communist agitation, it suppressed communist activities not only inside the army but also outside the army, on the grounds that the JCP's national and international scope endangered domestic peace and security as well as the army. The Kenpeitai increased its surveillance of non-military movements involving workers, farmers, students and intellectuals and began interfering in areas formerly entrusted to the police exclusively.[71] For example, while Abe Genki was Tokkô division chief, the Shibuya Kenpeitai became involved in mediating a labour dispute at a munitions factory, a task that fell under the Tokkô's jurisdiction. The Keishichô did not object, but when the Kenpeitai was unable to obtain a settlement and an Army Ministry officer asked Abe to join Kenpeitai mediation efforts, Abe refused and expressed his outrage at Kenpeitai involvement in a labour dispute. Not only did he point out that labour dispute mediation lay outside the Kenpeitai's jurisdiction, but since both sides usually ended up dissatisfied with the settlement, he also warned that public criticism would hurt the army. Subsequently, the Kenpeitai pulled out of the dispute completely and asked the Tokkô to take over, which it did successfully.[72] In this case police officials could feel smug about the Kenpeitai's eventual acknowledgement of their superior skills, but in general the Kenpeitai's encroachment into the police's jurisdiction was successful.[73] With the shift to wartime conditions in the late 1930s, the Kenpeitai interfered more and more in control of speech, meetings and labour disputes, justifying intervention by the need to control anti-military and anti-war movements.[74]

The police's peace preservation role was also compromised during the 1930s by the army's insistence on its sole authority to judge military personnel. The Kenpeitai at least possessed some legitimate authority to concern itself with civilian matters because it was responsible for maintaining public peace and order. The police, in contrast, had no authority in military matters. Traditionally, it did handle soldiers committing offences outside their barracks, turning over anyone arrested to the Kenpeitai. However, after the Manchurian Incident the army increasingly asserted its institutional autonomy in clashes between police officers and soldiers and made them into issues of army honour.

The Go-Stop Incident of 1933 was the most renowned of such clashes between the police and Kenpeitai over institutional prestige. It began as a trivial encounter between an Osaka traffic patrolman and an off-duty soldier. When the police officer reprimanded the soldier for ignoring a traffic signal, the soldier insolently refused to listen and was forcefully taken to the police box. A scuffle ensued, though stories vary on who struck the first blow. Kenpeitai officers then arrived on the scene in response to a phone call reporting that a policeman was giving a soldier a hard time. Finding the soldier with his uniform in disarray, his lip bleeding slightly, and exchanging hostile looks with the police officers, they took the soldier into custody and accepted his version of the incident. When they reported the incident to the regiment and army division headquarters to which their unit was attached, they described it as a matter concerning the honour of the imperial army and thereby transformed a minor conflict into a major confrontation between civil and military authorities. The division commander's report to the Army Minister expressed anger with the police's use of violence against an unresisting soldier in front of the public. The report was followed by the division commander's formal protest to the Osaka government authorities, demanding an apology. The police retaliated with countercharges. The army asked the chief district procurator to mediate, but negotiations broke down. The dispute stretched out over five months and received nationwide publicity before mediation efforts by the Hyogo prefecture governor finally resolved it. Police officials made apologies for the patrolman's improper actions, and the regiment commander expressed regrets that the soldier's inattention had been the cause.[75]

Intense institutional loyalties had contributed to turning the minor incident into a major conflict. The soldier, perhaps drunk, defied the police officer's warnings and retorted that he would take orders from the Kenpeitai but not from the police.[76] The Kenpeitai's actions also displayed strong institutional loyalties by going to the defence of the soldier and interpreting the affair as an insult to the army as a whole. Although the police initially tried to deal with the incident as a traffic matter, it immediately leaped to the challenge raised by the army's demand for an apology. Director of the Keihokyoku Matsumoto Manabu regarded the demand as perverse and insisted that the police must not surrender to the military.[77] He and other police leaders saw the army's actions as an attempt to place itself totally outside police authority. They viewed the outcome as a draw and expressed satisfaction with Osaka police leaders' protection of police prestige from military attacks.[78]

The conflict became especially serious because each side defended its authority and status on the basis of one of the imperial prerogatives. This reveals the extent to which imperial prerogatives had become institutionalised by the 1930s and the divisive effects of this institutionalisation.[79] The army had traditionally possessed pride in its special position as His Majesty's personal instrument. This was based on Article 11 of the Meiji Constitution declaring the emperor supreme commander of the army and navy and was institutionalised in the autonomous general staff system and the military's right to appeal directly to the throne. The 'prerogative of supreme command' was of particular concern to military personnel in 1933 because it had recently been made a major issue in the attempt of navy general staff officers to prevent ratification of the London Naval Disarmament Treaty.[80] The Kenpeitai's actions in the Go-Stop Incident accorded with general trends towards military assertiveness in politics. It is not surprising that on arrival at the police box the Kenpeitai officers demanded to know, 'What are you doing to an Imperial Army soldier?'[81] and then reported the incident as one involving the honour of the imperial army and, by extension, of the emperor himself. The army took the position that the police had damaged respect for the army uniform and caused a loss of prestige for His Majesty's soldiers.

The police responded to the army's appeals to the imperial symbol with an appeal of their own. In a postwar interview Matsumoto took credit for creating the phrase 'His Majesty's police officials' in order to counter army claims about 'His Majesty's soldiers'.[82] Adoption of this slogan heralded the emergence of the emperor's police ideology. This involved not only increased emphasis on police spirit in general, but also a deliberate effort to strengthen the national identification of the police, which was one reason for the growing prominence of the Tokkô at that time. Even at the peak of promotion of a people's police, police leaders had not abandoned the fundamental conception of the police as an institution of the state and especially the emperor. Consequently, the association of police officials with the emperor was not new, but the sloganeering was. The new phrase therefore indicated the amplified legitimising function served by the imperial symbol during the 1930s, when the plural political elites competed fiercely to fill the power vacuum created by the passing of the *genrô* generation of elder statesmen and the weaknesses of the established political parties.

The Go-Stop Incident and adoption of the slogan of 'His Majesty's police officials' strengthened the vertical integration of police officials with the nation, but this came at the expense of hindering development of horizontal relationships between the police and the people. The Go-Stop Incident alone did not have this effect, of course. It was the broader trend towards emphasising the position of police officials as officials of the emperor that contributed to the decline in emphasis on the police as officials of (or for) the people. However, conflicts with the Kenpeitai and police leaders' attitudes and actions in these conflicts encouraged police officials to think more of preserving their pride as His Majesty's police officials than of developing consciousness of belonging to a people's police. The Go-Stop Incident was the most well-known, but many other smaller incidents arose where army authorities demanded apologies from the police for alleged mistreatment or disrespect shown to a soldier. In one case Superintendent-General of the Keishichô Fujinuma Shôhei asked Tokyo Kenpeitai Commander Mochinaga Asaharu if the regiment commander would apologise to him if a similar incident occurred involving the army in reverse. Fujinuma reports that Mochinaga replied haughtily, 'We are the right-hand men of His Majesty and would not apologise'. Fujinuma then declared that he would not apologise either if a similar incident happened again.[83]

The immunity of military personnel from arrest by the police also became an obstacle to achieving the police's task of peace preservation, because military officers participated in right wing coup and assassination attempts, which were the chief threats to peace and order after the communist movement had been annihilated. Police leaders on the whole wanted to repress right wing violence because of a sense of professional responsibility, if not political beliefs or personal ties. For example, Superintendent-General of the Keishichô Maruyama Tsurukichi strongly criticised the Kenpeitai for protecting participants in the May 15 Incident. The new bureaucrats also were opposed to violent revolution as the means for changing the existing system, as borne out by their connections with the Tôseiha. Karasawa Toshiki claims that, while he was Director of the Keihokyoku, the extreme left had almost disappeared, so the Tokkô directed all its power to checking the extreme right but lacked the means to cope with movements including military personnel.[84]

Since the police adopted a strict hands-off policy towards military personnel, the burden of control fell on the Kenpeitai. Police officers limited their activities to prior detection where military people were involved, informing military authorities when they discovered military involvement in plots.[85] This policy resulted from both military pressure and police leaders' assessment of police capabilities. For some time police leaders debated whether or not to arm the police with machine guns, but they finally decided that, if the army took part in a rightist action, the police could not stop it even with machine guns.[86]

The Keishichô's official position during the 26 February 1936 rebellion provides a good illustration of this policy and shows how small a role the police came to play in domestic peace preservation once members of the military became involved in threats to public order. Before the rebellion Keishichô leaders sensed that an uprising was imminent, especially after the rebels had conducted a practice attack on the Keishichô. Tokkô Division Chief Abe Genki recalled that the Tokkô actively conducted surveillance and other secret inquiries but could not obtain an accurate report about the date set for the uprising.[87] In any case, according to the official history of the Keishichô, the police absolutely could not interfere with the military at that time except to send warnings to the Kenpeitai.[88] Keishichô division chiefs discussed arming the Special Defence Corps (Tokubetsu Keibitai) with machine guns. but Abe opposed it for fear that a police confrontation with the army might spread throughout the country. This same argument decided the Keishichô's policy once the rebellion broke out. Division and section chiefs met and agreed that pacification of the rebels would be left strictly to the military while the police would take responsibility for maintaining peace among civilians. One group, led by Tokkô Section Chief Môri Moto, felt responsible for not being able to prevent the uprising and disgraced by the rebels' occupation of Keishichô headquarters. Môri offered to lead a death corps of 300 men to recapture it, but first Abe and then Superintendent-General of the Keishichô Oguri Kazuo rejected the idea on the grounds that such an action would escalate into national disorder.[89] Môri's offer shows that police morale and police loyalty were strong in the mid 1930s despite military incursions on its sphere of authority. Nevertheless, the outsider's role played by the police in pacifying the rebellion paralleled the role played by civilians in general during the revolt and indicates the increased extent to which the military had become involved in domestic politics by 1936.

During the 1930s the Tokkô therefore suffered the progressive limitation of its actual sphere of operations due to the intrusion of the Justice Ministry and the army. It was no longer the central agency in the control of thought and social movements. At the same time, however, the conflicts with the Justice Ministry and the Kenpeitai served to expand the police's social and cultural role and to elevate its significance for the state and society. The Tokkô in particular was instructed to guide or redirect the people's thought into proper channels and to work actively for the welfare of the state and people as a whole. Its methods were by no means limited to negative repression, and its mission came to be valued as the most important and noble of police duties for the future of the state.

The emergence of the new bureaucrats in top police positions gave further impetus to the redefinition and enlargement of the police's role and to the exaltation of its national mission. They argued that the national crisis required police and other government officials, as His Majesty's officials, to work actively for improvement of the state and the collective welfare of the people, not merely to follow the orders of their superiors.[90] On the one hand, they therefore promoted expansion of an active social and cultural role for the police, such as the Tokkô's guidance of thought into proper channels. On the other hand, their emphasis on state and imperial service was intended to end police involvement in partisan politics, especially its interference in elections. Their efforts to establish police impartiality in politics included abolition of the higher police (the branch responsible for election control) and the free appointment system for the posts of Director of the Keihokyoku and Superintendent-General of the Keishichô. Particular attention was given to maintaining the Tokkô's impartiality and independence from political parties and social classes.[91] These reforms no doubt contributed to the absence of police interference in the 1936 general election. However, by that time the parties no longer had a chance of holding power so the achievement of police impartiality in elections was politically inconsequential. Of greater relevance to the police's role in prewar Japanese society were byproducts of these reform attempts. By stressing service to the state and emperor, rather than one party, faction, class or locality, the new bureaucrats reinforced the national identification of the police and especially the Tokkô. This strengthening of police officials' vertical ties with the emperor and state brought about a weakening of horizontal ties with the people.

Inter- and intra-institutional relationships in this way explain the emergence of the emperor's police ideology during the early and mid 1930s. Conflicts with the Justice Ministry and army contributed to the feeling among police leaders that definition of the police function must be expanded and made to serve more closely the interests of the state, nation and emperor. These developments took place in an atmosphere of national and international crisis. It is this sense of crisis that suggests a broader explanation for the emergence of the emperor's police ideology and the nature of the Tokkô's role in repression during the prewar period.

The origins and functions of the emperor's police ideology

Explanations for the origins and function of ideology fall into three major categories.[92] One emphasises promotion and protection of social and political interests as the motivation for creation of an ideology. A second views ideology as both a symptom and remedy for socio-psychological dislocation. A third approaches ideology as indicating the existence of a challenge to fundamental cultural values. The first approach is least helpful for explaining the emergence and function of the emperor's police ideology in prewar Japan. Viewing ideology as a weapon of individuals or groups that is systematically manipulated in the pursuit of political power roots the emperor's police ideology in the interests of particular social and political groups in prewar Japanese society. However, reducing social action to a mere struggle for power overlooks the role played by ideologies in 'defining (or obscuring) social categories, stabilising (or upsetting) social expectations, maintaining (or undermining) social norms, strengthening (or weakening) social consensus, relieving (or exacerbating) social tensions'.[93]

Consequently, the emperor's police ideology was not formed simply for the conscious pursuit of interest; it was also a symptom of the malintegration of society that appears on the individual level as personal insecurity. The ideology may therefore be explained as a response to psychological strains generated by social disequilibrium. The emergence after the First World War of social and political movements composed of industrial workers, tenant farmers, *eta* (outcastes), consumers and other non-elite groups demanding a greater share in the economic and political processes disturbed existing patterns of social, economic and political relations. The movements were manifestations of socio-political dislocation brought about by industrialisation, urbanisation and social differentiation. Their threat to the legitimacy of the existing social and cultural order became evident when it had to be defended by the Peace Preservation Law and open thought countermeasures. The emperor's police ideology was therefore a symptom of socio-psychological strains. It also functioned as a remedy. It eased the strains by providing a legitimate object of hostility and by uniting and sustaining the morale of threatened social and political groups. At the same time it restored conceptual order to a political world in which the established values and authority were being questioned. Ideology therefore was also a response to cultural strain.

We can understand what Home Ministry and police leaders consciously and unconsciously perceived as under challenge by examining their image of the enemy, the targets of Tokkô control. All social thought and social movements fell under Tokkô control, but police authorities differentiated among them according to the degree of danger they posed. During the early 1920s they judged both anarchism and communism dangerous enough to require repression, but it was the formation of a communist party movement that pushed previously reluctant Home Ministry and police leaders to support new peace preservation legislation. By the late 1920s communism came to be singled out as the most dangerous thought and social movement.

Its violent revolutionary methods obviously made communism an immediate object of police repression. Police leaders did not deny the worth of Marxist theory completely and even praised it for pointing out the defects of capitalism, a necessary activity leading to social progress, but they felt that they could by no means tolerate communist methods of what they considered 'thoughtless destruction'.[94] The methods employed by social democrats, anarchists and various nationalists also shaped the police's policy towards them. Social democrats denied capitalism and hoped to realise socialism as communists did; but because they favoured parliamentarism and legalism, police leaders recommended vigilance and not immediate and complete annihilation as they did for communism.[95] Anarchists' resort to direct action and terrorism elicited prompt police suppression, but their lack of organisation and decline in popularity by the mid 1920s made them the less of a danger than communists in the eyes of the police.[96] The violent methods of nationalist movements brought them to the attention of the Tokkô. Police officials regarded the aims of nationalist movements as compatible with the *kokutai*, although they expressed mixed feelings about the dangers of national socialist attacks on capitalism and disagreed with fascists' denial of the parliamentary system. What police leaders could not condone, however, was nationalists' disturbances of the peace by direct action and terrorism.[97] Consequently, while their basic sympathetic attitude towards right wing movements remained unchanged during the 1930s, in practice the Tokkô stepped up its surveillance of such groups, expanded its organisations dealing with them and pressed for new legislation to control their actions. The Tokkô never denied their very right of existence, however, as it did with communist organisations, nor did it try to repress the 'thought' behind them.[98]

As suggested by Tokkô attitudes towards right wing movements, revolutionary methods were not the most important consideration for measuring the dangerousness of social movements. They did not give the danger of communism its distinctive characteristics. Means did not constitute a factor for establishing crimes under the Peace Preservation Law; and even when communists employed legal methods and organisations, police leaders responded with appeals for all the more thorough efforts aimed at their eradication.[99] Any individuals or groups associated with communism were drawn into the scope of Tokkô repression. For example, the Communist Party's various front organisations, such as the National Labour Unions Council of Japan (Nihon Rôdô Kumiai Zenkoku Kyôgikai) and the proletarian cultural movement, came under police attack during the early 1930s.[100] In contrast, police supported nationalistic 'sound trade unions' such as the social democratic Sôdômei (Japan General Federation of Labour) and Congress of Japanese Labour Unions, participating regularly in a series of regional 'industrial cooperation conferences' sponsored by those unions in 1933 and 1934. Tokkô officers took pride in their ability to distinguish between cooperative trade unionists and dangerous communists.[101]

The Tokkô paid close attention to the labour, rural relief and *suihei* (social equality for *eta*) movements for fear of 'radicalisation' and communisation. While accepting strikes as legal and inevitable, they would not permit labour disputes to become 'rehearsals for the revolution'.[102] In the late 1930s certain non-communist individuals and academic groups, such as the Rônôha, lost their legality because they associated themselves with the communists by joining the Popular Front movement.[103]

The perception of extraordinary menace, which belied the party's small numbers, derived less from the communist movement's methods than from its multiple threat to the existing patterns of interests, power, social organisation and relationships, and values. The threat to interests and socio-political relationships is indicated by the points of the Communist Party program that police leaders labelled the most dangerous: abolition of the imperial system, confiscation without compensation of land, destruction of the private property system and institution of communism, abolition of the Diet and establishment of a worker–farmer dictatorship.[104] These presented a direct attack on the predominant economic, social and political groups in interwar Japan, which included the capitalists, landlords, aristocrats and educated elite dominating the parties, bureaucracy and military.

Contrary to certain Marxist interpretations of interwar developments, however, the government's response to the communists' threat was not simply a defence of capitalist interests.[105] Even in the early 1920s police authorities had acknowledged defects in society brought about by the advance of capitalism and industrialisation and praised socialism for pointing out these weaknesses. During discussion of the Peace Preservation Law bill, all those involved agreed that an attempt to destroy the private property system was a lesser crime than an attempt to change the *kokutai*. Interpellators in both houses questioned government spokesmen as to why the punishment was the same for both crimes, since, they said, attempting to change the *kokutai* was clearly a worse crime.[106] Nakamura Keijirô introduced an amendment that would have meted out heavier punishment for *kokutai*-related crimes. He argued that punishment should be differentiated because the *kokutai* was absolutely inviolable whereas the private property system was not and could be changed by legal means.[107]

Successive revisions of the Peace Preservation Law suggest the declining importance attached to protection of the private property system. The 1928 revision separated the crimes of denying the private property system and of attempting to change the *kokutai* and did not make penalties for the former as heavy as penalties for the latter. According to a model answer for a question appearing on police examinations, changing the *kokutai* was certainly impermissible, so that extreme punishment was appropriate, but acts attempting to change or deny the private property system, 'which is known to have evils', by moderate means were to be permitted and even supported.[108] The 1941 revision dropped the private property-related crimes altogether from the law.

While the desire to defend capitalism appears to have waned, the perceived need to defend the *kokutai* and the cluster of values that it represented became acute. From an external perspective it can be seen that the communists' advocacy of abolition of the imperial system struck not only at the political structures and practices of the state, but also at the moral principles and spiritual purposes that the Japanese considered unique to themselves as a nation and a people. The emperor made up the core of the *kokutai* and was intimately linked with Japan's distinctive mystical, historical and emotional qualities. The emphasis on social harmony and unity in the emperor's police ideology implied social disruption, but the vague mystical terms in which the communist threat was described indicate as well the crisis in national values. The police's response, although disproportionate to the political threat posed by the Communist Party, is nonetheless comprehensible in view of the ideological and cultural threat posed by communist doctrine.

Police depictions of the communist enemy exhibited many similarities to American nativists' images of their Masonic, Catholic and Mormon enemies during the second quarter of the nineteenth century, an example of the 'paranoid style of politics' that Richard Hofstadter has used to describe a recurrent mode of expression in American public life.[109] The 'paranoid disposition is mobilised chiefly by social conflicts that involve ultimate spheres of values and that bring fundamental fears and hatreds, rather than negotiable interests, into political action'.[110] American nativists perceived their enemies as a threat to American ideals and the American way of life. Exposure of subversion served as a means of promoting unity, clarifying national values and providing a sense of high moral sanction and righteousness. Emphasising the falsity of the enemy's claims helped to establish the legitimacy and just authority of American institutions during a period of bewildering social change.[111] The emperor's police ideology similarly helped to bolster the Japanese police against the communist challenge to its identity and legitimacy. However, while exposing the enemy, American nativists, like Japanese police officials, simultaneously sought to win converts among the rank-and-file members of the enemy camp. Since their foes were distinguished not ethnically nor racially but by their intellectual and emotional loyalty, no physical barrier stood in the way of apostasy.[112] For the same reason, those who renounced Marxism and the communist movement in Japan could be readmitted to social acceptability. The enemy was what existed in the mind, not the particular social or economic ends being sought by communists.

The Japanese police similarly portrayed communism as an inverted image of Japanese ideals as well as a threat to the established political and socio-economic system. Its internationalism and support for Japan's historical and current enemy, the Soviet Union, showed its lack of patriotism—hence police officials' epithet 'Red traitors'.[113] Its 'classism' was anathema to a value system extolling cooperation and a harmonious family state. Police leaders did not deny the existence of classes or of class exploitation in the past. However, they did deny the inevitability of class struggle and its determining influence on history. As one writer declared, 'cooperation is always the law of life, and competition is always the law of death'.[114] Communism was also viewed as anti-national in its theory of the class state. Police officials found its explanation of the state as class exploitation unacceptable for Japan, though it might apply to Western European countries. Such a view of the state contradicted the ideal of the family state headed by a parental emperor representing no class or other subnational interests.[115]

In addition, communism's advocacy of revolution by 'thoughtless destruction' revealed both its reckless anti-social quality and its lack of realism. In the eyes of the police, revolution itself was uncivilised, for it meant the destruction of existing culture. Moreover, police leaders felt that communists were trying to destroy the existing society without a concrete plan for establishing the new society. They dismissed the vision of communism as no more than an ideal, for they believed that humans are born with differences that made equal work and distribution of production an impossibility.[116]

In projecting their anxieties on communism, the police imitated the enemy in many respects and attributed great strength and intelligence to it. There is a remarkable similarity between the views of social conditions held by communists and police authorities, to the extent that police leaders even adopted Marxist terminology. Both traced the emergence of social movements to the growth of 'class consciousness' among workers and tenant farmers, which they regarded as a natural attempt to remove or correct the evils and 'contradictions' arising from the development of capitalism. Both saw socialism as a means of solving these social problems. However, police leaders opposed socialism for it meant the destruction of capitalism, which they believed formed the basis of Japan's economic organisation despite its present weaknesses. If they destroyed this foundation, they would also destroy the Japanese nation. This was of course unthinkable to them. Consequently, they favoured expanded state actions, including the role of the police, and improved social policies as an alternative to socialism.[117]

While supporting social reforms by the state, police officials simultaneously insisted on eradication of communism and constant vigilance against its revival, for communists were portrayed as extremely clever and skilful in their propaganda and agitation tactics. Police leaders credited the communists with extensive success, as in the early 1930s when they saw the hand of the party reaching in among elementary school teachers. They saw the Comintern policy of a popular front as a tactic even more skilful than earlier ones. Communists' clever use of legal methods and mass movements called forth instructions for devising all the more clever and thorough investigative techniques.[118]

The emergence of the ideology of the emperor's police was therefore a response to social and cultural strain as well as to threats against social and political elites. The communists' advocacy of abolition of the imperial system was particularly dangerous because the emperor symbolised both the existing socio-political structure and existing values. An unbroken line of emperors was simultaneously the equivalent of both the state and the *kokutai*. Therefore, abolition of the imperial system meant changing the state, which in turn meant changing the *kokutai* or vice versa. This inseparability of state and *kokutai* underlies the expansion of Tokkô repression to certain religious groups. Ômotokyô members, for example, were accused of aiming at political and economic, not simply spiritual, reform and of denying the legitimacy of the emperor's right of supreme rule in favour of that of their leader.[119] The emperor's dual symbolism also explains why the police was 'especially fearful in pursuing the least mistakes in conduct in one's attitudes towards the Throne'.[120]

Along with factors discussed in previous chapters, the breadth and profundity of the perceived communist threat and the position of the police in the front line of defence, especially with the ideology of the emperor's police, help to account for the severity and persistence of the suppression of communism and its spread to other groups as the sense of external as well as internal crisis grew during the 1930s. In particular, these two factors help to explain the use of torture and other police abuses, which assumed their worst form against suspects of crimes related to the state and *kokutai*. Police officers learned from textbooks and directives that a thought crime was 'the most evil and anti-social act', endangering both the state and the *kokutai*. Unlike even the worst ordinary crime, murder, it affected millions of people, not just one or several.[121] Police authorities repeatedly called for the 'all-out annihilation' of communism and any other evil thought or illegal radical social movement.[122] When such strong words were put into action, it is not surprising that police officers were sometimes brutal even in the absence of specific directives from their superiors. After all, communists were traitors. Legislation reinforced a feeling of moral righteousness on the part of the Tokkô officer participating in eradication of a terrible enemy. The 1928 revision of the Peace Preservation Law made changing the *kokutai* a capital crime. Even though that sentence was not imposed until 1944, the wickedness of the crime was instilled in the minds of ordinary Tokkô officers.[123]

Changing tactics of the JCP beginning with the election campaign of February 1930 gave the dangerous image of the communists a reality for the ordinary Tokkô officer. The party's central committee approved formation of 'Red self-defence bodies' to oppose 'white terror'. In Tokyo these squads of armed men went into the streets to distribute handbills and hang posters calling for 'armed strikes, arson and the destruction of factories'. They also tried to incite and intimidate workers and to clash openly with the police. According to JCP specialists George Beckmann and Okubo Genji, 'the communists of course invited police retaliation' by coming out into the open.[124] In late February the Osaka police caught several party leaders after a gun battle. Violent incidents multiplied, culminating in the party's call for a worker uprising and an armed march on the Diet on May Day.

Violent tactics continued during the next few years in reaction to the Manchurian Incident, right wing violence and infiltration by police spies. In October 1932 police arrested party members involved in the armed robbery of an Omori bank. Meanwhile, Tokkô officers had been outfitted with bulletproof equipment and used it in the arrest of party leaders at Atami that same month. The more notorious incidents of police brutality occurred during the next few months, including the deaths of Iwata Yoshimichi and Kobayashi Takiji. At the same time as the communist movement was becoming more violent, violence from right wing movements broke out. Violence became common enough for a contemporary foreign journalist to describe Japan as 'government by assassination'.[125] Studies of the police in other countries suggest that, in such times when violence seems endemic, the police often turns to violence as well. Moreover, in an atmosphere of high political tension accompanied by violence, police violence becomes tolerated even if not in-institutionalised.[126]

However, forceful suppression was not the only means of control; guidance of thought into proper channels was equally important. In practice as well as theory, *tenkô* became the police's goal, and thousands of successful cases were achieved without torture. This policy was one that evolved from the 1920s to 1930s. It did not emerge clearly and consistently from the beginning but rather as the result of the resolution of conflicts among groups both within the police and between the police and other institutions. Consequently, for some time there remained a lack of clarity and consensus in thought control policy, which no doubt caused confusion for the ordinary Tokkô officer. However, in the midst of the general atmosphere of crisis and an array of proposals for a solution to the crisis, the imperial structure established by the Meiji Constitution was never questioned, nor was the role of police officials as defenders of that system.

Through the process of defending the imperial system against the communist challenge, the social and political role of the police and Tokkô in particular grew. Based on the German social policy approach, Tokkô officers became increasingly involved in the daily lives of the Japanese people as the preventive aspects of their tasks were emphasised. The Tokkô's pervasiveness of Japanese society went beyond the regulatory aims of the eighteenth-century *Polizeistaat*. Nevertheless, competition with the Justice Ministry and the Kenpeitai curbed its domination of the political system as a whole.

6

THE JAPANESE POLICE STATE

'The Tokkô is *not* a reactionary police like Bismarck's.... *The Tokkô promotes strong points of social movements, corrects weak points and encourages those truly useful to the development of society and the state.* In this sense, the Tokkô is a guiding police.'

Aoki Sadao, 1937[1]

'The aim of safeguarding the security of the people and the state is the only standard for the National Socialist political police ... it is unlimited in the choice of its measures.'

H. Schlierbach, 1938[2]

'We can achieve nothing unless we use terror.'

V. I. Lenin, 1918[3]

The interwar period witnessed notable, if not revolutionary, changes in the role of the Tokkô in Japanese politics and society. During the early 1920s and even at the time of passage of the Peace Preservation Law, the Tokkô was but one element in the police system, assigned the tasks of detecting, keeping watch and, if necessary, arresting those whose actions threatened the existing social and political order. Taking a relatively tolerant view of emerging social movements, Tokkô leaders concentrated harsh suppressive measures on the radical left wing. A people's police ideal dominated police rhetoric. By the middle of the 1930s, however, the Tokkô had become the ideological core and elite of the police system, and its tasks had grown to include labour and agricultural dispute arbitration, the supervision of Marxist converts, and other social and cultural activities designed to prevent as well as curtail the harmful effects of 'dangerous thought' on the social and political order. Victims of Tokkô repression were no longer limited to members of communist and other radical socialist organisations; they also included liberal intellectuals, students and members of right wing and religious organisations. 'The emperor's police' replaced 'the people's police' as the prevailing slogan, and 'protection of the *kokutai*' became the highest mission of all police officers, not just the Tokkô.

These changes derived in part from the historical and legal legacies of the police institution, background factors that continued to shape police leaders' responses to changing social and political conditions during the 1920s and 1930s. In addition, a series of immediate factors arising from a complex interaction of the police with its social-political-cultural environment affected repression policies and the definition as well as actual scope of the police's role. Historical tradition, the legal environment, problems of professional role definition and competition with other agencies determined the role of the police in the prewar Japanese political system. They also provide a framework for analysis of other police and the roles they play in their respective political systems. Comparative analysis in turn contributes to a final assessment of the Japanese police and its social and political role.

Comparison of the Tokkô with the political police of Nazi Germany and Stalinist Russia provides a particularly useful means of understanding the nature of the interwar Japanese police system. Assessment of claims by critics of prewar Japanese society that Japan was 'totalitarian' or 'fascist' in fact requires such an explicit comparison. In addition to these general interpretive points, the international perspective offers another angle from which to view the position of the Tokkô in the police institution and its relationship to other institutions in the political structure. In particular, it helps to delineate the role of police terror in the prewar Japanese state.

The domestic context of the Japanese police state

In the case of the Japanese police, historical traditions provided especially strong models for attitudes and behaviour because its organisation and functions had not altered fundamentally since the Meiji period. Structurally, the Japanese police remained centralised, with the Tokkô representing the most extensive development of this element in the tradition in both ideal and practice. The choice of a centralised police system reflected the Meiji founders' concerns with preventing disintegration of the new central authority. A centralised police system was intended to contribute to political integration in general. Later police leaders worked for ever more centralisation because they believed that it would increase efficiency and ensure the use of police power for national goals.

American intelligence and Occupation officials viewed this centralised structure as a major obstacle to democracy and consequently considered decentralisation an urgent and necessary reform. MacArthur concluded, perhaps accurately, that 'the dominant character' of modern totalitarian dictatorships is a strongly centralised police bureaucracy headed by a chief executive official beyond popular control.[4] There does seem to be a rough historical correlation between a centralised police system and an authoritarian political system. At least, governments tend to resort to a centralised police system to end civil disorder and strengthen central authority. The British, for example, departed from their usual police practices and principles of decentralisation to deal with disorder in Ireland during the nineteenth century.[5] More recently, certain American police administrators recommended consolidation and centralisation of police forces as a means of rectifying defects made apparent in their handling of civil discord and strife during the 1960s.[6]

However, centralisation does not necessarily ensure efficiency. Centralised bureaucratic hierarchies may develop autonomously and in competition with one another. In prewar Japan bureaucratic sectionalism became evident in the rivalry between the Tokkô and other branches of the police and between the military and civil police during the 1930s. Rather than increasing efficiency, competition frequently resulted in breakdowns in communications among police agencies. The police system in Nazi Germany became even more centralised than in Japan; in 1936 the police agencies of both the state and party were brought together under one person: Heinrich Himmler. Nevertheless, this did not eliminate the confusion of overlapping jurisdictions among them.[7]

Centralisation does not automatically lead to totalitarianism nor decentralisation to democracy, but the question of whether a police system is centralised or decentralised provides an avenue to understanding the purposes of a given police institution. Furthermore, a centralised organisation is more easily brought under the control of a single individual or small group of individuals than a decentralised one. System-wide reforms for whatever purpose could be planned and implemented in the interwar Japanese police to an extent impossible even to contemplate in a decentralised police system such as the American one.

In addition to continuity in organisation, there was continuity in the conception of the functions that Japanese leaders expected the police to carry out. From the early Meiji period the police was associated with modern techniques and entrusted with authority to enforce the government's policies of economic modernisation as well as political centralisation. Like its centralised structure, the delegation of extensive tasks and powers to an administrative police followed continental European rather than Anglo-American models. It gave the Japanese police a much larger social and political role than that of the British or American police. In Japan police responsibilities went far beyond crime prevention and detection and the maintenance of peace and order. The open assignment of political functions also derived from French and German models, as indicated in the borrowing of the name 'higher police' for the political police, but it had precedents in the Tokugawa police system as well.

All countries have a political police. What is significant for the nature of a political system is whether or not it is publicly and legally affirmed. Where a political police is illegal, restriction of civil liberties may still occur, but this is regarded as an abuse of the system. Postwar critics of the Tokkô may be right in their assertion that the source of Tokkô high-handedness and arrogance is to be found in the establishment in the first place of a higher police.[8] A political police is established to stabilise, maintain and strengthen the existing political system and often to protect a particular regime. By definition it must look warily and with hostility on any disagreement or opposition to the government. In prewar Japan exaltation of the task of protecting the state and *kokutai* above other police duties added to Tokkô officers' sense of superiority. The openness of thought control revealed an assumption that an individual's thinking lay within the government's concerns. It showed the lack of separation between public and private spheres that characterised prewar Japanese society.

Hopefully, the abolition of an open legal political police during the Occupation will help to insure against revival of a Tokkô-like organisation in the future, which a number of postwar Japanese have feared.[9] As in the prewar period, the majority of cases of postwar police brutality have occurred against leftists, and many citizens perceive the police as biased towards the right.[10] However, these incidents have been rare (far fewer than in the United States, for example) and highly celebrated as abuses of the system. Certain foreign observers have in fact praised the riot police for their ability to cope with provocative demonstrations without recourse to firearms.[11] Generally exemplary police behaviour in the postwar period, despite continuities in centralised organisation and even personnel from the prewar period, suggests the great importance of role definition and of the designated purpose of the police in the actual operation and conduct of the police in any society.

The third element inherited by the interwar Japanese police was a tradition of service to the state and paternalism towards the people. Service to the state dated back to the Tokugawa period, but with the establishment of a police system based on Western models during the Meiji period it no longer meant simply exploitation of the people on the behalf of a limited ruling class. The 'nursemaid' ideal expounded by Kawaji Toshiyoshi made police officials protectors and teachers of the people as well as political emissaries of the state. It placed them in an intermediary position between the emperor and the people in a hierarchical family state. Consequently, the Meiji legacy regarding ideal police relations with the state and the people was somewhat ambiguous. On the one hand, the paternalism outlined by Kawaji provided the seedbed for growth of the people's police ideal in the 1920s, which was an extension of Kawaji's efforts to improve police–public relations and to direct police activities towards promoting the public welfare. On the other hand, the long history of state service and poor police–public relations was not easily overcome. The adoption of first a people's police ideal in the 1920s and later an emperor's police ideal in the 1930s demonstrates the flexibility of historical traditions as models for attitudes and behaviour. While tracing the historical roots of the interwar police shows strong continuities in the development of the institution, it was specific conditions of the 1920s and 1930s rather than the traditional models themselves that affected the manner and degree to which police officials accepted them.

Among the immediate factors determining police behaviour were the specific laws and ordinances that police officers were responsible for enforcing and that gave them authority for carrying out their tasks. The review of peace preservation laws and general procedural laws shows the wide range of political activities and powers of the interwar Japanese police. Investigation of the police's legal environment involves more than examining the content of legislation and regulations, however. Because police officials had discretion in applying laws, it is also necessary to understand their concepts of and attitudes towards the role of law.

The rule by law ideal, rather than the rule of law ideal, was accepted by 'liberal' constitutional scholars as well as police officials in interwar Japan. It meant that law was viewed as an instrument of administration, which included the police. Law was regarded neither as an immutable standard of justice nor as an absolute limitation on administrative authority. Within the rule by law framework police officials did not contradict themselves when they insisted on both the requirement of law for their actions and the flexibility of laws. As revealed by this view of law, the constitutionalism they supported was premised on the existence of an absolute sovereign authority. Therefore, while introducing the necessity of a legal basis for exercise of police authority, the rule by law ideal intrinsically inhibited the development of responsible administration.

Understanding police officials' self-image and role expectations in addition to their attitudes towards law contributes to an explanation of their behaviour. A clarification of the outlook and ethos that police leaders tried to instil among their subordinates also reveals the social and political role pursued by the police as an institution. The Japanese police, like other twentieth-century police, aspired to be professional. Through their recruitment, training and promotion policies police leaders sought to develop a corporate body of police officials who utilised their specialised expertise on the behalf of society as a whole. During the 1920s and 1930s the Japanese police took strides towards professionalism, as recruitment criteria became more stringent, formal training programs were lengthened and expanded, and modern scientific methods and technology were adopted. Police leaders and educators attempted to arouse a sense of unity and pride in being police officials by stressing the importance of developing police spirit. In response to the mounting sense of national crisis during the early 1930s, these efforts increased, and there was a shift in emphasis in discussions of police relations with the people. Rather than promoting a people's police that emphasised the necessity of police officials' becoming protectors of the people, police leaders concentrated on strengthening police officials' consciousness of serving the emperor and defending the state and *kokutai*. Tokkô duties became elevated above other police duties, the suppression of the communist movement reached the peak of its violence, and the net of police repression spread over non-communist individuals and groups.

Although the increase in police violence during the 1930s is partially explained by inadequate professionalisation, the examination of the role requirements of prewar Japanese police officers suggests that harsh, if not brutal, handling of citizens might have occurred even if professionalism had been achieved. Instructions to ordinary police officers on how to treat imperial subjects concurred with the paternalism of the nursemaid ideal and followed from its premise that police officers were officials of the state, not servants of the people. Police officers were told to be kind and courteous to the people, but not overfriendly or fawning. While guiding and protecting the people, they were not to compromise justice or harm the dignity of the police. They needed, therefore, to use 'common sense'. Putting such instructions into practice was difficult, as is suggested by similar problems encountered by American police departments. A study of New York City police training in the 1960s revealed that police officers had trouble executing the precept to 'be firm but courteous', which they learned at the police academy, and tended to err on the side of firmness. They received the same admonition as Japanese police officers to use their common sense and also found it problematic.[12] Such difficulties are related to the general problem of police role conflicts faced by all police forces. The conflicts stem from the fact that the police role actually combines the multiple roles of peace keeping, crime fighting and social service, which require different and sometimes inconsistent attitudes and behaviour. It is difficult for a single individual to perform all these roles.[13]

Careful training and socialisation help to clarify role expectations and overcome role conflicts, but the occurrence of police brutality at the same time that the police was becoming more professional in prewar Japan suggests that professionalisation does not necessarily ensure community control or more cooperative police–public relations. Professionalisation has positive aspects of increased efficiency and competence through the development of specialised knowledge and skills among police officials and the establishment of higher and more uniform standards for recruitment, training and promotion. In prewar Japan and Vollmer's Berkeley it also meant introduction of an ethic of public service and political impartiality, which upgraded the occupation of policing. However, the processes of rationalisation, centralisation, specialisation and spiritual unification, which contribute to professionalism, may have negative as well as positive implications for police relations with the people. They may reinforce elitism and make police officials unresponsive to suggestions or criticism from outside the profession.[14] The Tokkô became the most professionalised branch of the prewar police. Its members were recruited for their superior talents and expertise, display of police spirit and desire to serve the nation. Its organisation was the most centralised among police branches and kept detached from partisan politics. However, these very features made it an elite insulated from public pressures. Police leaders warned Tokkô officers that their actions would receive criticism from all sides but assured them of the nobility and righteousness of their mission.

This does not mean that the prewar Japanese police became totally immune to outside influence. Relations with other institutions, especially the Justice Ministry and the army, had important consequences for both the definition of the police's role and its actual sphere of operations. The Justice Ministry successfully challenged the Home Ministry's traditional monopoly over control of political and thought movements, while the Kenpeitai gradually stepped out of its traditional auxiliary role in domestic peace preservation and performed tasks among civilians previously carried out solely by the police. The police's competition with the Justice Ministry and the Kenpeitai reflects the more active political role played by bureaucrats and military men during the 1930s. The Kenpeitai's encroachment on the police's sphere of operations corresponded to the ascendance of the army in that larger power struggle.

Although conflicts with the Justice Ministry and the army resulted in a contraction of the police's share of peace preservation and thought control, they at the same time brought about an enlargement of that peace preservation and thought control role. The adoption of *tenkô* and administrative use of the law shifted the emphasis in Tokkô work from arrests and other punitive methods to persuasion and other preventive means. Promotion of an active police role in guiding thought therefore meant an expanded social and cultural role for the police. Conflicts with the Kenpeitai reinforced the tendency for this new activism to be directed towards state interests. In response to the challenge posed by the army during the Go-Stop Incident, police leaders fashioned a new slogan of 'the emperor's police' to go with the vital national mission of defending the *kokutai*.

While conflicts between the police and other institutions over peace preservation policy provided the occasions for redefinition and magnification of the police's social and political role, the broader social and cultural explanation must be sought in the background of national and international crisis. The sense of domestic crisis resulted from economic depression, social dislocation caused by industrialisation and urbanisation, and political uncertainty accompanying the emergence of social movements appealing to the masses and the expansion of the electorate. Police leaders supported universal manhood suffrage and the growth of social movements but sought to prevent the social disorder that might result from them. They favoured peaceful and orderly social and political change, not revolution in either methods or aims. Harsh suppressive actions were directed against communists not only because they threatened established political and social interests and power relationships, but also because they rejected values regarded as unique to the Japanese.

Examination of police leaders' image of their communist enemy suggests that repression policies did not derive simply from capitalist class interests as many Marxist studies have claimed. Although the police regarded the capitalist system as the economic foundation of existing Japanese society, they also saw weaknesses in the system. Their approach to social problems was based in part on this critique of capitalism. Moreover, their commitment to maintaining capitalism came second to preserving the mythic *kokutai*. The existence of serious differences between police and Justice Ministry officials also shows that repression policies were not forged by a united single-minded government. For these reasons Marxist interpretations of prewar Japan as fascist are inadequate explanations of developments in Japanese society and politics.[15]

The Japanese police state in comparative perspective

A comparative approach focused on the political police provides insights into the functioning of the prewar Japanese political system as a whole. From this perspective, prewar Japan bore a closer resemblance to the eighteenth and nineteenth-century police states of Germany, Austria and France than to its twentieth-century contemporaries in Nazi Germany, Mussolini's Italy and Stalinist Russia. Like the German *Polizeistaat*, the prewar Japanese state demonstrated a commitment to rationality and order in administration and society and to use of the state's machinery to mobilise and develop all economic and social resources for the welfare of the nation-state. Its concern for social problems and dedication to protection of the population manifested the paternalism characteristic of the *Polizeistaat*. Like Joseph II of Austria, prewar Japanese leaders left the need to control public opinion as well as political opposition groups and therefore extended the administrative functions of the centralised police force to all aspects of life and its intelligence-surveillance functions to all classes of society. The Tokkô was known for its ubiquitousness through informers, spies and double agents as well as through open surveillance and censorship. Like the French police created by Joseph Fouché, the Japanese police in its thought control activities became the moral guide and arbiter of society as well as its protector and censor. As in the French system, concern with political matters and the 'thought' problem turned the 'higher police' into the core of the police system.

Police states like Nazi Germany or the Soviet Union may emerge when there is 'deliberate, embracing and concerted attempt to subvert the existing institutions and political principles of government' by either a government undertaking to change society or 'an opposition claiming to possess revealed truths'.[16] The Japanese Communist Party (JCP) certainly represented such a challenge, wielding Marxism-Leninism as its body of revealed truths. Subsequently, the Tokkô did expand its numbers, the scope of its role, and the methods and powers at its command. It became dreaded and notorious for its disregard of legal restrictions.

The Tokkô went beyond its eighteenth and nineteenth-century models in its offensive character. Tokkô officers numbered in the thousands rather than the dozens or hundreds in political police forces under enlightened absolutism. Their equipment and technology indicates the more advanced stage of industrialisation Japan had achieved by the 1930s, which along with an expanded state bureaucracy enabled the Tokkô to penetrate Japanese society to a much greater degree than its early modern European models. The Tokkô's role in preventing social discord, re-educating and reintegrating Marxist converts and otherwise mobilising support for the government's policies reflected Japan's position as a latecomer to industrialisation whose leaders could see the political and social effects of industrialisation and post-French Revolution political ideas.

Nevertheless, Japan of the 1930s remained significantly different from the police states of Nazi Germany and Stalinist Russia. This is evident from a comparison of the organisational position and degree of independence of their political police, the police's relationship to law, the purpose of the police, and the scale and purpose of terror. In German historical scholarship the view of a monolithic Nazi state has been modified, as has a similar view of prewar and wartime Japan. Notably, the Schutzstaffel (SS) is now described as a 'complex heterogeneous institution'.[17] Nevertheless, although the SS perhaps did not achieve a state within a state as once portrayed in the 1950s and 1960s, its leader, Heinrich Himmler, did attempt and to a large degree succeeded in establishing an independent structure separate from or superseding the regular government administration, a development that cannot be found in the history of the prewar Japanese police. The Gestapo was the political intelligence branch of the SS, which is frequently compared with the Tokkô by Japanese critics. It emerged under Hermann Göring as a Prussian political police agency with independent executive authority symbolised by its physical separation from the rest of the Prussian police force.[18] In 1936 Hitler recognised it as a special police organisation with jurisdiction over the entire Reich, thus making it the first unified police in German history. Himmler's appointment that same year as Reichsführer SS and Chief of the German Police at the Ministry of the Interior highlights the institutional expansion and unification of the Nazi police. While nominally under the Minister of the Interior, Himmler had access to the Reich cabinet in all police matters, which in 1937 was denied to the Minister cf the Interior.[19] A ministry circular in May also recognised the powers of the Chief of Police as equal to those of the minister. Himmler's fusion of party and state police agencies was replaced by Himmler's assignment to Reinhard Heydrich of the dual command of the Sicherheitsdienst (or SD, which was an SS and Party organisation) and the Security Police (which was a state agency comprised of the Gestapo and Criminal Police).[20]

The Nazi police's independence from the state administration and judiciary derived from the nature of sovereignty and power in the Führer state. It was the Führer rather than the state that embodied national sovereignty, and political power correlated with proximity to the Führer. Consequently, in conflicts over police matters the Reichsführer SS, who was also Chief of Police, had priority over the Minister of the Interior because he was personally and directly subordinate to the Führer. As a direct organ of the Führer the police stood above both state and party. In practice, Hitler bypassed the minister when sending instructions to the SS leader and Chief of Police.[21]

Law similarly derived from the Führer. In the later years of the Third Reich, a command of the Führer came to override all written law to the contrary. The police acted legally not only when in accordance with existing laws and regulations, but also when carrying out the Führer's will. According to Werner Best, the legal expert of the SD, legal rules were unnecessary for police work because Hitler's will 'created law and altered existing law'.[22] Therefore, the courts were incapable of reviewing actions of the Gestapo. Only a complaint to higher authorities within the Gestapo itself offered a means of obtaining redress.[23]

Neither the Gestapo nor the larger SS became omnipotent vis-à-vis the regular courts, but they did make incursions on judicial authority, which Japanese police leaders never advocated. In 1933 an emergency decree 'For the Protection of People and State' empowered the police to place citizens under 'preventive arrest' or 'preventive custody' in a concentration camp. With the Gestapo as the highest authority for issuing preventive arrest warrants, the police became independent of the courts. Chief of the Security Police Reinhard Heydrich instructed the Gestapo in 1937 to use 'preventive arrest' rather than regular police arrest 'so as to avoid the necessity for subsequent examination by the courts of measures taken by the police'.[24] In 1942 the Minister of Justice, Otto Thierack, conceded the Reich Security Main Office (RSHA)[25] the privilege of 'correcting' sentences of the courts by means of Gestapo 'special treatment'. Moreover, persons sentenced by normal courts to more than eight years' imprisonment were thereafter handed over to the police. The Security Police received complete judicial responsibility for Poles and Jews in 'reincorporated Eastern Territories', and the following year all Jews under German sovereignty also came under RSHA jurisdiction.[26]

Hostility and a sense of competition characterised SS relations with the army, especially as the war continued and the SS's military division, the Waffen-SS, expanded and played a larger role in actual combat. In 1941 on the eve of the Soviet invasion, the Waffen-SS numbered 160 000. It took a prominent role in the invasion and from 1942 received the latest equipment available. This distribution of modern weapons represented a reversal of priority vis-à-vis the Wehrmacht. In 1944 the SS took over the Wehrmacht's intelligence service, the Abwehr.[27]

This institutional independence and translegal status corresponded with Nazi police leaders' vision of the police and its purpose. According to Himmler:

'... the powers of the National Socialist police force are directed towards implementing the will of the leaders of the state and the protection of the people and the state; they are therefore necessarily based not upon detailed laws but upon the realities of the National Socialist Führer state and upon the duties allotted to it by the leadership. The powers of the police force cannot therefore be restricted by formal regulations, since such limitations would impede fulfillment of the tasks given to it by the leadership.'[28]

The powers of the police became limitless in the eyes of police leaders 'in order to suppress and avert any disturbance of governmental order in the Third Reich, even though an infringement of law and order may not, or not yet, have taken place'.[29] In contrast to the police of previous eras, the Nazi political police moved from being a defensive organisation to being an offensive one, an omnipotent purifier of the nation's thought. Whereas earlier political police had been satisfied to act when some definite danger could be detected, the Gestapo aimed to catch enemies of the state before even their thinking could undermine the Führer system.[30]

Moreover, police officers were exhorted to take forceful action. Göring, for example, issued the following directive:

'Police officers who make use of firearms in the execution of their duties will, without regard to the consequences of such use, benefit by my protection; those who out of a misplaced regard for such consequences fail in their duty will be punished in accordance with the regulations.... Every official must bear in mind that failure to act will be regarded more seriously than an error due to taking action.'[31]

Police leaders claimed historical necessity to justify harsh suppression. Heydrich, in a 1936 pamphlet, urged severe repressive measures even at the expense of justice:

'To preserve our people, we must be hard on our opponents, even if we run the danger of perchance harming an individual opponent and of possibly being decried as unrestrained ruffians by a few no doubt well-meaning persons. For if, as National Socialists, we do *not* fulfill our historic task because we are too objective and humane, we will nevertheless not be credited with mitigating circumstances. It will simply be said: In the judgment of history, they did not fulfill their task.'[32]

The mass scale of terror under Nazi rule follows from this totalitarian vision of the police with its encouragement of ruthless action. The number of victims is nevertheless overwhelming. Raul Hilberg estimates that the number of Jews murdered in areas under SS control totaled 5 100 000. This included 250 000 in Germany (50 per cent of the Jewish population), 3 000 000 in Poland (90 per cent of the Jewish population) and 900 000 in the Soviet Union (28 per cent of the Jewish population).[33]

The mass scale of terror in Stalinist Russia is as well known as that of Nazi Germany. Forced collectivisation alone sent millions to prison, banishment or forced labour between 1929 and 1933. One official document mentions 800 000 in prison, which would not include those in labour camps or colonies.[34] The party purges of the later 1930s reduced the membership from 3 500 000 in 1933 to 2 000 000 in 1938. Most were liquidated, if the case of the Kiev region is at all representative. There, 54 per cent of the members were arrested and most executed by the end of May 1937.[35] By 1941 'a highly conservative' Western estimate suggests that the forced labour population had reached 3 500 000.[36]

With the camps, terror became institutionalised as a means for the 'development of Communism'. Torture was explicitly permitted and justified as follows by the Party Central Committee in 1937:

'It is known that all bourgeois intelligence services use methods of physical influence against the representatives of the socialist proletariat and that they use them in their most scandalous forms.

The question arises as to why the socialist intelligence service should be more humanitarian against the deadly enemies of the working class and of the collective farm workers. The Party Central Committee considers that physical pressure should still be used obligatorily, as an exception applicable to known and obstinate enemies of the people, as a method both justifiable and appropriate.'[37]

Even before 1937, in fact since its beginnings as the Cheka in 1918, the Soviet police had possessed extra-judicial powers, including the authority to send people to corrective labour camps and to impose the death sentence.

The justification of terror followed from the envisioned purpose of the police under the Soviet regime. Felix Dzerzinsky, head of the Cheka, explained in a press interview that the Cheka stood for organised terror, which was 'an absolute necessity during times of revolution'. Furthermore, he declared that:

'... we terrorize the enemies of the Soviet Government in order to stop crime at its inception .... The Cheka is not a court. The Cheka is the defense of the Revolution as the Red Army is. And just as in the civil war the Red Army cannot stop to ask whether or not it may harm individuals ... the Cheka is obliged to defend the Revolution and conquer the enemy, even if its sword does by chance sometimes fall upon the heads of the innocent.'[38]

Stalin similarly described the State Political Administration (GPU) as:

'... more or less analogous to the Committee of Public Safety set up during the Great French Revolution. It punishes primarily spies, plotters, terrorists, bandits, profiteers and counterfeiters. It is something in the nature of a military-political tribunal set up for the purpose of protecting the interests of the revolution from the counter-revolutionary bourgeoisie and their agents.'[39]

As defender of the revolution the Soviet police could do no wrong, and its activities did not need to be restrained by legal or other considerations. As in Nazi Germany, the requirements of history were invoked when the police were instructed not only that they had enemies to deal with, but also that they must not be squeamish in doing their duty and could ignore all existing laws and regulations, for 'there are stages in the history of man, and in our lives, when the laws are seen to be obsolete, and one must push them aside'.[40]

Though few statistics are available on the Soviet police, especially after the mid 1930s, a list of subordinate departments given in the 1934 decree setting up the the GPU's successor, the People's Commissariat of Internal Affairs (NKVD), shows the wide range of responsibilities delegated to the police: State Security, Worker-Peasant Militia, Border and Internal Guard, Fire Guard, Corrective Labour Camps and Labor Colonisation, Acts of Civil Status, Administrative-Economic Administration. Departments related to forestry, transport, defence and archives were later added. Attached to the NKVD was also a so-called Special Board which, unfettered by the legal codes or other procedural restraints, could sentence 'socially dangerous' persons to exile, deportation and confinement in labor camps. This Special Board became one of Stalin's chief instruments in the party purges of the mid and late 1930s. During that period the political police became elevated above even the Communist Party.[41]

The extensive responsibilities of domestic administration of the Soviet and Nazi police resemble those of the Japanese Home Ministry of which the police was a part. However, the Home Ministry did not represent the culmination of police institutional expansion as did the NKVD or SS of the late 1930s. Although police authorities claimed a larger social and cultural role for the Tokkô and police as a whole during the 1930s, police duties and functions remained essentially the same as those established during the Meiji period. These followed the French model and therefore extended beyond those of the British and American police, but they did not approach the range of those of the Nazi and Soviet police. The Tokkô was elevated but did not achieve domination of the entire police structure or become the sole protective force in society. Notably, the Japanese police never came to administer a system of concentration camps.

In contrast to the Nazi and Soviet police, the Japanese police did not free itself from all legal restraint or judicial control. Police officials continued to show a concern for proper procedures and the limits of the law, even though they often violated them. Although the police made extensive use of its administrative and quasi-judicial powers, it did not neutralise the judiciary by establishing its own judicial institutions. It did not acquire extra-judicial powers except for traditional ones of summary jurisdiction for misdemeanours such as vagrancy. Rather, the police lost some jurisdictional control in the competition with Justice Ministry institutions. Until the mid 1920s the Tokkô had exclusive control over political and thought movements, but after that it gradually had to share control with the thought procurators in the Justice Ministry.

No Japanese leader ever claimed, as Himmler or Stalin did, that the police were above and beyond the law. The rule by law ideal remained operational in that police leaders sought legislative changes to ratify police practices. The revisions of the Peace Preservation Law represent such ratifications of what police considered changing administrative needs and desires. When the emphasis in Tokkô and Justice Ministry officials' treatment of thought criminals shifted to achieving conversions, the Home and Justice Ministries sought both new legislation to establish a supervisory system over converts and a revision of old legislation to legalise preventive detention of confirmed Marxists. The former was achieved in 1936 but the latter not until 1941, which shows that the police did not automatically get its way in the 1930s.

The Japanese police also differed from the SS in its relations with the army, as represented by the Kenpeitai. It did not develop its own paramilitary forces as did the SS. These already existed in the Kenpeitai, but unlike the Waffen-SS the Kenpeitai fell under the Army Ministry. Therefore, when called on to assist the police in civil peace preservation, the Kenpeitai did so as an independent organisation. During the 1930s the Kenpeitai also began to exercise its authority in peace preservation without waiting requests for assistance from the police. Jurisdictional clashes between the police and Kenpeitai became frequent and reverberated to the highest levels of civil and military administration. In particular, the Tokkô was forced to share control of right wing movements with the Kenpeitai because of the involvement of military personnel in those organisations.

The scale of terror and abuses of the law in Japan paralleled the police's comparative limitations in institutional independence and power. There are no estimates of torture victims to be found in either official or unofficial histories of Tokkô repression. However, it is clear that police terror did not reach a mass scale as in Germany or the Soviet Union, since even critical studies of the Tokkô refer only to specific cases and no system of concentration or forced labour camps existed in either prewar or wartime Japan. The difference in scale is significant if analysing the political system as a whole, for it means that in Japan police brutality never became institutionalised and therefore was never officially condoned. In several cases, such as Kobayashi Takiji's, where public allegations of torture were made, police authorities denied the occurrence. Nevertheless, while police brutality was thus left unpunished, it was not justified or encouraged by police leaders as in Germany or the Soviet Union.[42]

Moreover, by 1933 conversions rather than judicial punishment became the object of applying the Peace Preservation Law. This is evident in the increasing number of stays of execution and probationary releases without prosecution. As a result a relatively small percentage of those arrested went to court or to prison.[43] Japanese leaders concerned with political criminals apparently believed that proper guidance and supervision could still turn them into loyal respectable citizens. Torture was used in some cases, but psychological and familial pressure proved to be more common tools for achieving conversions.[44] Tokkô leaders also realised that thought criminals differed from ordinary criminals in the strength of their convictions and their higher educational and social backgrounds. Consequently, they explicitly recruited officers for the Tokkô who had not only demonstrated nationalist zeal but also could speak articulately. Tokkô interrogators were expected to be able to argue persuasively against Marxist theory in order to achieve successful conversions.[45]

The emphasis on *tenkô* suggests a different attitude towards crime and punishment and a different view of the role of ideas from those of the West, which continue to be evident in contemporary Japanese policing and judicial practices.[46] The Japanese attitude towards crime and punishment is based on a belief in the mutability of character. It therefore emphasises rehabilitation and, concomitant to that, an attempt to obtain an offender's repentance for his crime. Concern for the latter sometimes seems to outweigh concern for arriving at a just punishment for the crime, as suggested by the low prosecution rate of thought crime suspects and by Tokkô and thought procurators' preoccupation with *tenkô*. Even Tokkô torture may be partially explained by the traditional necessity to obtain a confession, an acknowledgement of guilt. Underlying the approach to thought criminals was the assumption that ideas or 'thought' possess a palpability and that what goes on in the mind is important for determining actions and hence the state of society. Like the Chinese the Japanese believe that re-education of the mind is possible as well as desirable. This palpability is clear in the way in which Tokkô and other authorities talked about 'thought worsening' and 'controlling thought with thought'.

The differences in scale of terror and attitudes towards the law between Japan on the one hand, and Nazi Germany and Soviet Russia on the other, also derive from differences in the purpose of police terror and repression. As historian George Mosse points out in a discussion of the Nazi police, 'violence against individuals was always possible as an abuse under ordinary police procedure, but violence against masses of the population required basic changes in organisation and purpose'.[47] Although there was a shift in emphasis from a people's police in the 1920s to the emperor's police during the 1930s, this did not constitute a basic changes in either the organisation or purpose of the police. The new bureaucrats aimed at restructuring political institutions, but not by revolutionary means.

Consequently, although police repression increased during the 1930s, it was still used for conservative ends, to preserve the existing social, political and, to some extent, economic system. In contrast, police terror and repression were used and justified as a means of revolution for changing the existing system in Nazi Germany and the Soviet Union. Logically, the Tokkô had fewer possible objects of repression since it was not its prescribed mission to change the fundamental structure of society, for fewer individuals or groups were likely to need elimination or change than under a revolutionary regime.

This difference in police purpose reflects the greater homogeneity and integration of Japanese society compared to German or Russian society. When the Tokkô began expanding in the 1920s, Japan was undergoing social and economic strains, but there remained a consensus on preserving the *kokutai*. Diet opponents of the Peace Preservation Law, for example, never opposed the *kokutai* phrase in principle. As one said, 'no one in Japan would want to destroy the *kokutai*'.[48]

This statement suggests that the prewar Japanese state in its ideology more closely resembled the early modern European police state than its twentieth-century contemporaries and wartime allies. In the police states of enlightened absolutism, the police were intended to impose restraints on the powerful, who were not, however, necessarily regarded as enemies of the state. 'The police and its opponents still shared the greater part of their world in common.'[49] The Tokkô's Marxist opponents may not appear to fit in this category, but the extent to which they did may help to explain the comparatively limited scale of terror. To begin with, although the Tokkô's opponents in the radical left were not powerful politically, they were part of the nation's elite because of their high social and educational backgrounds. Consequently, they were not handled like common criminals. Marxism did not share the same view of the world as the Tokkô. In fact it was potentially very disintegrative, which is a major reason for the harshness of its repression. However, perhaps it was not harsher or carried out on a mass scale because *tenkô* efforts were very successful. The success of *tenkô* in turn indicates that the Tokkô and its opponents did in fact continue to share the greater part of their world in common. This applies even more strongly to the relationship between the Tokkô and less radical opponents of the existing system.

Why did prewar Japan not become a police state like Nazi Germany or the Soviet Union in the face of the communist challenge? One reason lies in the weakness of that challenge. For various reasons the left remained organisationally weak so that it never grew into a potent political force. Its ideas therefore constituted the main threat, and despite the government's fears they lacked mass appeal. The program insisted on by the Comintern attacked key national symbols, such as the emperor, that the vast majority of individuals and groups in Japanese society accepted and supported. Moreover, Marxian socialist theory did not in general seek emancipation of the largest dissatisfied group in prewar Japan: the farmers.

Related to the first reason is the strength of national identification, especially the national symbol of the emperor. Horizontal integration among members of the political system was weak, as exemplified by the conflicts within the police and Home Ministry, between the police and Justice Ministry, and between the police and Kenpeitai. Yet even in these conflicts strong identification with the nation or its symbol, the emperor, is visible. Police and Justice Ministry officials debated heatedly over means of controlling communists and anarchists, but they displayed fundamental agreement on the necessity of controlling them and on the goal of protecting the basic institutions and values then predominant in Japanese society. In addition, the appeal of both the police and army to imperial sanction in the Go-Stop Incident showed the significance of the imperial institution as a unifying and legitimising force.

What might be called the 'Old Right' as opposed to the 'New Right' thus remained strong in interwar Japan.[50] Hiranuma and Suzuki's Justice Ministry faction clearly falls under this designation. The new bureaucrats of the police and Home Ministry differed somewhat from the classical conservatives of Hiranuma's group. They looked to contemporary Nazi Germany for models,[51] but their state social policy approach evolved from the vantage point of historical hindsight. It was Bismarck's Germany more than Hitler's Germany that most influenced this approach.[52] Consequently, while seeking institutional reforms and greater mobilisation of popular support for governmental policies than any early modern *Polizeistaat*, the new bureaucrats remained part of the Old Right in their rejection of the New Right's radical revolutionary aims and ruthless political style.

In Europe fascism achieved its greatest successes where the Old Right was too weak to stand its ground alone against the Marxist left. 'It was not the strength of the right but its relative weakness, its fears, and its fits of panic, which created one of the essential conditions of fascist success.'[53] In Japan the Old Right, in its varied forms represented among the Tokkô and thought procurators, maintained a solid social and institutional base and drew upon traditional sources of authority to face challenges presented not only by the Marxist left but by the fascist right as well.

The outcome of the police's competition with the Kenpeitai suggests another reason for the comparatively limited role of the political police in prewar Japan. The military had traditionally occupied a special position in Japanese society. During the early 1920s it had not been politically prominent because the domestic and international situation favoured disarmament and democracy. However, as the sense of domestic social and economic crisis grew, public opinion expressed through the press and the platforms of opposition movements blamed the two established political parties, politicians, big businessmen and bureaucrats for the various problems. Radical right wing reform proposals envisioned the military as the initiator and leading agent for change, and during the 1930s military officers, such as the 'young officers', stepped forward to assume the role of national saviour. Despite the police's claims of being the emperor's police, by custom and law the military rather than the police occupied the closer position to the emperor and received his attendant status and prestige. Therefore, when the threat of war compounded the dangers of the national crisis, the military rather than the police became the chief protective force in Japanese society.

Nevertheless, the police exemplified the sense of crisis pervading prewar Japanese society. Economic depression, the communist challenge and international friction constituted the main elements in that crisis. The police and Tokkô in particular were directly responsible for resolving the second of these problems and indirectly responsible for dealing with the social and political disruptions arising from the other two. In the eyes of police leaders, the national and international dilemmas of the late 1920s and 1930s demanded an end to selfish individualism and *laissez faire* governmental policies. In police policy a corresponding shift away from a people's police ideal towards the emperor's police ideal reflected the 'new age' requirements of collectivism and active state intervention to mobilise all the nation's resources.

However, through its very response to the national crisis the police helped to create as well as reflect the climate of opinion. Given the traditional view of the police as nursemaids of society rather than mere agents of the law, eliminating the communist menace was regarded as only one of the Tokkô's designated tasks. Restoring social order and harmony through the 'proper guidance of thought' became an equally important task. As the foreign crisis mounted, the mission of protecting the *kokutai* raised the Tokkô to the apex of the police institution. By bringing the Tokkô into contact not only with those on the ideological fringe, but also with the lives of ordinary Japanese people, it gave the Tokkô a crucial role in forging the national unity desired by government leaders as they embarked on a course towards war.

APPENDIXES

Appendix I: The Tokkô chain of command in the 1930s

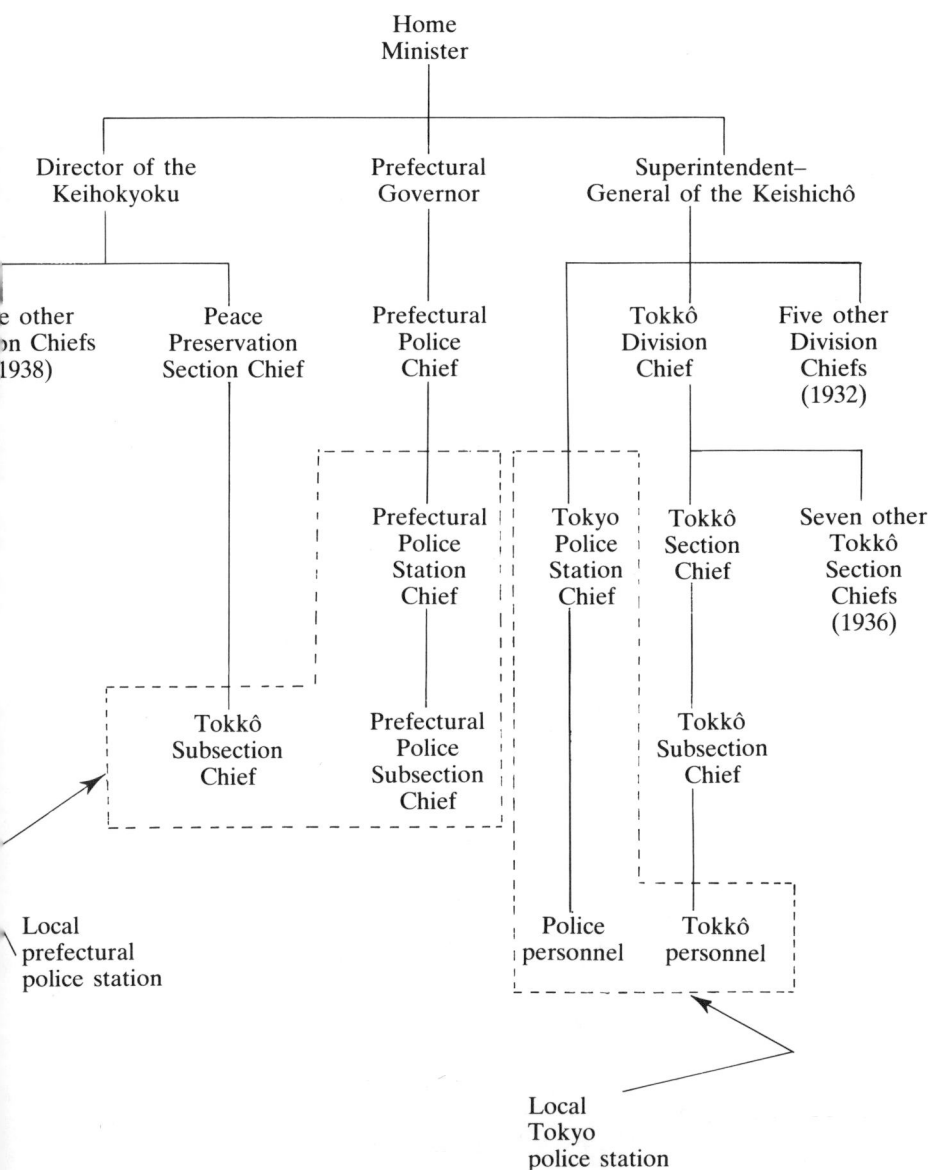

Appendix II: Disposition of Peace Preservation Law violations

	Arrests	Prosecutions	Stays of prosecution	Action withheld	No charge
1928					
Left wing	3 426	525	16		168
Independent	—	—	—		—
Religious	—	—	—		—
Total	3 426	525	16		168
1929					
Left wing	4 942	339	27		2
Independent	—	—	—		—
Religious	—	—	—		—
Total	4 942	339	27		2
1930					
Left wing	6 124	461	292		38
Independent	—	—	—		—
Religious	—	—	—		—
Total	6 124	461	292		38
1931					
Left wing	10 422	307	454	67	4
Independent	—	—	—	—	—
Religious	—	—	—	—	—
Total	10 422	307	454	67	4
1932					
Left wing	13 938	646	774	717	24
Independent	—	—	—	—	—
Religious	—	—	—	—	—
Total	13 938	646	774	717	24
1933					
Left wing	14 622	1 285	1 474	1 016	22
Independent	—	—	—	—	—
Religious	—	—	—	—	—
Total	14 622	1 285	1 474	1 016	22
1934					
Left wing	3 994	496	831	626	17
Independent	—	—	—	—	—
Religious	—	—	—	—	—
Total	3 994	496	831	626	17
1935					
Left wing	1 718	113	269	186	9
Independent	—	—	—	—	—
Religious	67	—	—	—	—
Total	1 785	113	269	186	9

	Arrests	Prosecutions	Stays of prosecution	Action withheld	No charge
1936					
Left wing	1 207	97	154	53	11
Independent	—	—	—	—	—
Religious	860	61	174	3	7
Total	2 067	158	328	56	18
1937					
Left wing	1 292	210	298		15
Independent	7	—	—		—
Religious	13	—	4		—
Total	1 313	210	302		15
1938					
Left wing	789	237	381		43
Independent	—	3	1		1
Religious	193	—	—		—
Total	982	240	382		44
1939					
Left wing	389	163	381		24
Independent	8	—	3		—
Religious	325	225	56		16
Total	722	388	440		40
1940					
Left wing	713	128	231		6
Independent	71	12	8		3
Religious	33	89	76		12
Total	817	229	315		21
1941					
Left wing	849	205	291		53
Independent	256	29	60		9
Religious	107	2	4		5
Total	1 212	236	355		67
1942					
Left wing	332	217	317		95
Independent	203	62	179		41
Religious	163	60	52		9
Total	698	339	548		145
1943					
Left wing	87	18	39		8
Independent	53	15	34		13
Religious	19	19	15		—
Total	159	52	88		21

Source: Okudaira (1973: 646–9)

Appendix III: Disposition of right wing related cases

	Cases	Prosecutions	No prosecution	Under investigation
1935	147	132	15	
1936	37	22	15	
1937	49	8	41	
1938	15	12	3	
1939	61	39	22	
1940	61	40	21	
1941	53	31	22	
1942	39	21	16	2
1943 (Jan.–Apr.)	7	7		

Source: Okudaira (1973: 651)

NOTES

Introduction
1. Takagi (1954: 118).
2. Akashi and Matsuura (1975: 10).
3. Ogino (1984: 454). The television series was entitled 'Oshin'. 'Seiji kyôiku to keisatsu' (1990).
4. Eleanor Westney has done a study of organisational transfer of Western police models to Meiji Japan. James Leavell emphasises the centralisation of the Meiji police. A few other studies of the Japanese police exist but deal with the postwar system. See Ames (1981), Bayley (1976), Leavell (1984), Nakahara (1955), Parker (1984), Sugai (1957), Westney (1982 and 1987), Winant (1971).
5. For example, Bickerton (1934: 30–4), Chamberlain (1937: 31–6), 'No left turn' (1936: 95–100ff), Ward (1925: 289–90), Wildes (1927), Young (1938).
6. United States, War Department, Office of Strategic Services, Research and Analysis Branch (1945: v, 12, 44).
7. Supreme Commander for the Allied Powers, Government Section (1949: 298, 705).
8. *Ibid.* pp. 292–6, 298.
9. For example, Beckmann and Okubo (1969), Colbert (1952), Scalapino (1967), Swearingen and Langer (1952), Totten (1966).
10. Mitchell (1976 and 1983).
11. Skashi and Matsuura (1975: 9), Hironaka (1974: 9–21), Kondô (1957: 16), Ôno (1973: 28–35), Takagi (1954: 111, 118–19).
12. Ôno (1973: 53–4), see also Kaino (1960: 57), Matsumoto (1964: 198–9, 202–3).
13. Keishichô Shi Hensan Iinkai (ed.) (1959–62, early Shôwa: 107–8),

ex-Tokkôbuchô Abe Genki in Kobayashi (1952: 3(foreword), 34–5), Ôhashi (1967: 30), Taikakai (1971, v.1: 751–2), Taki (1974: 149), Yamagata, (1968: 13–16). A rare exception to this pattern of views was expressed by former Home Ministry official Sugimoto (1952).
14 Notably, Ebashi (1976), Ogino (1984).
15 Ogino (1984: 456).
16 For example, de Polnay (1970), Kohn-Bramstedt (1945).
17 Exceptions include Monas' study of the Tsarist Russian police, Knight's study of the Soviet security police (KGB) and Reith's and Gorer's studies of the British police. Gorer speculates on the possible influence of police on national character. Reith goes beyond speculation, arguing that the nature of a regime is determined by the character of its police. Monas (1961), Gorer (1955), Reith (1952). Knight points out that abandonment of the totalitarian model of Soviet politics has turned attention away from the political police as a subject of research, so that 'the KGB has been virtually ignored by Western experts'. Knight (1988: xvi).
18 Even a proponent of police history categorically stated that 'as an institution they [police] are wholly dependent upon the values and the social structure of a particular society'. Mosse (1975 b: 1).
19 For example, Bowden (1973), Hoffmann (1973), Johnson (1972), Richardson (1972), Squire (1968), Swanson (1972), Tamuno, (1970), Tobias (1972).
20 For example, Banton (1963), Wilson, (1968). Anthropologist Walter Ames' study of the Japanese police has a comparative interest, but it is to examine the Japanese police as a possible model for contemporary American police forces. His focus is therefore on the present rather than the past. Ames (1981).
21 For example, the essays collected in Bayley (1977).
22 For example, Bayley (1969), Potholm (1969), Weed (1970), Young (1965).
23 Dawson and Prewitt (1969: 36–8, 79).
24 For example, see LeVine (1963), Verba (1965).
25 Deutsch does mention middle-level police officials, but is interested in them as middle-level administrators rather than as police officials *per se*. Deutsch (1966).
26 Bayley (1975).
27 Wilson (1968: 231).
28 See Broeker (1970), Tobias (1972: 214–19).
29 Chapman (1970: 125).
30 Weed summarizes similarities and differences between police and military forces and argues that the differences give the police a greater influence in modernization than the military. Weed (1970: 7–8).
31 Schafer (1974: 20).
32 Bayley (1969: 14).
33 Spaulding (1971: 36).
34 Wilson (1968: 7). See also Bayley (1969: 19–25).

35 Almond and Verba (1965).
36 Bayley (1969: 25–7).
37 Chapman (1970: 99–100).
38 Quoted in Emsley (1983: 4).
39 Chapman (1970: 101).
40 Beckmann (1971: 148).
41 On the import of police history and traditions for the Weimar and American police systems during the 1920s and early 1930s, see Richardson (1972: 262). For the Brazilian police, see Jakubs (1977: 102).
42 For examples of leading definitions, see Allardyce (1971), Gregor (1969), Laqueur (1976), Laqueur and Mosse (1966), Nolte (1966), Turner (1975). See also Gavan McCormack's article surveying theories of fascism, especially as applied to Japan. McCormack (1980).
43 McCormack (1980: 132–3).
44 For example, Duus and Okimoto (1979), Wilson (1968). Reviewing Olavi Fält's *Fascism, Militarism or Japanism?*, Richard Mitchell referred to "Beating the Dead Horse of Fascism" to indicate the now widespread dissatisfaction among scholars with the term's applicability to prewar Japan. See Mitchell (1985). However, Hilary Conroy has argued against abandonment of the study of Japanese fascism so that the '*results* of Japanese fascism are not obscured or forgotten'. Conroy (1981).
45 Fletcher (1979: 59).
46 Maruyama (1963: ch. 2, 5).
47 For example, Garon (1987), Mitchell (1976). In his book on censorship Mitchell compared the Meiji system with censorship systems of other 'highly authoritarian regimes' but also used Marc Raeff's concept of a 'well-ordered police state'. Mitchell (1983: 362, 364). He later refined his view of prewar Japan, concluding that '"well-ordered paternalistic police state" is a more precise label'. Mitchell (1985: 448).
48 The term 'regulative state,' is from Dorwart (1971: 4).
49 Monas (1961: 22–3).
50 Raeff (1975: 1225). See also Raeff (1983).
51 Dorwart (1971: 5), Chapman (1970: 15–18).
52 Chapman (1970: 20–5). See also Donald Emerson's study of the Hapsburg's use of the political police during the nineteenth century. Emerson (1968).
53 Lévy (1966: 488).
54 Chapman (1970: 29).
55 Roach (1985: 109).
56 Chapman (1970: 33–46).
57 Aside from the Japanese critics of the Tokkô cited earlier in this chapter, a similar analogy has been made by Brian Chapman, who has constructed useful typologies of different kinds of police states. He

categorizes pre-1945 Japan as a 'totalitarian' police state on the basis of its police apparat occupying 'a similar position as guardian of ideology as in Hitler's Germany or Stalin's Russia ...' *Ibid.* p. 120.

Chapter 1
1. Swearingen and Langer (1952: 58).
2. Beckmann and Okubo (1969: 1–2), Scalapino (1967: 1–2), Totten (1966: 22–3, 27).
3. Beckmann and Okubo (1969: 5), Kublin (1964: 147–8), Notehelfer (1971: 62–5), Scalapino (1967: 3).
4. Matsuo (1971: 90–1).
5. Beckmann and Okubo (1969: 22–3), Totten (1966: 33).
6. Beckmann (1971: 151).
7. For example, Ebashi (1976: 70), Ikeda (1939: 3), Watanabe (1976: 25).
8. Ebashi (1976: 69), Taki (1974: 119, 124). On censorship, see Mitchell (1983: 177–8).
9. Ebashi (1976: 70–2), Nihon Kindai Shiryô Kenkyûkai (1968: 10), Ogino (1984: 115–23).
10. Ebashi (1976: 69), Watanabe (1976: 25).
11. Mitchell (1976: 45), Watanabe (1976: 25–7).
12. Matsuo (1971: 107).
13. *Ibid.* p. 108, Tsunoda (1956: 57).
14. Matsuo (1971: 111). See also Duus (1968: 227).
15. Mitchell (1976: 53).
16. Keishichô, Sôkan Kanbô Bunshoka (1919–37: 1922–4)
17. Matsuo (1971: 121).
18. For interpretations of the connection between passage of the two laws, see Ayusawa (1966: 143–4), Beckmann (1971: 150), Mitchell (1976: 58–62), Tamura (1932: 147–8), Watanabe (1976: 18–19), Wildes (1925: 419) On the universal manhood suffrage law, see Griffin (1972).
19. Okudaira (1975: 102–3).
20. *Ibid.* xx, Furuta (1925: 6, 9), Mitchell (1976: 67–8), Miyake (1931: 186–7), Wildes (1925: 418).
21. Mitchell (1976: 73), Okudaira (1973: 63).
22. Katô (1972: 5), Okudaira (1975: x). According to Henry Smith, the full force of police repression of the student movement came with the 15 March 1928 arrests. Smith (1972: 131, 187).
23. Kawasaki Takukichi Denki Hensankai (ed.) (1961: 304–5), Mitchell (1976: 72–3), Okudaira (1973: 63).
24. Satô (1937: 27), Taki (1974: 151).
25. Hôjô (1956: 27–8), Kôketsu (1955: 58–9), Matsumoto (1965: 219–21, 226).
26. Colegrove (1928: 404–5), Hôjô (1956: 28–9), Mitchell (1976: 81–2), Maeshima (1969: 15–16), Okudaira (1973:64), Swearingen and Langer (1952: 30).
27. Hayashi (1975: 175), Matsuzaka (1965: 46), Mitchell (1976: 86).

Notes   163

28 Keishichô, Sôkan Kanbô Bunshoka (1919–37: 1928–9).
29 Judicial police authority refers to the authority to carry out post-arrest functions of interrogation and investigation. It may also include authority to render certain punishments, such as fines for minor offenses.
30 Suzuki Kisaburô Sensei Denki Hensankai (1955: 274).
31 Naimushô, Keihokyoku (1926–41: 1929).
32 After 1930 this publication was superceded by the monthly *Tokkô geppô* and yearly *Shakai undô no jôkyô*.
33 Okudaira (1977: 94), Suzuki Kisaburô Sensei Denki Hensankai (1955: 274).
34 Ebashi (1976: 79–80).
35 Okudaira (1975: 646–9). For a Keishichô report on arrests made after 15 March, see 'Keishisôkan no kenkyo ni kansuru tsûhô' (1965).
36 Okudaira (1962: 12).
37 Keishichô Shi Hensan Iinkai (1959–62, early Shôwa: 266–8), Yamamoto and Arita (1950: 209–10). A 1934 Keihokyoku report shows that fifteen Keishichô police officials and ten in other areas had received wounds from extreme leftists. Naimushô, Keihokyoku (1934c).
38 The 1932 Tokkô budget included funds for 200 sets of bulletproof equipment. Ogino (1984: 229).
39 For example, Ôno (1973: 28–9, 35, 52), Takagi (1954: 118).
40 For example, Keishichô Shi Hensan Iinkai (1959–62, Shôwa: 107–8), Ôhashi (1967: 30), Taikakai (1971, v.1: 751–2), Taki (1974: 149), Yamagata (1968: 15–16).
41 *Tokkô Monthly Report* reported Kobayashi's death from a heart attack and in addition, the JCP's accusations and plans for mass protest demonstrations. Naimushô, Keihokyoku, Hoanka (1930–44, Mar. 1933: 9–10).
42 Descriptions of the wounds go on like this for at least a page. For example, see Matsuo (1971: 172–3), Ôno (1973: 24–6). For other accounts of the case, see Eguchi (1974), Matsumoto (1965, v. 5: 302).
43 Beckmann and Okubo (1969: 237). *Tokkô Monthly Report* attributed Iwata's death to pulmonary tuberculosis and beriberi heart disease, while also reporting *Red Flag's* denunciation of his death due to Keishichô 'butchery' and its call for a mass protest movement. Naimushô, Keihokyoku, Hoanka (1930–44, Dec. 1932: 19). Other accusations of torture appeared during the argument for a unified public trial of communists arrested in 1928 and 1929 and during the trial itself. Matsuo (1971: 154), Tamaki (1946: 12–13, 26, 28, 34, 36, 38).
44 Not long after his interpellation Yamamoto was killed by a member of an organisation planning to assassinate many left wing Diet representatives whom they considered disrespectful. Excerpts of his interpellation may be found in Maeshima (1969: 19–22), Matsumoto (1965, v.5: 251–3), Matsuo (1971: 149–53), Ôno (1973: 95).
45 Beckmann and Okubo (1969: 235).

46 For a socio-psychological analysis of *tenkôsha*, see Steinhoff (1969).
47 Miyashita, Itô, and Nakamura (1978: 97, 108–9).
48 Ogino (1984: 229).
49 Beckmann and Okubo (1969: 244).
50 For an example of police recognition and sharing of this sense of crisis, see Naimushô, Keihokyoku, Toshoka (1936: 1, 365–6). On the depression, see Downard (1976). On the establishment of the Tokkôbu, see Ishii (1932: 20–4), Ogino (1984: 225–32).
51 Naimushô, Keihokyoku, Hoanka (1930–44, May 1932: 102).
52 Ebashi (1976: 85).
53 Keishichô Shi Hensan Iinkai (1959–62, Shôwa: 849–50, 852).
54 Keishichô, Sôkan Kanbô Bunshoka (1919–37: 1931–2).
55 Several charts of Home Ministry actions appear in Mitchell (1983: 267–71). See also Borton (1940: 109n).
56 Okudaira (1976: 50).
57 Okudaira (1975: xxvii, 220; for the text of the proposals, 198–203).
58 *Ibid.* pp. 197, 220. See also Ogino (1984: 253–9).
59 Okudaira (1976: 57). On the bill, see also Mitchell (1976: 121–5).
60 Matsuo (1971: 11), Mitchell (1976: 140–1), Okudaira, (1975: xiii), Okudaira (1973: 51).
61 Steinhoff (1969: 7, 12–13).
62 On the affair and academic purge, see Miller (1965: 196–253).
63 Naimushô, Keihokyoku, Hoanka (1930–44: 1935).
64 'Jihen to keisatsukan' (1937: 1), Onuki (1937), Sudô (1937).
65 Naimushô, Keihokyoku (1926–41: 1929), Richardson (1972: 269), Yashiro (1934: 41).
66 Dore and Ôuchi (1971: 187). A chart in the 1928 *Keishichô tôkei sho* also shows that police numbers increased and decreased in proportion to changes in population for the 1919–1928 period. Keishichô, Sôkan Kanbô Bunshoka (1919–37: 1928)
67 Ogino (1984: 210).
68 Ônô (1973: 54, 89–90, 100), Shinobu et al. (1960: 205), Watanabe (1976: 19, 22, 32).
69 This is a common view among Japanese Marxist scholars, for example, 'Chian iji hô' (1952: 4), Nakayama (1970: 17–21), Ônô (1973: 53–4).
70 For example, Ebashi, Mitchell, Okudaira.
71 Furuta (1925: 1–2).
72 For example, Wakatsuki's statements during the Diet debates. Okudaira (1975: 51–2, 57, 60, 65). Former Director of the Keihokyoku Karasawa's statement shows that this was clear in the minds of police leaders. 'Chian iji hô' (1952: 77).
73 The quote that begins this chapter expresses this single-mindedness as effectively as any of the following examples. See also Naimushô, Keihokyoku (1934–43: Frames 386132–3), Ibarakiken (June 1934–39: Frames 382004, 382436), Nakagawa (1934: 210).
74 Wald (1949: 203–4), Young (1938: 281).
75 Ôtani (1971: 51).

Notes 165

76 Beckmann (1971: 148), Colbert (1952: 3), Nakamura (1958: 337–8).
77 Beckmann (1971: 160), Scalapino (1967: 45).
78 Also the conclusion reached by contemporary American observer, Hugh Byas. Byas (1932: 195).

Chapter 2
1 Matsui (1933: 4).
2 Taki (1974: 59).
3 Regarding the influence of tradition on the American and Berlin police, see Richardson (1972: 262); on the British police, see Tobias (1972: 202–5); on the Brazilian police, especially its violent and repressive behaviour, see Jakubs (1977: 85–106).
4 Yamamoto (1937: 1).
5 Japanese historians usually emphasize the continuities in the police system since the Meiji period; for example, Saitô (1974: 13–14).
6 The *ken* refers to prefecture and is not to be confused with Kenpeitai (Military Police). Matsui (1933: 77), Naimushô, Keihokyoku (1927a, v.1: 2–3), Tamura (1932: 1–4).
7 Kuroda (1963: 194, 212–14), Tamura (1932: 5–7), Yamamoto (1937: 146–7).
8 Keishichô Shi Hensan Iinkai (1959–62, Meiji: 28, 30).
9 Naimushô, Keihokyoku (1927a, v.1: 4–5).
10 On the origins of American and English police forces, see Hacker (1977), Miller (1977).
11 Quotations can be found in Yamamoto (1937: 128–31). See also, Kuroda (1963: 195–9), Matsui (1933: 28, 33), Saitô (1974: 18), Taki (1974: 60).
12 Westney (1987: 41).
13 Keishichô Shi Hensan Iinkai (1959–62, Meiji: 31), Naimushô, Keihokyoku (1929a, v.1: 5), Tamura (1932: 11, 13).
14 Brown (1966: 204–5), Hackett (1971: 71–102).
15 Ôno (1973: 49).
16 Brown (1966: 205).
17 Kawaji's petition is quoted in Kuroda (1963: 199–202), Naimushô, Keihokyoku (1927a, v.1: 11–15), Taikakai (1971: v.1: 575–7), Tamura (1932: 17), Yamamoto (1937: 132–4).
18 Taikakai (1971, v.1: 584–5). See also Matsui (1933: 15, 124). Critics, in contrast, have made the opposite value judgment. They agree that a unified national organisation contributed to police strength, but to them this only helped achieve a deplorable end, the consolidation of a police state serving the interests of the state rather than the people. See Kainô (1960: 52), Ôno (1973: 56–8).
19 Fosdick (1916: 23).
20 *Ibid.* pp. 18–20, 23–5.
21 *Ibid.* pp. 18–19.
22 Kainô (1960: 71), Ôno (1973: 42). Compared to Germany, the executive in Japan retained even larger lawmaking power. See Chapter 3.
23 Abe (1956: 617).

24 For a concise outline of this organisation in English, see Nakahara (1955: 583); in Japanese, see Taikakai (1971, v.1: 583–4).
25 Taikakai (1971, v.1: 619).
26 Nakahara (1955: 584).
27 *Ibid.* p. 583. On the Paris Prefect of Police, see Payne (1966). For details on adoption of the French model see Westney (1987: 45–72).
28 Keishichô Shi Hensan Iinkai (1959–62, Meiji: 124), Saitô (1974:23), Taikakai (1971, v.1: 589), Tamura (1932: 29–31), Yamamoto (1937: 205–6).
29 Keishichô Shi Hensan Iinkai (1959–62, Meiji: 123), Saitô (1974: 24).
30 Tamura (1932: 36–8).
31 Hackett (1971: 79).
32 Keishichô Shi Hensan Iinkai (1959–62, Meiji: 135, 139).
33 Hackett (1971: 79).
34 Keishichô Shi Hensan Iinkai (1959–62, Meiji: 161–4).
35 Kuroda (1963: 259), Naimushô, Keihokyoku (1927a, v.1: 270, 274), Taikakai (1971, v.1: 564, 589).
36 Taikakai (1971, v.1: 589).
37 *Ibid.* p. 564.
38 Hackett (1971: 103), Matsumoto (1964: 199), Taikakai (1971, v.1: 642).
39 Hackett (1971: 102–3), Matsumoto (1964: 200).
40 Taikakai (1971, v.1: 921).
41 Matsui (1932c: 194–6), Yamamoto (1937: 135). See also Hackett (1971: 103), Matsumoto (1964: 200), Taikakai (1971, v.1: 643).
42 Hackett (1971: 103–4), Matsui (1933: 32), Taki (1974: 61). This distribution of police boxes in rural and metropolitan areas continues today and is regarded by many foreign observers as a strength of the present Japanese police system. See Ames (1981: Ch.1 and 2), Bayley (1976: Ch. 2).
43 Taki (1974: 62).
44 *Ibid.*
45 The author gives no indication of whether or not the Japanese followed these particular suggestions. *Plus ça change* ... *Ibid.* p. 63.
46 *Ibid.* pp. 63–4.
47 Taikakai (1971, v.1: 614).
48 The *Naimushô shi* gives the 1892 election as an example of egregious police interference, but claims that the police were impartial in several other elections during the 1890s. *Ibid.* p. 692.
49 Keishichô Shi Hensan Iinkai (1959–62, Meiji: 437), Takeno and Akaeda (1946, pt 4: 126–7).
50 Takeno and Akaeda (1946, pt 4: 127).
51 Keishichô Shi Hensan Iinkai (1959–62, Meiji: 437–41), Taikakai (1971, v.1: 592).
52 Taikakai (1971, v.1: 594), Takeno and Akaeda (1946, pt 4: 127–8).
53 Kainô (1950: 87, 93), Keishichô Shi Hensan Iinkai (1959–62, Meiji: 10–11).
54 Taikakai (1971, v.1: 568).
55 Takeno and Akaeda (1946, pt 2: 133).

56 Chapman (1970: 27–9).
57 Koike (1968: 96), Taikakai (1971, v.1: 598).
58 Keishichô Shi Hensan Iinkai (1959–62, Meiji: 476), Taikakai (1971, v.1: 750).
59 Kurihara and Ogata (1932: 2–3).
60 Taikakai (1971, v.1: 750–1).
61 Yamagata Tamezô, a former police station chief and Tokkô official, is an example of these defenders. Yamagata (1968: 15). The *Naimushô shi* is a semi-official history pointing out the Tokkô's centralised character. Taikakai (1971, v.1: 751). So do both a neutral source, Sugimoto (1952, Kan: 38), and a critical source, Ônô (1973: 63).
62 Abe (1978: 89), Sugimoto (1952, Kan: 38), Taikakai (1971, v.1: 751), Yamagata (1968: 15).
63 Ônô (1973: 63), Saitô (1974: 14, 30), Sugimoto (1952, Kan: 38).
64 Taikakai (1971, v.1: 751).
65 Keishichô (1935), Okudaira (1975: 451).
66 Kamiyanagi (1925: 18–19), Taikakai (1971, v.1: 917–18).
67 Taikakai (1971, v.1: 575), Naimushô, Keihokyoku (1927a, v.1: 11–15), Tamura (1932: 17).
68 Hironaka (1974: 3–4), Taki (1974: 59), Toyama (1933: 32).
69 Tamura (1932: 28).
70 *Ibid.*; see also Matsui (1933: 125–6).
71 From excerpts of 'Hand and Eye of the Police' in Hironaka, (1974: 4–5). Kondô Takanosuke, a postwar journalist, goes further in concluding that Kawaji's aim was to create a police state. Kondô (1957: 10).
72 See Chapter 3.
73 Akamatsu (1974: 9–11), Tanaka (1956: 4–5).
74 Takeno and Akaeda (1946, pt 3: 124).
75 Akamatsu (1974: 8, 81–2, 128–30).
76 *Ibid.* pp. 38–9.
77 *Ibid.* pp. 50–3; Totten (1966: 229).
78 Maeda (1948: 331).
79 Naimushô, Keihokyoku (1927a, v.1: 492), Taikakai (1971: v.1: 565, 611–15, 746–9).
80 Kuroda (1963: 232–3).
81 Tamura (1932: 9), Yamamoto (1937: 155–6).
82 Matsui (1933: 30–1), Ônô (1973: 30–3), Taki (1974: 60), Wildes (1928: 392–5).
83 Akamatsu (1974: 58).
84 Keishichô Shi Hensan Iinkai (1959–62, Meiji: 429), Taikakai (1971, v.1: 817–24), Tsunoda (1956: 29).
85 For example, Matsui (1933: 17–20, 83, 120), Matsumoto (1934: 5–6).

Chapter 3
1 Shôkadô (ed.) (1932, v.2: 6).
2 Matsui (1933: 172).
3 Henderson (1968: 415), Takayanagi (1963: 15, 38).

4 Henderson (1968: 415). See Hashimoto for a similar definition of rule of law as understood by postwar Japanese jurists. Hashimoto (1963: 241).
5 Henderson (1968: 400–3).
6 *Ibid*. pp. 390, 394–5, 404–5; Minear (1973: 4–5).
7 Henderson (1968: 412).
8 *Ibid*. p. 39.
9 Takayanagi (1963: 39).
10 Von Mehren (1963: 427).
11 There were 61 recidivists between 1925 and 1933, including 37 who had served their full prison terms and presumably had not converted. For a chart, see Shakai Bunko (ed.) (1965: 257–8). Only 1 per cent of the 13 000 people handled by the supervision centres between 1936 and 1938 were repeaters. Mitchell (1976: 139).
12 Henderson (1968: 431–3).
13 *Ibid*. p. 415.
14 Hashimoto (1963: 240), Henderson (1968: 423), Kainô (1960: 71). Even a severe critic of the prewar police system notes these differences between the premodern and modern Japanese police systems. Ôno (1973: 40, 42).
15 Henderson (1968: 416, 420, 423).
16 Kido (1928: 21). See also Takayanagi (1963: 38).
17 Fosdick (1916: 18–19).
18 Ishihara (1928: 11). See also Matsui (1937: 137), Von Mehren (1963: 426–7).
19 Quoted in Patricia Steinhoff (1969: 66).
20 For discussions of the imperial ordinance power, see Miller (1965: 86–94), Nakano (1923).
21 Payne (1966: 9–10).
22 Pittau (1967: 194).
23 Watanabe and Ishikawa (1933: 240).
24 Those stating the need for a statute include Hirata (1926: 8), Shimizu and Wataru (1932: 3), Shôkadô (1932, v.2: 6–7). Those disagreeing include Kido (1928: 30–1), Mitamura (1930: 10–11).
25 Shimizu and Wataru (1932: 3), Shôkadô (1932. v.2: 6–7).
26 Henderson (1968: 419).
27 Mitchell (1983: 46–8). See also Matsuo (1971: 22–4), Tamura (1932: 108–9), Taki (1974: 87–91).
28 Mitchell (1983: 51), Taikakai (1971, v.1: 688).
29 Mitchell (1983: 49).
30 Nakayama (1970: 29–30).
31 Public Meeting Rules (Shûkai kisoku), Dec. 9, 1878. See Naimushô, Keihokyoku (1927a, v.1: 222).
32 Public Meetings Control Law (Shûkai torishimari hô), Dec. 4, 1978. See *ibid*. pp. 220–1.
33 *Ibid*. p. 258; Matsuo (1971: 26–7), Ôno (1973: 79), Tamura (1932: 116–7).
34 Mitchell (1983: 87).

35 Naimushô, Keihokyoku (1927a, v.1: 396–7, 559), Taikakai (1971, v.1: 688–90).
36 Hackett (1971: 105–6), Matsuo (1971: 32–3), Naimushô, Keihokyoku (1927a, v.1: 558), Ôno (1973: 82), Taikakai (1971, v.1: 680–1), Tamura (1932: 128–30).
37 See Naimushô, Keihokyoku (1927a, v.1: 658–9, 600–1).
38 Taikakai (1971, v.1: 690).
39 Ôno (1973: 83).
40 Nakayama (1970: 36).
41 Kôchiken, Tokubetsu Kôtôka (1929: 19), Taikakai (1971, v.1: 707), Takeno and Akaeda (1946, pt 3: 119), Tamura (1932: 136).
42 Kinoshita (1933: 57).
43 Kainô (1960: 85), Matsui (1933: 72), Tamura (1932: 149–50, 273).
44 The criminal code divided crimes according to the severity of their penalties into major crimes, minor crimes, and *ikeizai*. *Ikeizai* included all crimes punishable by detention or fine. *Keisatsuhan* referred to a violation of a police ordinance, which usually but not exclusively carried a detention or fine penalty. Kinoshita (1933: 195–6).
45 Hironaka (1968: 17–18).
46 Mitchell (1983: 140–4).
47 Kinoshita (1933: 57).
48 For a full text of the bill, see Okudaira (1975: 51) or Shakai Mondai Shiryô Kenkyûkai (ed.) (1972: 1–2).
49 For example, definitions given by Home Minister Wakatsuki Reijirô and Committee Chairman Maeda Yonezô during the House of Representatives proceedings. Okudaira (1975: 57, 92–3). This was also the definition provided to police officials at the Police Training Institute and to all police officials via the *Police Association Magazine* 'Chian iji hô kakujô gikai' (1925: 60). Furuta (1925: 8–9).
50 Furuta (1925: 11).
51 Shakai Mondai Shiryô Kenkyûkai (ed.) (1972: 7–8).
52 Okudaira (1975: 100–1).
53 Shakai Mondai Shiryô Kenkyûkai (ed.) (1972: 18). Wakatsuki was applauded after stating this opinion.
54 *Ibid.* pp. 2–3, 13. Justice Ministry officials reiterated these assurances. *Ibid.* pp. 360–1, 572.
55 *Ibid.* pp. 10–12, 24; Okudaira (1975: 51–2, 56–8, 60). Furuta made the same explanations in his lecture on the new Peace Preservation Law at the Police Training Institute. Furuta (1925: 1–5).
56 Okudaira (1975: 71). Shakai Mondai Shiryô Kenkyûkai (ed.) (1972: 84–5).
57 Okudaira (1975: 57).
58 Shakai Mondai Shiryô Kenkyûkai (ed.) (1972: 86–8). Honda was not worried about Justice Ministry officials' use of the law, only the possibility of police abuses since the police were subject to the political pressures of changes in government.
59 *Ibid.* pp. 91–2; Okudaira (1975: 72–5).
60 For example, ideological motive distinguished the organisation of an

association crime (*kesshazai*) in Article 1 from the crime of rebellion (*nairanzai*) in the criminal code. Determination of the former involved no question of means while the latter required use of violence. Furuta (1925: 23–4). On the newness of this aspect of the law, see 'Chian iji hô' (1952, pt 2: 9), Ikeda (1939: 1, 23).
61 Okudaira (1975: xxi).
62 Okudaira (1977: 54).
63 Shakai Mondai Shiryô Kenkyûkai (ed.) (1972: 315–16, 477, 576).
64 The 'traditional' school 'emphasized the divinity of the emperor and rejected a secular approach to the state.' It retained traditional Japanese biases against the concept of law in general and the implications of Western law in particular. The 'liberal' school 'emphasized a secular approach to the state and the emperor at the expense of the imperial mystique.' It adopted the Western conception of law as well as its veneration for law. The conflict between the two schools was more political than methodological, as will be made evident by the discussion of differences within the 'liberal' school later in this chapter. The quotations are from Minear (1970: 6). See also Miller (1965: 285–6). Minobe Tatsukichi initially opposed the use of '*kokutai*' as a legal term because it was usually used as an historical and psychological concept, but after passage of the Peace Preservation Law and the 1929 and 1931 Supreme Court decisions, he also accepted this legal definition. Tsuneishi (1960: 168), Yokota (1949: 164–7).
65 For descriptions of the two types of definitions, see Tsuneishi (1960: 165–9), Yokota (1949: 154–71, 185–6).
66 Okudaira (1975: xx).
67 Naimushô, Keihokyoku (1934a: Frame 385038), Okudaira (1976: 58–9).
68 Miyake (1931: 188) Miyake was an active judge when he wrote this article. It may be considered an official interpretation, for it was published in place of one critical of the law that was banned and was frequently cited in books for police officials. The banned article was published after the war in Kazahaya (1948). See also Kurihara and Ogata (1932: 228), Satô (1937: 31–2).
69 Sasaki (1922: 304, 338).
70 Mitchell (1983: 151).
71 For example, the Publication Law, Article 19 states that 'when a book is published which he considers harmful to the public peace and order or detrimental to public morals, the home minister can prohibit its sales and distribution and seize the printing press and printed copies.' Ôtake (1933: Appendix 15).
72 Mitchell (1983: 151).
73 Okudaira (1962: 46–7), Taikakai (1971, v.1: 757). The *Naimushô shi* authors argue that these guidelines constituted rules with concrete categories, while Okudaira considers them to be only loose, general instructions.
74 'Chian iji hô' (1952, pt 2: 10), Hironaka (1974: 16–18), Kazahaya (1948: 2), Taikakai (1971, v.1: 610).

75 Mitamura (1930: 45–9), Sugimoto (1933: 150), Yamaguchi (1933: 93–8). On the attempt of certain Diet members to prohibit repeated detentions for the same reason, see 'Jinken jûrin mondai ni kansuru Kiyose-Hitomatsu ryôdaigishi no enzetsu yôshi' (1933: 38–9).
76 Hironaka (1974: 17), Ôno (1973: 103–4).
77 Okudaira (1967: 180–3), Okudaira ((1962: 53–4).
78 Yamagataken, Tokubetsu Kôtôka (Oct. 1939: Frame 381187).
79 Taikakai, (1971, v.1: 757–8).
80 For example, Aketa (1934: 6, 128, 146), Kinoshita (1933: 6, 296), Kurihara and Ogata (1932: 9–13), Miyake (1931: 185), Yamagata (1968: 56–8).
81 Matsui (1933: 172).
82 *Ibid.* p. 171; Akiyoshi (1935: 7).
83 Buchheim (1965: 188).
84 The quote from *Police Training Book* at the beginning of this chapter is an example of these. See also, Futagawa (1925: 36), Kido (1928: 31), Shimizu and Wataru (1932: 2), Shôkadô Henshûbu (1934: 4), Yamaguchi (1933: 43).
85 For example, Keisatsu Kenkyûkai (1931: 75–6), Kinoshita (1933: 6 296), Kurihara and Ogata (1932: 9–11).
86 Furuta (1925: 6–7, 40–1), Miyake (1931: 212–13, 221–3). Miyake concluded his article by advising, 'in applying this law do not forget to have a tolerance which will transcend the age' (p. 223).
87 Miyashita Hiroshi recalls in his memoirs that police recruits studied mostly law at the police training school. Miyashita, Itô and Nakamura (1978: 25).
88 Examples of test questions appeared periodically in *Keisatsu Kyôkai zasshi*. See also Shôkadô Henshûbu (1934).
89 Takahashi (1927: Preface). Seki (1928: Preface 1) also noted that books interpreting police laws and regulations were common.
90 For example, Dôjinsha Hensanbu (1932), Irokawa (1931).
91 Fleisher (1941: 319).
92 Miyake (1931: 185).
93 Ebashi (1976: 80), Okudaira (1975: x–xi), Ôtake (1933: 81).
94 Okudaira (1976: 52). Mitchell also points out that Justice Ministry officials wanted to strengthen and rationalise the conversion and rehabilitation system. Mitchell (1976: 121–2). For an explanation of the law for supervision of thought criminals, see Moriyama (1936: 13–17).
95 Okudaira (1976: 63–4), Okudaira (1975: xvi, xviii).
96 In 1936 a professor at the Police Training Institute wrote an article arguing against the past practice of defining the police from an exclusively legal point of view. Suzuki (1936: May 77–98, June 63–78).
97 Minobe is well-known for his theory of the emperor as an organ, albeit the supreme organ , of the state. During the 1920s it was the generally accepted and established view among constitutional scholars, but in 1935 it became the subject of attack by civilian and military rightists in the midst of their demands for clarification of the *kokutai*. As a result, Minobe was forced to resign from the House of

Peers and Tokyo Imperial University. The 'Minobe affair' or 'organ theory affair' is often considered to be symbolic of the defeat of prewar liberalism.

Sasaki taught constitutional law and administrative law at Kyoto Imperial University from 1913 to 1933. Acting on his liberal political views and in defense of academic freedom, he submitted his resignation in protest against the forced resignation of a fellow law faculty colleague, Takikawa Yukitatsu, in 1933. Sasaki then became a professor at the Kobe University of Commerce. In 1935 he was indefinitely suspended from teaching constitutional law as part of the general academic purge accompanying the 'organ theory affair.' Although not dismissed, he remained under continual scrutiny. Karasawa (1956: 122–6), Miller (1965: 159, 196–253, 312).

Good discussions of the debate over the concept of the police are provided by Nomura (1939: 323–5), Sugai (1937: 590–602).

98 Sasaki (1922: 113, 115–16). For other passivist views, see Ichimura (1911: 728–31), Shimamura (1939: 367), Watanabe (1935: 60–1).
99 Minobe (1932: 5–6) (the 1st and 2nd editions contain less elaborate expositions of the same view); Minobe (1931: 2–3). For another activist view, see Shimizu (1935: 216, 218).
100 Minobe (1932: 5).
101 Miller (1965: 52–3).
102 The debate among scholars continued into the late 1930s, but official and semi-official police sources indicate that the official police position was leaning towards the activist one. A long series of articles by Minobe on the concept of the police appeared in the official police journal, *Keisatsu kenkyû*, due to popular demand. No passivist view was published. The authors of many police textbooks explained the debate but adopted the activist position for themselves. Minobe (1931a: 1–8). Supporters of the activist view include Hôsei Jihôsha (1933: 47), Katô (1936: 37–8), 'Keisatsuken on genkai, keisatsu gyôsei no shokuiki no mondai ni tsuite' (1935: 41–2), Kido (1928: Preface by Director of the Keihokyoku Yamaoka Mannosuke and 5–6, 12–13), Kuwabara (1930: 221, 225, 231–6), Matsumoto (1934: 2), Shimizu and Wataru (1932: 1), Shôkadô Henshûbu (1934: 6), Shôkadô (1932: 3, 8), Tamura (1932: 219), Torigoe and Matsuo (1931: 16), Toyama (1933: 4–6). One exception supporting the passivist view is Yamaguchi (1933: 3).
103 Kido (1928: 29–31).
104 On German liberalism and the *Rechtsstaat*, see Krieger (1957: 252–61).
105 For example, on France see Payne (1966: 10).
106 Hashimoto (1963: 240), Henderson (1968: 426–8), Hirata (1926: 65–70), Irokawa (1931: 198), Kido (1928: 30–1), Minobe (1932: 58, 90).
107 Irokawa (1931: 204–5), Minobe (1932: 91).
108 Okudaira (1973: 51).
109 Shakai Bunko (1965: 9–14).

Notes   173

110 Abe (1956: 332–3).
111 Shakai Bunko (1965: 9–14).

Chapter 4

1   From Yamamoto's instructions at the 16 May 1934 prefectural police chiefs meeting. Naimushô, Keihokyoku (1934–43: Frame 386003).
2   Matsui (1921c: 3).
3   Matsui (1937: Preface 1).
4   Cyert and MacCrimmon (1968: 587), Gross et al. (1958: 17), Sarbin and Allen (1968: 506).
5   Though at least one has in retrospect. Naisei Shi Kenkyûkai (1967: 17).
6   The following typology is derived from Becker (1970: 17–23), Carte and Carte (1975: 1–4, 85–97), Huntington (1957: 8–10), Reiss (1971: 122–3), Rubin (1972: 21–3).
7   Westley (1970: xvi).
8   Carte and Carte (1975: 4, 105–7).
9   Westley (1970: xvi). See also Bent (1974: 155).
10 For example, Matsui (1923: 5), Toyama (1933: 54–5). On Vollmer, see Carte and Carte (1975: 2–3).
11 Keishichô Shi Hensan Iinkai (1959–62, Taishô: 186–9), Naimushô, Keihokyoku (1927a, v.1: 398), Taikakai (1971, v.1: 623).
12 Miyashita, Itô and Nakamura (1978: 24–5).
13 Matsui (1932c: 131, 232).
14 Hiraga (1919: 1), Matsui (1932c: 232).
15 Taikakai (1971, v.1: 637–9).
16 Naimushô, Keihokyoku (1926–41: 1932, p. 22).
17 Hiraga (1919: 1).
18 Yokoyama (1928: 251).
19 *Ibid.* pp. 54, 265–6; Keishichô Keisatsu Renshûjo (1923: 94), Matsui (1932c: 133).
20 Keishichô, Sôkan Kanbô Bunshoka (1919–38: 1919–29).
21 *Ibid.* See also Chûô Shokugyô Shôkai Jimukyoku (n.d.).
22 Wray (1973: 49–50).
23 See Westney (1987: 76–80) on Meiji police training.
24 The Police Association was founded in 1900 to encourage scholarship and military arts among police officials as well as to foster morality and improvements in the police. All police officials in the country belonged to the organisation and received its publication, *Keisatsu Kyôkai zasshi. Catalogue of Items, Connected with the General Police System in Japan* (1904: 8), Ishihara (1932: 126–32), Keishichô Shi Hensan Iinkai (1959–62, Meiji: 367–8), Taikakai (1971, v.1: 669), Yokoyama (1928: 275).
25 Ishihara (1930: 271–2), Taikakai (1971, v.1: 645–8).
26 Carte and Carte (1975: 26).
27 Futagawa (1925: 83–4), Matsui (1932c: 3), Matsui (1920a: 15).

28 Futagawa (1925: 83–4), Matsui (1932c: 3, 160–2).
29 Matsui (1932c: 160).
30 *Ibid.* p. 162; Hiraga (1919: 20–2).
31 Bayley (1976: 56).
32 Matsui (1932c: 161–2). Interestingly, this was also the length of training received by Tokyo police recruits in the 1970s. Bayley (1976: 56).
33 For example, Home Minister Mizuno Rentarô's speech at the Sept. 1923 police division chiefs meeting. Naimushô, Keihokyoku (1927b: 85).
34 Gotô (1921: 2), Hiraga (1919: 4–5), Matsui (1932c: 4, 78–96, 133–57, 165, 178–91), Matsui (1921a: 8, 10–11), Yamagata (1921: 20–37).
35 Matsui (1921a: 6). Another writer saw a trend from a competitive to cooperative civilisation accompanying rising consciousness of social justice and social service. Accordingly, he envisioned an active police role in promotion of social welfare. Agata (1921: 5–6).
36 Matsui (1921a: 6).
37 Futagawa (1925: intro. 5–6), Gotô (1921: 1–2), Kamata (1921: 1–5), Matsui (1932c: 40–1), Matsui (1921c: 3), Naimushô (1927b: 80), Shibusawa (1921: 6), Yokoyama (1928: preface 3), Yubara (1921: 15–16).
38 Keishichô Keisatsu Renshûjo (1923: 20–3), Matsui (1928: 14), Naganoken, Keisatsubu (1922: 2–4), Oka (1921: 3), Yuasa (1924: 10), Yubara (1921: 15).
39 Gotô (1921: 1–2), Yuasa (1924: 11).
40 Matsui (1920: 24). See also Yamagata (1921: 33).
41 Naimushô (1927b: 93–4), Oka (1921: 2), Shimada (1921: 10).
42 Keishichô Keisatsu Renshûjo (1923: 33–4), Kuroda (1937: 291–2, 298).
43 Stead (1977: 75, 78–9).
44 Futagawa (1925: 75), Keishichô Keisatsu Renshûjo (1923: 1–2), Matsui (1932c: 47–8).
45 Keishichô Keisatsu Renshûjo (1923: 23), Matsui (1932c: 4), Matsui (1921b: 55), Wada (1920: 1), Yokoyama (1928: 5 (preface), 1, 231–40).
46 Naganoken Keisatsubu (1922: 2, 75), Yokoyama (1928: 3 (preface), 9–10).
47 Kamata (1921: 3), Matsui (1923: 4), Matsui (1932c: 31), Matsui (1921a: 7), Matsui (1921c: 7, 9), Oka (1921: 2–3), Shibusawa (1921: 1–2, 4), Yokoyama (1928: 4).
48 'Minshû no keisatsuka' along with 'keisatsu no minshûka,' Oka (1921: 3).
49 Matsui (1920b: 23). See also Keishichô Keisatsu Renshûjo (1923: 247), Matsui (1923: 5–6), Shibusawa (1921: 6).
50 Futagawa (1925: 84–5).
51 Stead (1977: 76).
52 Keishichô Shi Hensan Iikai (1959–62, Taishô: 160–9), Keishichô Keisatsu Renshûjo (1923: 4–7, 87, 94), Yokoyama (1928: 53).
53 For example, Hiraga (1919: 2–3), Keishichô Keisatsu Renshûjo (1923:

8–9, 19, 27–31, 37–8), Nakatani (1921: 13, 15–16, 19), Yokoyama (1928: 6–7 (preface), 13, 19–35, 45, 51, 183–217).
54 Nanba (1924: 188–9), Yokoyama (1928: 4 (preface), 10–14, 18–19).
55 Yokoyama (1928: 5, 37–8).
56 Adachi (1929: 2–3), Keishichô Shi Hensan Iinkai (1959–62, Meiji: 481–3), Keishichô Shi Hensan Iinkai (1959–62, Taishô: 197–203), Keishichô Shi Hensan Iinkai (1959–62, Shôwa: 142, 145, 147–54), Naganoken Keisatsubu (1922: 2), Taikakai (1971, v.1: 651), Yokoyama (1928: 72–3). The annual tournament continued to be held until 1937. Two more imperial inspection tournaments were held in 1934 and 1940. Skill in martial arts also figured in recruitment of patrolmen and brought special privileges. For example, Mase Toshirô writes in his memoirs that he failed to meet the weight minimum, but the examiner passed him because he was a second grade kendo. At training school and later he received recognition and certain privileges for his kendo skills. Mase (1971: 1–2, 4, 17).
57 The January and February 1931 issues of *KKZ* included a series of articles on police reforms.
58 Naimushô (1934–43: Frame 386003).
59 Shimizu (1930: 36–40), Yamamoto (1937: 361).
60 Keishichô, Sôkan Kanbô Bunshoka (1919–38: 1930–8).
61 Ishihara (1932: 159), Matsui (1933: 91–2). This was the case for a former Tokkô official whom I interviewed, Ôhashi Hideo. Ôhashi entered the Keishichô in late 1928 with both a military and a technical school education because he needed a job. He remembered that it became more competitive to enter the police as the depression worsened, especially around 1935. Interview with Ôhashi Hideo, Sept. 1975. Keishichô figures show that only 526 out of 10 056 applicants were accepted in 1935. Keishichô Sôkan Kanbô Bunshoka (1919–38: 1935).
62 Ishihara (1932: 127, 240–2), Toyama (1933: 18).
63 Yamamoto (1937: 361).
64 Ishihara (1930a: 127–37), Ishihara (1930b: 274–8).
65 Ôhashi Hideo said that he never received any formal supplemental training, but studied independently to learn about social movements and to pass the police sergeant and assistant inspector exams. According to Ôhashi, introductory textbooks outlining Tokkô matters were used mainly by police officers outside Tokyo since Tokyo officers could learn from first-hand experiences with social movements. Consequently, Ôhashi concentrated on studying the original writings of Marxists, anarchists, communists, etc. Interview with Ôhashi Hideo, Sept. 1975 and letter from Ôhashi Hideo, Oct. 1975.
66 Ishihara (1930a: 37–8, 90–3), Takahashi (1930: 15–16), Toyama (1933: 43).
67 Matsui (1933: 177, 182–4), Toyama (1933: 42).
68 Interview with Ôhashi Hideo, Sept. 1975. See also Matsui (1933: 93), Yamagata (1968: 47). Japanese police officials in the 1970s still work very long hours. See Bayley (1976: 22–3).

69 Salaries for Keishichô police officials consistently averaged 6–7 yen more than the national average. Naimushô, Keihokyoku (1926–41: 1930–7).
70 Toyama (1933: 122–3).
71 Matsui (1933: 92–3, 101–4). In 1933 both houses of the Diet passed resolutions favouring improved compensation of police officials and honours for those who performed meritorious service. 'Teikoku gikaini ni okeru keisatsukan yûgû ni kansuru kengi' (1933).
72 Toyama (1933: 122–3, 138–9).
73 *Ibid.* p.17; Matsui (1933: 81).
74 Keishichô Shi Hensan Iinkai (1959–62, Shôwa: 112–16).
75 Typically the rank of section, subsection, and police station chiefs.
76 Ishihara (1930a: 56–9).
77 Matsui (1933: 124–5), Nakagawa (1934: 22).
78 Taikakai (1971, v.1: 659).
79 Keishichô Shi Hensan Iinkai (1959–62, Shôwa: 193–4).
80 Taikakai (1971, v.1: 659).
81 Naimushô (1934–43: Frame 386037), Ibarakiken (June 1934–39: Frames 382116, 382393–5), Yokomizu (1928: 20).
82 This use of tear gas brought forth protests from four proletarian parties. Maruyama (1955: 215).
83 Kobayashi (1952: 134–5), Miyashita, Itô and Nakamura (1978: 99).
84 Naisei Shi Kenkyûkai (1967b: 97–8), Ogino (1984: 229).
85 For example, Keisatsu Kenkyûkai (1932: 1 (preface), 8).
86 Naimushô, Keihokyoku, Hoanka (1930–44, Apr. 1933: 134).
87 Ibarakiken (June 1934–39: Frames 382099, 382101, 382525–6), Ishihara (1930b: 43–4, 83–93), Nakagawa (1934: 19, 30–1, 113–16, 122–6), Ogata (1933: 258–9).
88 Kurihara and Ogata (1932: 17–18), Naimushô, Keihokyoku, Hoanka (1935, pt 2: 3), excerpts reprinted in Okudaira (1975: 445–64), Nakagawa (1934: 4 (intro.), 17).
89 Aketa (1932: 3–4), Kobayashi (1952: 153), Nakagawa (1934: 16, 32–3, 36), Sone (1930: preface 2–3), Yamaguchi (1933: preface 3). Former Tokkô officers Ôhashi Hideo and Satô Shigeru agreed that only police officers with superior scholarly knowledge and abilities could enter the Tokkô. Interviews with Ôhashi Hideo and Satô Shigeru, Sept. 1975.

Miyashita Hiroshi denied that Tokkô officers possessed superior knowledge and scholarly abilities, pointing to himself as a typical example. But this is belied by the fact that when Miyashita entered the Tokkô, he had already passed the exam for assistant inspector. Moreover, he says that after joining the Tokkô he began reading leftist periodicals in addition to less radical pubications such as *Kaizô* and *Chûô Kôron* that he had been reading previously. Miyashita, Itô and Nakamura (1978: 61–2).

For examples of official guidelines on ways to obtain *tenkô*, see Naimushô, Keihokyoku (1921–36: Frames 166–202).

90 Interview with Ôhashi Hideo, Sept. 1975. See also Ishihara (1930b: 46), Nakagawa (1934: 18).

91 Miyashita, Itô and Nakamura (1978: 73–4).
92 *Ibid*. p. 73.
93 Bent (1974: 8–9), Reiss (1971: 150).
94 Ishihara (1932: 73), Ogata (1933: 258).
95 See Chapter 3, note 89.
96 Aketa (1934: 164–6), Aoki (1937: 1, 5–6, 12–23), Hôsei Jihôsha (1933: 224–6), Jônan (1932: 131–2, 177–8, 183–4), Keisatsu Kenkyûkai (1931: 1–2), Kinoshita (1933: 3–4), Matsumoto (1934: 43), Naganoken Keisatsubu (1922: 52), Naimushô (n.d: Ch. 1, Sec. II, 1), Ogata (1933: 3–6), Sone (1930: 9–10), Tachibana (1929: 351), Yamamoto (1934: 315–17, 336–7).
97 Hôsei Jihôsha (1933: 195–6), Keisatsu Kenkyûkai (1931: 107), Matsui (1933: 131, 234), Nakagawa (1934: 12), Ogata (1933: 23, 261), Sasaki (1933: 6), Sone (1930: 7–8), Yamaguchi (1933: 16).
98 Keisatsu Kenkyûkai (1931: 144, 146, 152), Kuwabara (1930: 212), Yamamoto (1934: 340–1).
99 Ogino (1984: 277–80).
100 Such intervention was not always welcomed, especially by employers who referred to it as 'saber mediation'. Garon (1987: 206–7).
101 Hôsei Jihôsha (1933: 195), Ishihara (1932: 85–6), Ishihara (1930b: 226), Takahashi (1924: 24).
102 Naimushô Keihokyoku, Hoanka (1935: 2), Naimushô, Keihokyoku, Hoanka (1939: 22), Ogata (1933: 261), Sone (1930: preface 1), Yamamoto (1934: 334–6).
103 Yamagata (1968: 53).
104 Jônan (1930: 15–16), Matsui (1937: 131, 133), Sone (1930: 6), Tsunajima (1937: 40). Directives tried to eliminate use of such rude forms of address as 'oi oi' (hey!). Jônan (1933: 26–8). However, these were so commonly used by prewar police officers that a postwar critic dubbed them the 'oi kora' police. Hironaka (1974: 2).
105 For example, Gotô (1935: 2–6), Katô (1935a: 21–6), Katô (1935b: May 28–31, June 58–62), Naimushô, Keihokyoku (1934b: 11–20), Naimushô, Keihokyoku, Keimuka, Kaigigakari (1935: 19), [Naimushô], Keihokyoku, Keimuka, Kaigigakari (1936: 55), Tatebayashi (1936: 8).
106 Ishihara (1930b: 226, 228–9, 232–5, 256–7), Matsui (1932a: 4, 7), Matsui (1933: 16, 122–3), Sugimoto (1933: 216).
107 Aketa (1934: 73), Matsui (1933: 122), Matsui (1934: 3). For other discussions of these traditional elements, see Ishihara (1930b: 259, 262–9, 287–8), Keisatsu Kenkyûkai (1931: 113), Matsumoto (1934: 7–9), Toyama (1933: 30–1).
108 It is difficult to find a single appropriate translation for *tadashii*. Possibilities include righteous, just, proper, lawful.
109 Aketa (1934: 2, 8–25, 61–2), Katô (1936: .1), Nakagawa (1934: 10–12).
110 Aketa (1934: 74–6, 79–86, 99–100, 104, 108–23), Hôsei Jihôsha (1933: 72–3), Naimushô (n.d: Ch. 1, Sec. I.1), Nakagawa (1934: 1–3 (intro.), 10–12), Tatebayashi (1935: 19–27).
111 Aoki (1937: 4), Ishihara (1930b: 45, 47), Nakagawa (1934: 13–15).

112 Naimushô (n.d.: ch. 1, Sec. I.3.1), Naimushô, Keihokyoku, Hoanka (1935: 2).
113 Ishihara (1930b: 46–7, 49), Kurihara and Ogata (1932: 8–9), Nakagawa (1934: 9–10, 13, 16–17).
114 Ishihara (1930b: 48), Keisatsu Kenkyûkai (1931: 84), Nakagawa (1934: 16–17).
115 Miyashita, Itô and Nakamura (1978: 69–70). In interviews during September 1975 Ôhashi Hideo and Satô Shigeru also expressed a clear perception of the Tokkô's purpose as being protection of the imperial institution and *kokutai* rather than the people. Ôhashi distinguished the Tokkô from other police in this respect, saying that the criminal police, for example, worked to protect the people rather than the emperor.
116 Aoki (1937: 3–4), Matsui (1932b: 5), Ibarakiken (June 1934–9: Frames 382111–6, 382126), Shôkadô Henshûbu (1934: 16), Yamamoto (1934: 314–15, 333).
117 'Aristocracy' and 'favourite child' are the words of police officials themselves. Ishihara (1932: 73), Kinoshita (1933: preface 1).
118 Matsui (1937: 1–2 (preface), 1–2, 56–65).
119 Kuwabara (1930: 215), Matsui (1933: 5, 175–6), Sugimoto (1933: 259).
120 Keisatsu Kenkyûkai (1931: 80), Matsui (1937: 161), Nakagawa (1934: 28–9), Nanba (1924: 222–3), Satô (1937: preface 1–2), Ibarakiken (June 1934–9: Frames 382109–16), Sone (1930: 1), Tottoriken (1932–41: Frame 380977), Toyama (1933: 109).
121 The Shinpeitai was a group consisting mainly of civilians from right wing labour parties which plotted a coup involving assassination of the cabinet and other leading politicians and *zaibatsu* businessmen. See Shillony (1973: 42–3, 107–8).
122 Naisei Shi Kenkyûkai (1967a: 68, 71). The extent of secrecy in Tokkô reporting is also indicated in the memoirs of former Tokkô officer Ôhashi Hideo. Ôhashi says that while assigned to the Nakano Tokkô subsection, he made very few written reports on the military and civilian right wing because he was ordered to make direct oral reports to the Keishichô Tokkô subsection chief in charge of right wing control. He based these reports on personal notes, so only a few people knew their contents. Ôhashi (1967: 43).
123 Abe (1978: 91–2), Keishichô Shi Hensan Iinkai (1959–62, Shôwa: 405–6), Kobayashi (1952: 325–6), Naisei Shi Kenkyûkai (1967a: 34, 56–7), Tosawa (1965: 35–6).
124 Kawamura (1974: 164–5), Kobayashi (1952: 193), Ogino (1984: 233).
125 For example, in the mid 1930s the Keishichô Tokkô division was so enraged by the Keihokyoku's release of information from Tokkô reports to the newspapers that Abe Genki presented a letter of resignation for his department to the Keishichô Superintendent-General, who then made a protest to Director of the Keihokyoku Fujinuma Shôhei. Fujinuma (1957: 196).
126 Silberman (1974: 206–11), Spaulding (1967: 317–20).
127 Hayashi (1969: 71).

128 Fujinuma (1957: 25), Hayashi (1969: 70–1), Naisei Shi Kenkyûkai (1967a: 5), Naisei Shi Kenkyûkai (1967b, v.1: 7), Naisei Shi Kenyûkai (1967c: 7), Rikken Seiyûkai Suzuki Sôsai Hensanbu (1934: 188).
129 For example, Naisei Shi Kenkyûkai (1967a: 1–2), Naisei Shi Kenkyûkai (1967b, v.1: 8), Nagaoka (1939: 14).
130 Ôno (1973: 67–8), Saitô (1974: 14–15).
131 Silberman (1974: 208–9), Takeuchi (1930: 526).
132 Fujinuma (1957: 93, 95), Hayashi (1969: 94), Taikakai (1971, v.1: 612–15, 748).
133 Ishihara (1932: 156).
134 Ishihara (1930a: 56), Keishichô Shi Hensan Iinkai (1959–62, Shôwa: 115), Taikakai (1971, v.1: 621), Toyama (1933: 16).
135 Naimushô, Keihokyoku (1926–41: 1937–8), Toyama (1933: 16–17) Ôhashi Hideo said that out of the 98 who became patrolmen with him, only three became police sergeants. It took Ôhashi fifteen years to become an inspector. Interview, Sept. 1975.
136 Naisei Shi Kenkyûkai (1967a: 61–2). Tsuchiya Shôzô also blamed emphasis on expertise for the narrow field of vision of postwar police administrators, but he acknowledged problems associated with lack of expertise of prewar police administrators. Naisei Shi Kenkyûkai (1967c: 17–18).
137 Naisei Shi Kenkyûkai (1967c: 18).
138 Ibid. pp. 9, 12; Naisei Shi Kenkyûkai (1967b, v.1: 1).
139 Nagaoka (1939: 48).
140 Kobayashi (1952: 192–3), Yamagata (1968: 23–4).
141 Naisei Shi Kenkyûkai (1967a: 62–3).
142 Silberman (1974: 108–9), Takeuchi (1930: 526).
143 Maeshima (1969: 155).
144 Gotô Fumio was Director of the Keihokyku under the Katô Tomosaburô cabinet and Home Minister under the Okada Keisuke cabinet. Kawasaki Takukichi was the Director of the Keihokyoku when the Peace Preservation Law was passed and Home Vice-Minister under the second all-Kenseikai Katô Kômei cabinet. Ishihara Tsunejirô was Peace Preservation Section Chief under Keihokyoku directors Kawasaki and Matsumura Giichi. Maruyama Tsurukichi was Superintendent-General of the Keishichô under the Hamaguchi Osachi cabinet. Matsumoto Manabu was Director of the Keihokyoku under the Saitô Makoto cabinet.
145 Maeshima (1969: 158).
146 Maruyama (1955: 1, 3).
147 On the ideological and programmatic differences between the Kenseikai (Minseitô) and Seiyûkai, see Duus (1968: 135, 234–5, 248), Garon (1987: 55, 62–8, 136–43).
148 Kawamura (1974: 135–6, 175–6).
149 Both directors of the Keihokyoku under the Saitô and Ôkada cabinets, Matsumoto Manabu and Karasawa Toshiki respectively, were new bureaucrats. Naisei Shi Kenkyûkai (1967a: 82–3), Naisei Shi Kenkyûkai (1967b, v.1: 124–5).
150 Karasawa Toshiki had especially close relations with Nagata, who

came from the same hometown. Matsumoto (1965: 119), Naisei Shi Kenkyûkai (1967c: 112). For more details on the new bureaucrats, see Spaulding (1970).
151 Naisei Shi Kenkyûkai (1967a: 83), Naisei Shi Kenkyûkai (1967c: 111).
152 Yoshii Yoshizane, quoted in Ogino (1984: 291–2).
153 On the expansion of Home Ministry influence, see Berger (1977).
154 Wilson (1968: 138–9).
155 Another Tokkô commandment that may have been difficult to put into practice was the directive to pay careful attention to devising appropriate and reasonable methods without becoming lenient or losing strictness. Naimushô, Keihokyoku, Hoanka (1935: 1).
156 Suzuki (1936, pt 4: 84–97).
157 Westley (1970: xvi–xvii).
158 Carte and Carte (1975: 114–18).
159 Ishihara (1930b: 48, 243–9), Matsui (1933: 52, 108), Toyama (1933: 129–32).

Chapter 5
1 Nakagawa (1934: 13).
2 Geertz (1966: 64).
3 Okudaira (1973: 51).
4 Administrative conflict deriving from overlapping jurisdictions and procedures also characterised the Japanese police's model, the nineteenth century French police system. See Payne (1966: 26).
5 Naimushô, Keihokyoku (1927b: 97–8), Ogata (1933: 5–6), Sone (1930: 9), Hôsei Jihôsha (1933: 245–6). See also Chapter 4.
6 Jônan (1932: 178), Naganoken, Keisatsubu (1922: 52), Sone (1930: 9–10).
7 A career Justice Ministry bureaucrat who was Procurator-General from 1912–21, Justice Minister from 1922–3, Vice-President of the Privy Council from 1926–36, and Prime Minister in 1939. See Mitchell (1976: 36–8), Yasko (1973).
8 A career Justice Ministry bureaucrat who succeeded Hiranuma as Procurator-General in 1921, became Justice Minister under the Kiyoura cabinet (Jan.–May 1924), Home Minister under the Tanaka cabinet until censured for election interference (1927–8), and Seiyûkai president in the 1930s.
9 Suzuki Kisaburô Sensei Denki Hensankai (1955: 120–1, 211).
10 Berger (1977: 75–7, 143, 329).
11 Yasko (1973: 16, 21–5, 129–30).
12 Pyle (1974: 152).
13 Ibid. p. 162.
14 Ibid. pp. 143–4, 160–1.
15 Ibid. p. 144. See also Bernstein (1976: 55).
16 Naganoken, Keisatsubu (1922: 52–4), Wada (1921: 18).
17 Ebashi (1976: 73, 75), Hayashi (1969: 153), Izawa Takio Denki Hensan Iinkai (1951: 127–8).

18 Yoshino Sakuzô, the exponent of *minponshugi* (literally, the people as the base-ism), lectured at the Police Training School in 1919 on the theoretical basis of universal manhood suffrage. This seems to reinforce the picture of a 'progressive' clique dominating police circles during the early 1920s. For a different interpretation, see Mitchell (1976: 231–3).
19 Ebashi (1976: 73), Watanabe (1976: 24–5).
20 Ebashi (1976: 69), Taki (1974: 119, 124).
21 Fujinuma (1957: 56).
22 Naganoken, Keisatsubu (1922: 3).
23 Mitchell (1983: 251).
24 Ebashi (1976: 69), Taki (1974: 119), Watanabe (1976: 25).
25 Mitchell (1983: 252), Mitchell (1976: 39–44), Okudaira (1977: 21–2), Watanabe (1976: 25).
26 Okudaira (1977: 22).
27 Ebashi (1976: 75–6), Suzuki Kisaburô Sensei Denki Hensankai (1955: 105, 119).
28 Mitchell (1976: 44), Suzuki Kisaburô Sensei Denki Hensankai (1955: 255).
29 Okudaira (1977: 35).
30 Kawamura (1974: 134–5), Watanabe (1976: 25–8).
31 Hayashi (1969: 153), Izawa Takio Denki Hensan Iinkai (1951: 135), Okudaira (1975: 16–17, 21).
32 Ebashi (1976: 75), Hayashi (1969: 153), Izawa Takio Denki Hensan Iinkai (1951: 137–8).
33 For example, Home Minister Wakatsuki Reijirô and Director of the Keihokyoku Kawasaki Takukichi under the Katô Kômei cabinet (1924–6). Aoki (1958: 59), Kawasaki Takukichi Denki Hensankai (1961: 286), Wakatsuki (1950: 297).
34 Kawamura (1974: 200).
35 Kawasaki Takukichi Denki Hensankai (1961: 288).
36 Yuasa opposed the bill for having terminology just as vague and vast as the 1922 bill, for being even more severe, and for working in contradiction to the aim of universal manhood suffrage. He also feared police abuse of a law lacking in clarity. He did not oppose the goal of protecting the *kokutai*, but rather the way Article 1 seemed to equate an 'absolute' thing like the *kokutai* with the private property system which was not an absolute. Shakai Mondai Shiryô Kenkyûkai (ed.) (1972: 490–7).
37 During an interpellation a committee member referred to hearing this. Shakai Mondai Shiryô Kenkyûkai (ed.) (1972: 135).
38 Kawasaki Takukichi Denki Hensankai (1961: 178), Aoki (1958: 59), Suzuki Kisaburô Sensei Denki Hensankai (1955: 259–60), Wakatsuki (1950: 298), Watanabe (1976: 30–1).
39 See Diet proceedings in Okudaira (1975: 54–5) or Shakai Mondai Shiryô Kenkyûkai (ed.) (1972: 404). An *Asahi shinbun* editorial on 17 Jan. 1925 opposing the bill also declared that no one could disagree with or oppose the aim of the bill, which was to control radical

movements that sought to change the *kokutai*, subvert the constitution and laws of the state, or destroy the social structure. Okudaira (1975: 100).

40 Okudaira (1975: 56, 71, 92–3), Asahi Shinbunsha (1975: 110), Watanabe (1976: 31).
41 28 Apr. 1928 editorial reprinted in Okudaira (1975: 180).
42 Kawasaki Takukichi Denki Hensankai (1961: 297–8, 305), Okudaira (1973: 62–3).
43 Naisei Shi Kenkyûkai (1967b, v.1: 123), Suzuki Kisaburô Sensei Denki Hensankai (1955: 224).
44 Silberman (1974: 200), Spaulding (1967: 320).
45 The uniqueness of these characteristics of the 15 March arrests was pointed out by one of the six planners, then-Vice-Chief Procurator Matsuzaka Hiromasa, in a 1938 address to procuratorial officials. Matsuzaka (1965: 46–7, 55). See also Matsumoto (1965: 269, 276–7), Okudaira (1976: 40), Wagatsuma (1970: 133).
46 Ogino (1984: 171–2).
47 Okudaira (1977: 95), Okudaira (1973: 65).
48 For example, Ebashi (1976: 76). Suzuki's biographers, however, regarded Suzuki's resignation in mid 1928, followed by Vice-Minister Sugiyama and Director of the Keihokyoku Yamaoka, as the disappearance of the 'emergency advance guard' for eradication of the JCP. Suzuki Kisaburô Sensei Denki Hensankai (1955: 277).
49 For further details, see Mitchell (1976: 134–40).
50 Ebashi (1976: 89), Ibarakiken (June, 1934–9: Frames 382136, 382172), Ogino (1984: 308–9).
51 For example, in meetings of thought officials in 1937, 1940 and 1941. Okudaira (1975: 313, 373–4, 377–8). See also Naimushô, Keihokyoku (1934–43: Frame 386136), Ibarakiken (June 1934–9: Frames 382145, 382252–3), Tottoriken (1928: Frames 7–8).
52 Naimushô, Keihokyoku (1934–43: Frames 386130–1).
53 From the proceedings of the July 1941 thought administrators meeting. Okudaira (1975: 377–8).
54 Mitchell (1976: 126, 187).
55 *Ibid.* pp. 172–3.
56 *Ibid.* pp. 173–4; Okudaira (1973: 65).
57 For example, the regulations governing patrolman service. Keishichô Shi Hensan Iinkai (1959–62, Taishô: 163).
58 Naimushô, Keihokyoku, Hoanka (1935, pt 1: 5), reprinted in Okudaira (1975: 445–64).
59 Futagawa (1925: 446–52).
60 Keisatsu Kenkyûkai (1932: 82–3).
61 Miyashita, Itô and Nakamura (1978: 95).
62 *Ibid.* pp. 95–7.
63 Naimushô, Keihokyoku, Hoanka (1930–44, Jan. 1933: 6).
64 Ogino (1984: 250).
65 Mitchell (1976: 131–2).
66 *Ibid.* p. 131n.

67 Ogino (1984: 250).
68 Mitchell (1976: 131n).
69 For example, in 1935 the Hiroshima Tokkô section began holding special thought courses on the Japanese spirit for *tenkôsha*. Aoki (1936: 18–21).
70 Improvement of contacts and cooperation between the Tokkô and procurators and between the Tokkô and supervision centres for thought criminals was a common topic of discussion in Tokkô meetings. See Ibarakiken (June 1934–9: Frames 382259, 382397–401, 382432).
71 Ôtani (1966: 1, 29, 48–9).
72 Kobayashi (1952: 195), Naisei Shi Kenkyûkai (1967a: 38–40).
73 Former Keishichô Superintendent-General Fujinuma Shôhei gives another example of the Kenpeitai stealing a head start on the police and confiscating evidence related to the arrest of some JCP members before the investigation began. The police station sent an indignant report to Keishichô headquarters, but to Fujinuma's embarrassment, he did not learn of the incident until the Home and Justice Ministers mentioned hearing about a recent big arrest from the Army Minister at a cabinet meeting. Fujinuma (1957: 197).
74 Taikakai (1971: v.1: 772).
75 Kuroda (1963: 358–60), Naisei Shi Kenkyûkai (1967c, v.2: 92–3), Ôtani (1966: 114–16), Tateno (1963: 167), Tsunoda (1956: 98–105).
76 Kuroda, (1963: 358), Ôtani (1966: 115).
77 Naisei Shi Kenkyûkai (1967c, v.2: 93).
78 *Ibid.* pp. 90, 92–3; Kuroda, (1963: 358, 360). People associated with the military tend to see the incident ending in a victory for the army and in establishment of a hands-off policy towards active duty soldiers by the police.
79 Titus (1974: 98–100).
80 See Crowley (1966: 66–74), Itô (1969).
81 Tateno (1963: 167).
82 Naisei Shi Kenkyûkai (1967c, v.2: 91). In Miyashita Hiroshi's memory, he first heard a superior use the phrase in 1928. Prior to that time his police station chiefs had told patrolmen that they were part of the 'people's police.' The shift in emphasis to state service may thus have begun earlier, but Miyashita's retelling confirms that a shift occurred. Miyashita, Itô and Nakamura (1978: 54–5).
83 Fujinuma (1957: 177). For examples of other military-police friction, see Abe (1978: 99), Fujinuma (1957: 175–6), Naisei Shi Kenkyûkai (1967a: 39), Naisei Shi Kenkyûkai (1967c, v.2: 100–1).
84 'Chian iji hô' (1952, pt 2: 17), Fujinuma (1957: 175).
85 'Chian iji hô' (1952, pt 2: 17).
86 *Ibid.*
87 Abe (1978: 151).
88 Keishichô Shi Hensan Iinkai (1959–62, Shôwa: 447).
89 *Ibid.* pp. 446–63; Abe (1978: 171–2), Katô (1972: 143), Kobayashi (1952: 339–40, 344–50), Naisei Shi Kenkyûkai (1967a: 72–5).

90 Aketa (1934: 28–41).
91 Abe Genki claims that the Tokkô remained politically neutral until the war. He points out that it had no responsibilities for election control, and that unlike other police positions down to police station chief, the Tokkô section chief did not change with each cabinet. To maintain its neutrality in partisan politics, Abe successfully opposed the abolition of the higher police section in the Keishichô, saying that abolition would introduce the danger of political leaders turning to the Tokkô for election interference. Naisei Shi Kenkyûkai (1967a: 14, 36–7, 84–5). See also Aketa (1934: 169), Fujinuma, (1957: 191), Ishihara (1930b: 9–10, 26–31, 38–43), Kobayashi (1952: 198–200), Naisei Shi Kenkyûkai (1967c, v.2: 111), Nakagawa (1934: 9–10, 13–15).
92 The following general description and analysis of these theories is based on Barber (1971), Bluhm, (1974: 12–16), Geertz (1966: 52–64), Schulze (1973). Also helpful is Carol Gluck's definition of ideology and treatment of Meiji ideology as the product of an uncontrollable process rather than the product of only a small group of conscious ideologues. Gluck (1985).
93 Geertz (1966: 53).
94 Jônan (1932: 49–51), Ogata (1933: 53), Sone (1930: 3–4, 10), Tachibana (1929: 159, 163).
95 Aoki (1937: 245–6), Jônan (1932: 49, 60), Ogata (1933: 58), Sone (1930: 83), Tachibana (1929: 157). During the 1930s social democrats also shifted to support military preparations and actively extolled the *kokutai*. In return for collaboration in promoting 'industrial cooperation', the Home Ministry and Welfare Ministry (created in 1938 out of the Home Ministry's Social Bureau) realised some of the social democratic labour movement's long-standing legislative demands. Aoki (1937: 245), Garon (1987: 198), Naimushô, Keihokyoku, Chôsashitsu (1937), Totten (1966: 89–108, ch. 9–10).
96 Jônan (1932: 212), Ogata (1933: 69–70), Tachibana (1929: 340–1,.
97 Aoki (1937: 457–8), Kinoshita (1933: 12, 15, 16), Ogata (1933: 81–2, 107), Sasaki (1933: 3–4, 22–3), Ibarakiken (June 1934–9, Frames 382010), 382169), Sone (1930: 2, 131).
98 Ogino (1984: 270–6).
99 Aoki (1937: 165), Inomata (1937: 13–14), Ibarakiken (June 1934–9: Frames 382169–70, 382179, 382430), Sone (1930: 83–4).
100 Jônan (1932: 95–107), Ogata (1933: 191).
101 Garon (1987: 195, 207).
102 Jônan (1932: 210), Naimushô, Keihokyoku, Hoanka (1935, pt 2: 21), Sasaki (1933: 62).
103 Background factors, such as after-effects of the Minobe Affair and outbreak of war in China, no doubt contributed to the expansion of Tokkô operations to liberals and other non–communists, but the reasons given by official sources were agreement with Comintern policy and the possible existence of communist elements within legal popular front organisations. Aoki (1937: 281–2), Ibarakiken (June 1934–9: Frames 382169–70, 382179, 382430).

104 Futagawa (1925: 263), Hôsei Jihôsha (1933: 244), Ikeda (1939: 31), Jônan (1932: 2–3, 14–15, 91, 220–1), Katô (1972: 37–8), Naimushô, Keihokyoku (1927b: 97), Sone (1930: preface 1), Tachibana (1929: 263, 268–70).
105 Sheldon Garon's study of state labour policies points out considerable differences and even 'antipathy' between Home Ministry bureaucrats and capitalists. Garon (1987: for example, 78–82, 172–3, 207).
106 Shakai Mondai Shiryô Kenkyûkai (ed.) (1972: 386–7, 683).
107 *Ibid.* pp. 403–4, 531–2.
108 Shôkadô Henshûbu (1934: 125–6).
109 Davis (1960), Hofstadter (1965).
110 Hofstadter (1965: 39).
111 Davis (1960: 215–17, 224).
112 *Ibid.* pp. 212–13.
113 Kobayashi (1952: 41).
114 Kuwabara (1930: 259). See also Aketa (1934: 132–5), Jônan (1932: 32–3), Naimushô Keihokyoku (1927b: 97), Sone (1930: preface 1).
115 Jônan (1932: 40–3).
116 *Ibid.* pp. 49, 51; Sone (1930: 10), Tachibana (1929: 154).
117 Hôsei Jihôsha (1933: 250–1, 265), Ishihara (1930b: 128), Naganoken, Keisatsubu (1922: 52).
118 Matsui (1933: 227–8), Ibarakiken (June 1934–9: Frames 382169–70, 382179), Yamamoto (1934: 314).
119 Aoki (1937: 472–4), 'Chian iji hô' (1952, pt 2: 6), Jônan (1932: 216–17), Ogino (1984: 326), Okudaira (1977: 200), Ibarakiken (June 1934–9: Frames 382186, 382438), Tachibana (1929: 264–7).
120 Santaro (1924: 5).
121 Ishihara (1930b: 58), Nakagawa (1934: 7–8).
122 For example, Sasaki (1933: 2).
123 For a similar interpretation, see Ebashi (1976: 81).
124 Beckmann and Okubo (1969: 192).
125 Byas (1943).
126 For example, Jakubs (1977), Johnson (1978: 185–6).

Chapter 6
1 Aoki was the Tokkô Section Chief in Fukuoka prefecture at the time of writing. Aoki (1937: 5–6).
2 Burin (1952: 44n).
3 Conquest (1968: 15).
4 Supreme Commander for the Allied Powers, Government Section (1949: 705).
5 Broeker (1970).
6 For example, Garmire (1972: 9).
7 Crankshaw (1956: ch. 1–9).
8 Ôno (1973: 19, 55), Sugimoto (1952, pt 2: 38).
9 For example, Hironaka (1974: 143), Ogino (1984: 454). The Japanese lawyer Igarashi Futaba has described cases of injustice, particularly extended police detention, due to continued emphasis on obtaining a confession. Igarashi (1986).

10 Ames (1981: 143–4).
11 Bayley (1976: 177–9). Gavan McCormack, even while trying to expose the injustices of the contemporary police and judicial system, stated that the victims of injustice in the cases described had been freed and their complaints publicised, and that, therefore, Japan is 'not totalitarian or fascist'. McCormack (1986).
12 McNamara (1967: 176).
13 Recognition of this problem had led certain American police reformers in the 1970s to recommend structural reorganisation of police forces to enable specialisation in the different police functions. For example, see Garmire (1972: 6–8), Rubin (1972).
14 Carte and Carte (1975: 109–18), Westley (1970: xv–xvi), Wilson (1967).
15 For a good summary and critique of Marxist applications of the concept of fascism to Japan, see McCormack (1980), Wilson (1968: 401–4).
16 Chapman (1970: 137). Chapman has made virtually the only attempt to define 'police state' as a theoretical concept. Although his lack of knowledge of Japan leads him to the mistaken conclusion that Japan became a 'totalitarian' police state, his typologies are very useful in suggesting general categories for analysis.
17 Steiner (1976: 120). For clarification of the complex organisational relationships and personality types included in the Nazi police system, see Browder (1975). On the SS leadership, see Ziegler (1989).
18 Höhne (1969: 84) .
19 Reitlinger (1957: 90).
20 Buchheim (1972: 262). See also Browder (1975: 214–15). On the usurpation of state offices by party officials and the progressive erosion of the state apparatus, see also Mommsen (1976: 194, 201).
21 Buchheim (1972: 264). On the personal concept of politics, see Mommsen (1976: 195).
22 Quoted in Höhne (1969: 199). According to Steiner, this amounted to a 'state of legal lawlessness'. Steiner (1976: 144).
23 Buchheim (1972: 265), Reitlinger (1957: 89).
24 Höhne (1969: 174, 186, 200).
25 The RSHA, created in 1939 and commanded by Heydrich, represented the fusion of the Security Police and SD into a single body transcending both Party and state structures. Browder (1975: 221–4).
26 Höhne (1969: 402–3).
27 *Ibid.* pp. 463, 471, 482.
28 Buchheim (1965: 188).
29 Werner Best statement, Höhne (1969: 172).
30 Höhne (1969: 172–3), Bramstedt (1945: 101).
31 Crankshaw (1956: 32–3, 94).
32 Buchheim (1968: 47).
33 Höhne (1969: 656–7).
34 Conquest (1968: 17, 46).
35 Levytsky (1972: 128).

36 Conquest's description of the estimate. Conquest (1968: 81).
37 *Ibid.* p. 8.
38 *Ibid.* p. 15; similar translation in Levytsky (1972: 28). See also Knight (1988: 11–12).
39 Conquest (1968: 19).
40 *Ibid.* p. 7; Levytsky (1972: 119–20).
41 Knight (1988: 24–6).
42 In his memoirs a former Tokkô officer admitted knowledge of two cases of Tokkô brutality, but argued that organised terror was impossible since instructions from superiors never in his ten-year Tokkô career ordered the use of force but rather often instructed against its use. Yamagata (1968: 15–16).
43 Shakai Bunko (ed.) (1965: 2, 91).
44 Mitchell (1976: 142–5), Smith (1972: 248).
45 Aketa (1932: 3–4), Kobayashi (1952: 153), Nakagawa (1934: 16, 32–3, 36), Sone (1930: preface 2–3), Yamaguchi (1933: preface 3).
46 See Ames (1981: 135–6), Bayley (1976: 138–44).
47 Mosse (1975b: 4).
48 Shakai Mondai Shiryô Kenkyûkai (ed.) (1972: 7).
49 Monas (1961: 23).
50 For a summary of the differences between the Old Right and New Right in Europe, see Rogger (1966: 576, 579).
51 For example, for labour policies. Garon (1987: 189, 225).
52 On Bismarck's state socialism, see Briggs (1967), Dawson (1890), Fay (1950).
53 Sternhell (1976: 360).

BIBLIOGRAPHY

Abbreviation: *KKZ* = *Keisatsu Kyôkai zasshi*

Abe Genki (1978) *Shôwa dôran no shinsô* [The Truth about Shôwa Disturbances] Tokyo: Hara Shobô

Abe Haruo (1956) 'Self-incrimination—Japan and the United States' *Journal of Criminal Law, Criminology, and Police Science* 46, Jan.–Feb., 613–31

——(1963) 'The accused and society: therapeutic and preventive aspects of criminal justice in Japan' in Von Mehren (ed.) *Law in Japan* pp. 324–63

Adachi Kenzô (1929) 'Budô seishin no renma to keisatsu shiki no sakkô' [Cultivation of the spirit of martial arts and promotion of police spirit] *KKZ* 352, Dec., 2–3

Agata Shinobu (1921) 'Kyôsô bunmei no jidai kara kyôdô bunmei e' [From the age of competitive civilisation to cooperative civilisation] *KKZ* 255, Sept., 4–9

Akamatsu Katsumaro (1974) *Nihon shakai undô shi* [History of Japanese Social Movements] Tokyo: Iwanami Shinsho, originally 1952

Akashi Hirotaka and Matsuura Sôzô (eds) (1975) *Shôwa Tokkô dan' atsu shi* [A History of Special Higher Police Oppression during the Shôwa Period] v.1, Tokyo: Taihei Shuppansha

Aketa Takumi (1932) *Tokkô hikkei* [Handbook for the Special Higher Police] Tokyo: Shinkôkaku

——(1934) *Keisatsu seishin no shin kenkyû* [A New Study of Police Spirit] Tokyo: Shôkadô

Akiyoshi Toshirô (1935) 'Keisatsuken no genkai ni tsuite' [On the limits of police authority] *KKZ* 427, Dec., 5–13

Allardyce, Gilbert (ed.) (1971) *The Place of Fascism in European History* Englewood Cliffs: Prentice-Hall

Almond, Gabriel and Sidney Verba (1965) *The Civic Culture* Boston: Little, Brown
Ames, Walter (1981) *Police and Community in Japan* Berkeley: University of California Press
Aoki Sadao (1936) 'Shisôhan hogokai no sôritsu' [The establishment of societies to protect thought crimes] *KKZ* 435, Aug., 18–21
——(1937) *Tokkô kyôtei* [Special Higher Police Textbook] Tokyo: Shinkôkaku
Aoki Tokuzô (1958) *Wakatsuki Reijirô, Hamaguchi Osachi* Tokyo: Jiji Tsûshinsha
Asahi Shinbunsha (ed.) (1975) *Kussetsu no demokurashii* [Refracted Democracy] *Asahi shinbun* ni miru Nihon no ayumi series, v.5, Tokyo: Asahi Shinbunsha
Ayusawa, Iwao (1966) *A History of Labor in Modern Japan* Honolulu: East-West Center Press
Banton, Michael (1963) 'Social integration and police authority' *The Police Chief* Apr., 8–20
Barber, Bernard (1971) 'Function, Variability and Change in Ideological Systems' in Bernard Barber and Alex Inkeles (eds) *Stability and Social Change* Boston: Little Brown pp. 244–62
Bayley, David (1969) *The Police and Political Development in India* Princeton: Princeton University Press
——(1975) 'The police and political development in Europe' in Charles Tilly (ed.) *The Formation of National States in Western Europe* Princeton: Princeton University Press pp. 328–79
——(1976) *Forces of Order: Police Behavior in Japan and the United States* Berkeley: University of California Press
——(1977) *Police and Society* Beverly Hills: Sage
Becker, Harold (1970) *Issues in Public Administration* Metuchen: Scarecrow Press
Beckmann, George (1971) 'The radical left and the failure of communism' in Morley (ed.) *Dilemmas* pp. 139–80
Beckmann, George and Okubo Genji (1969) *The Japanese Communist Party, 1922–1945* Stanford: Stanford University Press
Bent, Alan E. (1974) *The Politics of Law Enforcement* Lexington: D. C. Heath
Berger, Gordon M. (1977) *Parties out of Power in Japan, 1931–1941* Princeton: Princeton University Press
Bernstein, Gail (1976) *Japanese Marxist: A Portrait of Kawakami Hajime, 1879–1946* Cambridge, Ma.: Harvard University Press
Bickerton, William (1934) 'Third degree in Japan' *Living Age* 347, Sep., 30–4
Bluhm, William (1974) *Ideologies and Attitudes: Modern Political Culture* Englewood Cliffs: Prentice-Hall
Bordua, David (ed.) (1967) *The Police: Six Sociological Essays* New York: John Wiley
Borton, Hugh (1940) *Japan since 1931: Its Political and Social Developments* New York: Institute of Pacific Relations

Bowdon, Tom (1973) 'The Irish underground and the war of independence, 1919–21' *Journal of Contemporary History* 8, Apr., 3–23
Bramstedt, E. Kohn- (1945) *Dictatorship and Political Police: The Technique of Control by Fear* New York: Oxford University Press
Briggs, Asa (1967) 'The welfare state in historical perspective' in Charles Schottland (ed.) *The Welfare State: Selected Essays* New York: Harper and Row, pp. 25–45
Broeker, Galen (1970) *Rural Disorder and Police Reform in Ireland, 1812–36* London: Routledge and Kegan Paul
Browder, George C. (1975) 'The SD: the significance of organization and image' in Mosse (ed.) *Police Forces* pp. 205–29
Brown, Sidney (1966) 'Ōkubo Toshimichi and the first Home Ministry bureaucracy, 1873–8' in Bernard Silberman and H. D. Harootunian (eds) *Modern Japanese Leadership: Transition and Change* Tucson: University of Arizona Press
Buchheim, Hans (1965) 'The SS—instrument of domination' in Helmut Krausnick et al. *Anatomy of the SS State* New York: Walker, pp. 127–302
——(1968) *Totalitarian Rule: Its Nature and Characteristics* Middletown: Wesleyan University Press
——(1972) 'The position of the SS in the Third Reich' in Hajo Holborn (ed.) *Republic to Reich: The Making of the Nazi Revolution* New York: Vintage
Burin, Frederic (1952) 'Bureaucracy and national socialism: a reconsideration of Weberian theory' in Robert Merton et al. *Reader in Bureaucracy* Glencoe: Free Press
Byas, H. (1932) 'Communist movement in Japan' *Contemporary Review* 141, Feb., 190–7
——(1943) *Government by Assassination* London: Allen and Unwin
Carte, Gene and Elaine Carte (1975) *Police Reform in the United States* Berkeley: University of California Press
Catalogue of Items, Connected with the General Police System in Japan (1904) Collected by the Police Association for the purpose of being exhibited in the St Louis Exposition, Tokyo: Tokyo Printing Co.
Chamberlain, William (1937) 'Japan's halfway house to fascism' *Current History* 46, May, 31–6
Chapman, Brian (1970) *Police State* New York: Praeger
'Chian iji hô' (1952) [The Peace Preservation Law] 2 pts *Jurisuto* no.13, 1 July, 26–46; and no. 14, 15 July, 2–25
'Chian iji hô kakujo gikai' (1925) [Exposition of the clauses of the Peace Preservation Law] *KKZ* 297, May, 59–66
Chûô Shokugyô Shôkai Jimukyoku (n.d.) *Keishichô junsa saiyô ni kansuru chôsa* [An Investigation of the Recruitment of Metropolitan Police Board Patrolmen] n.p.
Colbert, Evelyn (1952) *The Left Wing in Japanese Politics* New York: Institute of Pacific Relations
Colegrove, Kenneth (1928) 'The Japanese general election of 1928' *American Political Science Review* 22, May, 401–7

Conquest, Robert (1968) *The Soviet Police System* New York: Frederick A. Praeger
Conroy, Hilary (1981) 'Concerning Japanese fascism' *Journal of Asian Studies* 40:2, Feb., 327–8
Crankshaw, Edward (1956) *Gestapo* New York: Pyramid Books
Crowley, James (1966) *Japan's Quest for Autonomy* Princeton: Princeton University Press
Cyert, Richard and Kenneth MacCrimmon (1968) 'Organizations' in Lindzey and Aronson (eds) *Handbook* pp. 568–611
Davis, David Brion (1960) 'Some themes of counter-subversion: an analysis of anti-Masonic, anti-Catholic, and anti-Mormon literature' *Mississippi Valley Historical Review* 47, Sep., 205–24
Dawson, Richard and Kenneth Prewitt (1969) *Political Socialization* Boston: Little, Brown
Dawson, William H. (1890) *Bismarck and State Socialism: An Exposition of the Social and Economic Legislation of Germany since 1870* London: Swan Sonnenschein
De Polnay, Peter (1970) *Napoleon's Police* London: W. H. Allen
Deutsch, Karl (1966) *The Nerves of Government: Models of Political Communication and Control* New York: The Free Press
Dore, R. P. and Ôuchi Tsutomu (1971) 'Rural origins of Japanese fascism' in Morley (ed.) *Dilemmas* pp. 181–210
Dorwart, Reinhold A. (1971) *The Prussian Welfare State before 1740* Cambridge, Ma.: Harvard University Press
Downard, J. Douglas (1976) 'Tokyo: the Depression years, 1927–1933' PhD thesis, Indiana University
Duus, Peter (1968) *Party Rivalry and Political Change in Taishô Japan* Cambridge, Ma.: Harvard University Press
Duus, Peter and Daniel Okimoto (1979) 'Fascism and the history of pre-war Japan: the failure of a concept' *Journal of Asian Studies* 39, Nov., 65–76
Ebashi Takashi (1976) 'Shôwaki no Tokkô keisatsu' [The Special Higher Police during the Shôwa period] *Gendai shi* no. 7, June, 69–97
Eguchi Kiyoshi (1974) 'Takiji gyakusatsu' [The butchering of Takiji] in Kawaguchi Hiroshi (ed.) *Dokyumento Shôwa gojûnen shi* [A documentary history of 50 years of Shôwa] v.2, Tokyo: Sekibunsha, pp. 99–128
Emerson, Donald (1968) *Metternich and the Political Police: Security and Subversion in the Hapsburg Monarchy (1815–1830)* The Hague: Martinus Nijhoff
Emsley Clive (1983) *Policing and its Context 1750–1870* London: The Macmillan Press
Fay, Sidney B. (1950) 'Bismarck's welfare state' *Current History* 18, Jan., 1–8
Fleisher, Wilfrid (1941) *Volcanic Isle* Garden City: Doubleday, Doran
Fletcher, Miles (1979) 'Intellectuals and fascism in early Shôwa Japan' *Journal of Asian Studies* 39, Nov., 39–63
Fosdick, Raymond (1916) *European Police Systems* New York: The Century Co.

Fujinuma Shôhei (1957) *Watakushi no isshô* [My Life] Tokyo: Fujinuma Shôheicho *Watakushi no isshô* Kankôkai
Furuta Masatake (1925) *Chian iji hô* [The Peace Preservation Law] Keisatsu kyôyô shiryô series, no. 1, Tokyo: Keisatsu Kôshûjo Gakuyûkai
Futagawa Kiichi (1925) *Keisatsu no konpon kannen* [Basic Concepts of the Police] Tokyo: Shôkadô
Garmire, Bernard (1972) 'The police role in an urban society' in Steadman (ed.) *Police and Community* pp. 1–11
Garon, Sheldon (1987) *The State and Labor in Modern Japan* Berkeley: University of California Press
Geertz, Clifford (1964) 'Ideology as a cultural system' in David Apter (ed.) *Ideology and Discontent* New York: The Free Press, pp. 47–76
Gluck, Carol (1985) *Japan's Modern Myths* Princeton: Princeton University Press
Gorer, Geoffrey (1955) 'Modification of national character: the role of the police in England' *Journal of Social Issues* 11, 25–32
Gotô Fumio (1935) 'Keisatsu seishin no kakuritsu to tettei' [The establishment and perfection of police spirit] *KKZ* 420, June, 2–6
Gotô Shinpei (1921) 'Seiji keisatsu yori jichi keisatsu e' [From a political police to an autonomous police] *KKZ* 249, Mar., 1–2
Gregor, A. James (1969) *The Ideology of Fascism* New York: The Free Press
Griffin, Edward (1972) 'The universal suffrage issue in Japanese politics, 1918–25' *Journal of Asian Studies* 31, Feb., 275–90
Gross, Neal et al. (1958) *Explorations in Role Analysis* New York: John Wiley
Hacker, Andrew (1977) 'Safety last' *New York Review of Books* 24, 15 Sep., 3–8
Hackett, Roger (1971) *Yamagata Aritomo in the Rise of Modern Japan, 1838–1922* Cambridge, Ma.: Harvard University Press
Hashimoto, Kiminobu (1963) 'The rule of law: some aspects of judicial review of administrative action' in Von Mehren (ed.) *Law in Japan* pp. 239–73
Hayashi Shigeru (1969) *Yuasa Kurahei* Tokyo: Yuasa Kurahei Denki Hakkôkai
——(ed.) (1975) *Dokyumento Shôwa shi* [A Documentary History of the Shôwa Period] v.1, Tokyo: Heibonsha
Henderson, Dan Fenno (1968) 'Law and political modernization in Japan' in Robert E. Ward (ed.) *Political Development in Modern Japan* Princeton: Princeton University Press, pp. 387–456
Hiraga Makoto (1919) 'Keisatsu kyôyô ron' [An essay on police education] *KKZ* 227, Apr., 1–30
Hirata Kiyotsugu (1926) *Minshû keisatsu* [The People's Police] Tokyo: Taihei Shoin
Hironaka Toshio (1974) *Sengo Nihon no keisatsu* [The Postwar Japanese Police] Tokyo: Iwanami Shoten, originally 1968
Hoffmann, Peter (1973) 'Hitler's personal security' *Journal of Contemporary History* 8, Apr., 25–46

Hofstadter, Richard (1965) *The Paranoid Style in American Politics* New York: Knopf
Höhne, Heinz (1969) *The Order of the Death's Head: The Story of Hitler's SS* translated by Richard Barry London: Secker and Warburg
Hôjô Seiichi (1956) *Shôwa jiken shi* [A History of Shôwa Incidents] Tokyo: Masu Shobô
Hôsei Jihôsha (ed.) (1933) *Keisatsu tokuhon* [Police Reader] no. 2, Tokyo: Hôsei Jihôsha
Huntington, Samuel (1957) *The Soldier and the State* Cambridge, Ma.: Harvard University Press
Ibarakiken (June 1934–39) 'Shochô kaigi shorui tsuzuri, Tokkô kankei' [Bound documents of Police Station Chiefs meetings, related to the Special Higher Police] in Naimushô, Keihokyoku 'Documents' Reel 1/Item 2
Ichimura Mitsue (1911) *Gyôseihô genri* [Principles of Administrative Law] Tokyo: Hôbunkan
Igarashi Futaba (1986) 'Forced to confess' in McCormack and Sugimoto (eds) *Democracy* pp. 195–214
Ikeda Katsu (1939) *Chian iji hô* [The Peace Preservation Law] 2 pts, Shin hôgaku zenshû series, v.19, *Keiji hô* [Criminal laws] II, [Tokyo]: Nihon Hyôronsha
Inomata Keijirô (1937) 'Saikin ni okeru kyôsanshugi undô to Nichi-Doku bôkyô kyôtei' [The recent communist movement and the Japanese–German anti-Comintern pact] *KKZ* 440, Jan., 9–18
Irokawa Kôtarô (1931) *Musansha undô torishimari hôki suchi* [Necessary Knowledge of Laws and Regulations for the Control of Proletarian Movements] Kyoto: Kyôseikaku
Ishihara Tsunejirô (1928) *Hôgaku gairon* [An Introduction to Law] Tokyo: Keisatsu Kôshûjo Gakuyûkai
——(1930a) *Ichi kyôjû no omoide* [Recollections of a Professor] Tokyo: Shôkadô
——(1930b) *Shisô keisatsu gairon* [An Introduction to the Thought Police] Tokyo: Shôkadô
——(1932) *Keisatsu shinkan* [Commandments for the Police] Tokyo: Shôkadô
Ishii Masaichi (1932) 'Keishichô kansei no kaisei ni tsuite' [On the reform of the Metropolitan Police Board organization] *KKZ* 384, Aug., 20–4
Itô Takashi (1969) *Shôwa shoki seiji shi kenkyû* [A Study of Early Shôwa Political History] Tokyo: Tôkyô Daigaku Shuppankai
Izawa Takio Denki Hensan Iinkai (1951) *Izawa Takio* Tokyo: Izawa Takio Denki Hensan Iinkai
Jakubs, Deborah L. (1977) 'Police violence in times of political tension: the case of Brazil, 1968–1971' in Bayley (ed.) *Police and Society* pp. 85–106
'Japanese rarities: documents on thought control and other related subjects from the records of the Police Bureau, Ministry of Home Affairs, Tokyo, Japan' United States Library of Congress microfilm, MJ-144, 18 reels

'Jihen to keisatsukan' (1937) [The incident and police officials] *KKZ* 447, Aug., 1

'Jinken jûrin mondai ni kansuru Kiyose–Hitomatsu ryôdaigishi no enzetsu yôshi' (1933) [Major points from the speeches of representatives Kiyose and Hitomatsu concerning the problem of the trampling of human rights] *KKZ* 391, Mar., 38–9

Johnson, David R. (1978) *Policing the Urban Underworld: The Impact of Crime on the Development of the American Police, 1800–1887* Philadelphia: Temple University Press

Johnson, Richard (1972) 'Zagranichnaia Agentura: the Tsarist political police in Europe' *Journal of Contemporary History* 7, Jan.–Apr., 221–42

Jônan, Inshi (1930) *Keisatsu jôshiki* [Police Common Sense] Tokyo: Shôkadô

——(1932) *Tokkô kyôkasho* [Special Higher Police Textbook] Tokyo: Shôkadô Shoten

——(1933) *Fushin jinmon hikkei* [A Manual for Questioning] Tokyo: Shôkadô

Kainô Michitaka (1950) *Bôryoku—Nihon shakai no fuashizumu kikô* [Violence—The Fascist Structure of Japanese Society] Tokyo: Nihon Hyôronsha

——(1960) *Keisatsu ken* [Police Authority] Tokyo: Iwanami Shoten

Kamata Eikichi (1921) 'Kenryoku no daihyôsha ni arazu jiyû no hogosha nari' [Not representatives of power but protectors of freedom] *KKZ* 251, May, 1–5

Kamiyanagi Nobutarô (1925) 'Keisatsu seishin ni kansuru jakkan no kôsatsu' [Some comments related to police spirit] *KKZ* 293, Jan., 18–29

Karasawa Toshiki (1935) 'Tokkô gaiji keisatsu no jûyô naru shimei' [The important mission of the Special Higher Police and foreign affairs police] *KKZ* 421, July, 2–5

——(1956) 'Tennô kikansetsu no dan'atsu' [Suppression of the theory of the emperor as an organ] *Bungei shunjû* Tokushû: Tennô hakusho, Oct., 122–6

Katô Yûsaburô (1935a) 'Hijôji to Tokkô keisatsu' [The crisis and the Special Higher Police] *KKZ* 417, Apr., 21–6

——(1935b) 'Hijôji Tokkô keisatsu no shidô seishin to jissen no mondai' [The guiding spirit of the Special Higher Police in a time of crisis and the problem of its practice] *KKZ* 418, May, 28–31; and 420, June, 58–62

——(1936) *Hijôji ni okeru Tokkô keisatsu no ninmu* [Special Higher Police Duties during a Time of Crisis] Tokyo: Shinkôkaku

——(1972) *Ichi kanryô no mita Shôwa shi* [Shôwa History Seen by a Bureaucrat] Tokyo: Hara Shobô

Kawamura Teishirô (1974) *Kankai no hyôri* [The Ins and Outs of Official Life] Tokyo: Yûsankaku Shuppan, reprint of a 1933 edn.

Kawasaki Takukichi Denki Hensankai (ed.) (1961) *Kawasaki Takukichi* Tokyo: Kawasaki Takukichi Denki Hensankai

Kazahaya Yasoji (1948) *Seiji hanzai no shomondai* [Various Problems of

Political Crimes] Tokyo: Kenshinsha
Keisatsu Kenkyûkai (ed.) (1931) *Keisatsu jitsumu kyôhon, kôtô keisatsu hen* [Practical Police Affairs Textbook, Higher Police volume] Tokyo: Shôkadô
—— (1932) *Shakai undô ni chokumen shite* [Confronted by Social Movements] Tokyo: Shôkadô
'Keisatsuken no genkai, keisatsu gyôsei no shokuiki no mondai ni tsuite' (1935) [On the problem of the limits of police authority and the occupation of police administration] *KKZ* 424, Sep., 38–44
Keishichô (1935) *Tokkô keisatsu reiki* [Special Higher Police Regulations] pt 2 n.p.
Keishichô, Sôkan Kanbô Bunshoka (1919–38) *Keishichô tôkei sho* [Metropolitan Police Board Statistics Book] Tokyo: Keishisôkan Kanbô Bunshoka
'Keishichô Keisatsu Renshûjo (ed.) (1923) *Kun'iku kyôhon* [Moral Education Textbook] Tokyo: Keishichô Keisatsu Renshûjo
'Keishichô Shi Hensan Iinkai (ed.) (1959–62) *Keishichô shi* [A History of the Metropolitan Police Board] 3 v., Tokyo: Keishichô Shi Hensan Iinkai
'Keishisôkan no kenkyo ni kansuru tsûhô' (1965) [Metropolitan Police Board Superintendent-General's report on arrests] in Yamabe (ed.) *Shakaishugi undô* pt 3, pp. 65–70
Kido Tokuichi (1928) *Keisatsu daigaku, Keiseihen* [Police University, Police and Administration volume] v.2, Tokyo: Nihon Hôritsu Kenkyûkai
Kinoshita Eiichi (1933) *Tokkô hôrei no shin kenkyû* [A New Study of Special Higher Police Laws] Tokyo: Shôkadô
Knight, Amy (1988) *The KGB, Police and Politics in the Soviet Union* Boston: Unwin Hyman
Kobayashi Gorô (1952) *Tokkô keisatsu hiroku* [Confidential Record of the Special Higher Police] Tokyo: Seikatsu Shinsha
Kôchiken, Tokubetsu Kôtôka (1929) *Tokubetsu kôtô keisatsu kankei hôki kaigi shûroku* [Compilation of Laws and Regulations and Meetings Related to the Special Higher Police] Tokkô kyôyô shiryô series, no. 9, n.p., Mar.
Koike Yoshimi (1968) *Nihon no keisatsu* [The Japanese Police] Tokyo: Nihon Keisatsu Hensankai
Kôketsu Yazô (1955) 'Akairo sensen daikenkyo' [Mass arrest on the Red front] *Bungei shunjû* Rinji zôkan [Special issue], 33:16, Aug., 58–63
Kondô Takanosuke (1957) *Keisatsukan* [Police Officials] Tokyo: Nihon Hyôron Shinsha
Krieger, Leonard (1957) *The German Idea of Freedom: History of a Political Tradition* Chicago: University of Chicago Press
Kublin, Hyman (1964) *Asian Revolutionary: The Life of Katayama Sen* Princeton: Princeton University Press
Kurihara Ryûhei and Ogata Nakaba (1932) *Tokkô keisatsu yôkô* [An Outline of the Special Higher Police] Tokyo: Kokumeidô
Kuroda Shigeo (1963) *Nihon keisatsu shi no kenkyû* [A Study of the History of the Japanese Police] Tokyo: Reibunsha

Kuwabara Mikine (1930) *Keisatsu fûkei* [A View of the Police] Tokyo: Shôkadô
Laqueur, Walter (ed.) (1976) *Fascism: A Reader's Guide* Berkeley: University of California Press
Laqueur, Walter and George Mosse (eds) (1966) *International Fascism, 1920–1945* New York: Harper and Row
Leavell James (1984) 'The policing of society' in Hilary Conroy et al. *Japan in Transition: Thought and Action in the Meiji Era, 1868–1912* Rutherford: Fairleigh Dickinson University Press pp. 22–49
Le Vine, Robert (1963) 'Political socialization and culture change' in Clifford Geertz (ed.) *Old Societies and New States: The Quest for Modernity in Asia and Africa* New York: The Free Press
Levytsky, Boris (1972) *The Uses of Terror: The Soviet Secret Police, 1917–1970* New York: Coward, McCann and Geoghegan
Lindzey, G. and E. Aronson (eds) (1968) *The Handbook of Social Psychology* v.1, Reading, Ma.: Addison-Wesley
Maeda Renzan (1948) *Hoshi Tôru den* [Biography of Hoshi Tôru] Tokyo: Takayama Shoin
Maeshima Shôzô (1969) *Shôwa gunbatsu no jidai* [The Age of the Shôwa Military Clique] Kyoto: Mineruva Shobô
Maruyama Masao (1963) *Thought and Behavior in Modern Japanese Politics* London: Oxford University Press
Maruyama Tsurukichi (1955) *Nanajûnen tokorodokoro* [Seventy Years Here and There] Tokyo: Nanajûnen Tokorodokoro Hakkôkai
Mase Toshirô (1971) *Gyûho sanjûrokunen, keisatsu ni ikiru* [Thirty-six Years at a Snail's Pace, I Live in the Police] Tokyo: Tachibana Shobô
Matsui Shigeru (1920a) 'Kokumin to keisatsu' [The people and the police] *KKZ* 236, Feb., 12–21
——(1920b) 'Sengo no keisatsu ni tsuite' [On the postwar police] *KKZ* 242, Aug., 16–34
——(1921a) 'Sekaiteki kenchi yori mitaru keisatsu no minshûka' [The democratisation of the police seen from a world point of view] *KKZ* 251, May, 6–15
——(1921b) 'Tsumaranai shisô ni kanji somerenu yô' [Not influenced by worthless thought] *KKZ* 252, June, 52–5
——(1921c) 'Shakai to keisatsu' [Society and the police] *KKZ* 253, July, 1–13
——(1923) 'Keisatsu kannen no fukyû ni tsuite' [On spreading the concept of the police] *KKZ* 276, June, 1–23
——(1928) '*Junsa kara keishi made* o yomite' [Reading *From Patrolman to Superintendent*] *KKZ* 335, July, 12–17
——(1932a) 'Gunjin chokuyu to keisatsu seishin' [The Imperial Instructions to Soldiers and Police Spirit] *KKZ* 378, Feb., 2–12
——(1932b) 'Jikyoku to keisatsu seishin no sakkô' [The present situation and promotion of police spirit] *KKZ* 377, Jan., 2–9
——(1932c) *Keisatsu no konpon mondai* [Basic Problems of the Police] Tokyo: Keisatsu Kôshûjo Gakuyûkai, originally 1924
——(1933) *Keisatsu tokuhon* [Police Reader] Tokyo: Nihon Hyôronsha
——(1934) 'Keisatsu seishin sakkô mondai ni tsuite' [On the problem of

arousing police spirit] *KKZ* 408, July, 2-6
——(1937) *Kyôiku chokugo to keisatsu seishin no hatsuyô* [The Imperial Rescript on Education and the Promotion of Police Spirit] Tokyo: Shôkadô
Matsumoto Manabu (1934) *Keisatsu to minshû* [The Police and the People] Shakai kyôiku panfuretto, no. 196, Tokyo: Shakai Kyôiku Kyôkai
Matsumoto Seichô (1964) *Gendai kanryô ron* [An Essay on Modern Bureaucrats] v.2, Tokyo: Bungei Shunjû Shinsha
——(1965) *Shôwa shi hakkutsu* [Excavation of Shôwa History] v.2, 5, 7, Tokyo: Bungei Shunjû Shinsha
Matsuo Hiroshi (1971) *Chian iji hô* [The Peace Preservation Law] Tokyo: Shin Nihon Shuppansha
Matsuzaka Hiromasa (1965) 'San'ichigo, yon'ichiroku jiken kaiko' [Reminiscences of the March 15 and April 16 Incidents] in Yamabe (ed.) *Shakaishugi undô* pt 3
McCormack, Gavan (1980) '1930s Japan: fascist?' *Social Analysis* 516, Dec., 125-43
——(1986) 'Crime, confession, and control in contemporary Japan' in McCormack and Sugimoto (eds) *Democracy* pp. 186-94
McCormack, Gavan and Yoshio Sugimoto (eds) (1986) *Democracy in Contemporary Japan* Sydney: Hale and Iremonger
McNamara, John (1967) 'Uncertainties in police work: the relevance of police recruits' backgrounds and training' in Bordua (ed.) *The Police* pp. 163-252
Miller, Frank (1965) *Minobe Tatsukichi: Interpreter of Constitutionalism in Japan* Berkeley: University of California Press
Minear, Richard (1970) *Japanese Tradition and Western Law: Emperor, State, and Law in the Thought of Hozumi Yatsuka* Cambridge, Ma.: Harvard University Press
Minobe Tatsukichi (1931a) 'Keisatsu no gainen' [The concept of police] pt 1 *Keisatsu kenkyû* 2, June, 1-8
——(1931b) 'Keisatsu no mokuteki—keisatsu hô gairon, 2' [The purpose of the police—introduction to police law] *Keisatsu kenkyû* 2, July, 1-12
——(1932) *Gyôseihô satsuyô* [Essentials of Administrative Law] v.2, 3rd revised edn., Tokyo: Yûhikaku
Mitamura Takeo (1930) *Keisatsu kyôsei no kenkyû* [A Study of Police Coercion] Tokyo: Shôkadô
Mitchell, Richard (1976) *Thought Control in Prewar Japan* Ithaca: Cornell University Press
——(1983) *Censorship in Imperial Japan* Princeton: Princeton University Press
——(1985) Review of Olavi Fält *Fascism, Militarism or Japanism?* in *Monumenta Nipponica* 40: 4 Winter, 447-9
Miyake Shôtarô (1931) 'Chian iji hô' [the Peace Preservation Law] in *Gendai hôgaku zenshû* [A Complete Collection of Modern Law] v. 38, Tokyo: Nihon Hyôronsha, pp. 181-223
Miyashita Hiroshi, Itô Takashi and Nakamura Tomoko (eds) (1978) *Tokkô no kaisô* [Reminiscences of the Special Higher Police] Tokyo: Tabata Shoten

Mommsen, Hans (1976) 'National socialism—continuity and change' in Laqueur (ed.) *Fascism* pp. 179-210

Monas, Sidney (1961) *The Third Section* Cambridge, Ma.: Harvard University Press

Moriyama Takeichirô (1936) 'Shisôhan hogo kansatsu hô ni tsuite' [On the Law for Protection and Supervision of Thought Criminals] *KKZ* 435, Aug., 13-17

Morley, James (ed.) (1971) *Dilemmas of Growth in Prewar Japan* Princeton: Princeton University Press

Mosse, George (ed.) (1975a) *Police Forces in History* Beverly Hills: Sage

——(1975b) 'Police forces in history: introduction' in Mosse (ed.) *Police Forces* pp. 1-5

Naganoken, Keisatsubu (1922) *Bunbu kôshûkai kôenshû* [Collected Lectures from the Literary and Military Arts Course] Nagano City: Naganoken Keisatsubu

Nagaoka Ryûichirô (1939) *Kanryô nijûgonen* [Twenty-five Years of a Bureaucrat] Tokyo: Chûô Kôronsha

Naimushô (n.d.) *Tokkô keisatsu sôan* [Draft of the Special Higher Police] n.p.

Naimushô, Keihokyoku (1919-45) 'Documents on Japanese police activities, Tokyo' United States Library of Congress microfilm, Orientalia Japanica 38, 15 reels

——(n.d.) 'Kyôsanshugisha no tenkô hôsaku (miteikô)' [A plan for the conversion of communists (a rough draft)] in 'Japanese Rarities' Reel 7/Item 3.9/Frames 166-95

——(1921-36) 'Kyôsanshugi ni kansuru shorui tsuzuri' [Bound documents related to communism] in 'Japanese Rarities' Reel 7/Item 3.9

——(1926-41) *Keisatsu tôkei hôkoku* [Statistical Report on the Police] Tokyo: Naimushô Keihokyoku

——(1927a) *Chôfuken keisatsu enkaku shi* [A History of the Development of the Prefectural Police] 4 v., Tokyo: Naimushjô Keihokyoku

——(1927b) *Naimudaiji kunji yôshishû* [A Collection of Main Points from the Home Minister's Instructions] Keisatsu kenkyû shiryô series, v.4, Tokyo: Naimushô Keihokyoku

——(1934a) 'Chian iji hô kaisei hôritsuan, Dai rokujûgomen teikoku gikai ryôin honkaigi oyobi iinkai giji sokkiroku yôkô' [Bill for revision of the Peace Preservation Law, Important points from the stenographic record of the proceedings of the meetings of both houses and the committee of the 65th Imperial Diet] in Naimushô, Keihokyoku 'Documents' Reel 3/Item 5

——(1934b) 'Keisatsubuchô kaigi ni okeru chûshin gidai to shite no keisatsu seishin sakkô mondai' [The problem of arousing police spirit as the central topic for discussion in the Prefectural Police Department Chiefs Conference] *KKZ* 407, June, 11-20

——(1934c) *Kyokusa bunshi no buki shiyô ni yoru shôgai teido narabi ni sono bukibetsu shirabe* [An Investigation of the Degree of Injuries Due to Use of Weapons by Extreme Leftist Elements and of the Types of Weapons]

——(1934-43) 'Chihôchôkan keisatsubuchô kaigi kankei shorui' [Documents related to prefectural governors and police department chiefs conferences] in Naimushô, Keihokyoku 'Documents' Reel 4/Item 6

Naimushô, Keihokyoku, Chôsashitsu (1937) *Sayoku undô no nihonka* [The Japanisation of Left Wing Movements] n.p.

Naimushô, Keihokyoku, Hoanka (1930–44) *Tokkô geppô* [Special Higher Police Monthly Report]

——(1935) *Tokkô keisatsu reikishû* [A Collection of Special Higher Police Regulations] 3 pts

——(1939) *Tokkô keisatsu reikishû* [A Collection of Special Higher Police Regulations]

Naimushô, Keihokyoku, Keimuka, Kaigigakari (1935) 'Keisatsubuchô kaigi no gaikyô' [General conditions of the Prefectural Police Department Chiefs Conference] *KKZ* 420, June, 18–29

——(1936) 'Keisatsubuchô kaigi no jôkyô' [Conditions of the Prefectural Police Department Chiefs Conference] *KKZ* 434, July, 54–7

Naimushô, Keihokyoku, Toshoka (1936) *Shuppanbutsu o tsûjite mitaru go-ichigo jiken* [The 5–15 Incident Seen Through Publications] Shuppan keisatsu shiryô, v.7, Tokyo: Naimushô Keihokyoku Toshoka

Naisei Shi Kenkyûkai (ed.) (1967a) *Abe Genki shi danwa sokkiroku* [Stenographic Record of Conversations with Abe Genki] Naisei shi kenkyû shiryô series, 48–51, [Tokyo]: Naisei Shi Kenkyûkai

——(1967b) *Matsumoto Manabu shi danwa sokkiroku* [Stenographic Record of Conversations with Matsumoto Manabu] 2 v., Naisei shi kenkyû shiryô series, 52–5, [Tokyo]: Naisei Shi Kenkyûkai

——(1967c) *Tsuchiya Shôzô shi danwa sokkiroku* [Stenographic Record of Conversations with Tsuchiya Shôzô] Naisei shi kenkyû shiryô series, 59–60, [Tokyo]: Naisei Shi Kenkyûkai

Nakagawa Norikata (1934) *Shisô hanzai sôsa teiyô* [A Manual for Investigation of Thought Crimes] Tokyo: Shinkôkaku

Nakahara Hidenori (1955) 'The Japanese police' *Journal of Criminal Law, Criminology and Police Science* 46, Nov.–Dec., 583–94

Nakamura Kikuo (1958) *Shôwa seiji shi* [A History of Shôwa Politics] Tokyo: Keiô Tsûshin

Nakano, Tomio (1923) *The Ordinance Power of the Japanese Emperor* Baltimore: Johns Hopkins University Press

Nakatani Masaichi (1921) 'Heiso kôryô junbi subeki shoten' [Various points for general consideration and preparation] *KKZ* 254, Aug., 13–19

Nakayama Ken'ichi (1970) *Gendai shakai to chian hô* [Modern Society and Peace Preservation Laws] Tokyo: Iwanami Shinsho

Nanba Mokusaburô (1924) *Keisatsu tokuhon—Hijôshiki monogatari* [Police Reader—A Story of Lack of Common Sense] Tokyo: Shôkadô

Nihon Kindai Shiryô Kenkyûkai (ed.) (1968) *Taishô kôki Keihokyoku kankô shakai undô shiryô* [Historical Materials on Social Movements Published by the Police Bureau during the Latter Part of the Taishô Period] Nihon kindai shiryô sôsho series, A-1, Tokyo: Nihon Kindai Shiryô Kenkyûkai

'No left turn' (1936) *Fortune* 14, Sep., 95–100 ff.

Nolte, Ernst (1966) *Three Faces of Fascism* New York: Holt, Rinehart and Winston

Nomura Nobutaka (1939) *Gyôseihô taikô* [Outline of Administrative Law] Tokyo: Ganshôdô
Notehelfer, F. G. (1971) *Kôtoku Shûsui: Portrait of a Japanese Radical* Cambridge: Cambridge University Press
Ogata Nakaba (1933) *Tokkô keisatsu tokuhon* [Special Higher Police Reader] Tokyo: Shôkadô
Ogino Fujio (1984) *Tokkô keisatsu taisei shi* [A History of the Special Higher Police System] Tokyo: Sekita Shobô
Ôhashi Hideo (1967) *Aru keisatsukan no kiroku* [Record of a Police Official] Tokyo: Misuzu Shobô
Oka Kishichirô (1921) 'Keisatsu no minshûka to wa' [Democratisation of the Police] *KKZ* 255, Sep., 1–3
Okudaira Yasuhiro (1962) *Political Censorship in Japan from 1931 to 1945* n.p.: Institute of Legal Research, University of Pennsylvania
——(1967) 'Ken'etsu seido (zenki)' [The censorship system (all periods)] in Ukai Nobushige et al. (eds) *Nihon kindai hô hattatsu shi* [History of the Development of Modern Japanese Law] v.11, Tokyo: Kôsei Shobô, pp. 135–205
——(1973) 'Some preparatory notes for the study of the Peace Preservation Law in pre-war Japan' *Annals of the Institute of Social Science* no.14, University of Tokyo
——(ed.) (1975) *Chian iji hô* [The Peace Preservation Law] Gendai shi shiryô series, v.45, Tokyo: Misuzu Shobô
——(1976) 'Chian iji hô kaisei no rekishi' [History of the revision of the Peace Preservation Law] *Gendai shi* no. 7, June, 38–68
——(1977) *Chian iji hô shôshi* [A Short History of the Peace Preservation Law] Tokyo: Chikuma Shobô
Ôno Tatsuzô (1973) *Nihon no seiji keisatsu* [Japanese Political Police] Tokyo: Shin Nihon Shuppansha
Onuki Hiroshi (1937) 'Shisôsen to kokumin seishin sôdôin' [The thought war and the mobilisation of national spirit] *KKZ* 449, Oct., 15–22
Ôtake Takeshichirô (1933) *Shisô hanzai torishimarihô yôron* [An Outline of Laws for the Control of Thought Crimes] Tokyo: Shinkôkaku
Ôtani Keijirô (1966) *Shôwa kenpei shi* [History of the Shôwa Military Police] Tokyo: Misuzu Shobô
——(1971) *Gunbatsu* [Military Cliques] Tokyo: Tosho Shuppansha
Parker, L. Craig (1984) *The Japanese Police System Today: An American Perspective* New York: Kodansha International
Payne, Howard C. (1966) *The Police State of Louis Napoleon Bonaparte, 1851–1860* Seattle: University of Washington Press
Pittau, Joseph (1967) *Political Thought in Early Meiji Japan, 1868–1889* Cambridge, Ma.: Harvard University Press
'Police forces' (1972) *Journal of Contemporary History* 7, Jan.–Apr., 199–200
Potholm, Christian (1969) 'The multiple roles of the police as seen in the African context' *Journal of Developing Areas* 3, Jan., 139–57
Pyle, Kenneth (1974) 'Advantages of followership: German economics and Japanese bureaucrats, 1890–1925' *Journal of Japanese Studies* 1, Autumn, 127–64

Raeff, Marc (1975) 'The well-ordered police state and the development of modernity in seventeenth- and eighteenth-century Europe: an attempt at a comparative approach' *American Historical Review* 80, Dec., 1221–43
——(1983) *The Well-Ordered Police State: Social and Institutional Change Through Law in the Germanies and Russia, 1600–1800* New Haven: Yale University Press
Reiss, Albert (1971) *Police and the Public* New Haven: Yale University Press
Reith, Charles (1952) *The Blind Eye of History* London: Faber and Faber
Reitlinger, Gerald (1957) *The SS: Alibi of a Nation, 1922–1945* rev.edn., London: William Heinemann
Richardson, James (1972) 'Berlin police in the Weimar Republic: a comparison with police forces in cities of the United States' *Journal of Contemporary History* 7, Jan.–Apr., 261–75
Rikken Seiyûkai Suzuki Sôsai Hensanbu (ed.) (1934) *Suzuki sôsai* [President Suzuki] Tokyo: Rikken Seiyûkai Suzuki Sôsai Hensanbu
Roach John (1985) 'The French police' in John Roach and Jürgen Thomaneck (eds) *Police and Public Order in Europe* London: Croom Helm pp. 107–41
Rogger, Hans (1966) 'Afterthoughts' in Hans Rogger and Eugen Weber (eds) *The European Right: A Historical Profile* Berkeley: University of California Press pp. 575–89
Rubin, Jesse (1972) 'Police identity and the police role' in Steadman (ed.) *Police and the Community* pp. 12–50
Saitô Teruo (1974) *Keisatsuchô* [The Police Agency] Tokyo: Kyôikusha
Santaro (1924) 'Policemen and the people' *TransPacific* 11, 20 Dec., 5
Sarbin, T. R. and V. L. Allen (1968) 'Role theory' in Lindzey and Aronson (eds) *Handbook* pp. 488–567
Sasaki Sôichi (1922) *Nihon gyôseihô ron, kakuron* [An Essay on Japanese Administrative Law, Detailed Exposition] Tokyo: Yûhikaku
Sasaki Yoshizô (1933) *Tokkô keisatsu zensho* [A Complete Book about the Special Higher Police] Tokyo: Shôkadô
Satô Shôzô (1937) *Genka ni okeru Tokkô gaikan to zuikan zuisô* [An Outline of the Special Higher Police at the Present Time and Random Thoughts] Tokyo: Shinkôkaku
Scalapino, Robert (1967) *The Japanese Communist Movement, 1920–1966* Berkeley: University of California Press
Schafer, Stephen (1974) *The Political Criminal* New York: The Free Press
'Seiji kyôiku to keisatsu' (1990) [Political education and the police] *Asahi shinbun* 23 Mar. evening edn., p. 2
Seki Seitarô (1928) *Keisatsu jitsumu kôwa* [Lectures on Practical Police Affairs] Tokyo: Daigaku Shobô
Shakai Bunko (ed.) (1965) *Shôwaki kanken shisô chôsa hôkoku* [Reports of Thought Investigations by Authorities during the Shôwa Period] Shakai bunko sôsho series, v.5, Tokyo: Kashiwa Shobô
Shakai Mondai Shiryô Kenkyûkai (ed.) (1972) *Dai gojûkai teikoku gikai chian iji hôan giji sokkiroku narabi ni iinkai giroku* [Stenographic Record of the Diet and Committee on the Peace Preservation Bill of the Fiftieth Diet] Shakai Mondai Shiryô sôsho, dai 1-shû; Shisô kenkyû shiryô,

tokushû dai 7-go, Kyoto: Tôyô Bunkasha
Shibusawa Eiichi (1921) 'Kokumin to keisatsu to no sôgo ryôkai' [Mutual understanding between the people and the police] *KKZ* 248, Feb., 1–7
Shillony, Ben-Ami (1973) *Revolt in Japan: The Young Officers and the February 26, 1936 Incident* Princeton: Princeton University Press
Shimada Saburô (1921) 'Keisatsu wa kokumin no tomo de aru' [The police is the friend of the people] *KKZ* 248, Feb., 8–13
Shimamura Tasaburô (1939) *Gyôseihô yôron* [Outline of Administrative Law] Tokyo: Ganshôdô
Shimizu Chô (1935) *Nihon gyôseihô taii* [Outline of Japanese Administrative Law] Tokyo: Shimizu Shoten
Shimizu Nagao (1939) 'Junsa saiyô kisoku narabi junsa kyôshû gaisoku no kaisei ni tsuite' [On the revision of the rules for recruitment of patrolmen and rules for training of patrolmen] *KKZ* 357, May, 36–40
Shimizu Shigeo and Wataru Masami (1932) *Keimu taikei, Hôritsu hen* [An Outline of Police Work, Law volume] v.1, Tokyo: Keimu Kenkyûkai
Shinobu Seizaburô et al. (1960) *Gendai hantaisei undô shi* [A History of Modern Opposition Movements] v.2, Tokyo: Aoki Shoten
Shôkadô (ed.) (1932) *Keisatsu renshûsho* [Police Training Book] 2 v., Tokyo: Shôkadô
Shôkadô Henshûbu (ed.) (1934) *Keisatsu jûken zensho, Keisatsu hô hen* [A Complete Book on the Police Examination, Police Law volume] Tokyo: Shôkadô
Smih, Henry DeW. II (1972) *Japan's First Student Radicals* Cambridge, Ma.: Harvard University Press
Sone Chûichi (1930) *Tokkô keisatsu to shakai undô no gaisetsu* [An Outline of the Special Higher Police and Social Movements] Yamagata City: Yamagataken Keisatsubu Tokubetsu Kôtôka
Spaulding, Robert M. Jr (1967) *Imperial Japan's Higher Civil Service Examinations* Princeton: Princeton University Press
——(1970) 'Japan's "New Bureaucrats", 1932–45' in George M. Wilson (ed.) *Crisis Politics in Prewar Japan* Tokyo: Sophia University pp. 51–70
——(1971) 'The bureaucracy as a political force, 1920–45' in Morley (ed.) *Dilemmas* pp. 33–80
Squire, P. S. (1968) *The Third Department: The Political Police under Nicholas I* Cambridge: Cambridge University Press
Stead, Philip J. (1977) 'The new police' in Bayley (ed.) *Police and Society* pp. 73–84
Steadman, Robert (ed.) (1972) *The Police and the Community* Baltimore: Johns Hopkins University Press
Steiner, John M. (1976) *Power Politics and Social Change in National Socialist Germany: A Process of Escalation into Mass Destruction* The Hague: Mouton Publishers
Steinhoff, Patricia (1969) '*Tenkô*: ideology and societal integration in pre-war Japan' PhD thesis, Harvard University
Sternhell, Zeev (1976) 'Fascist ideology' in Laqueur (ed.) *Fascism* pp. 315–78

Sudô Tetsuomi (1937) 'Konji jihen ni saishi zenkoku keisatsu kanri ni nozomu' [What I expect of police officials throughout the country at the time of the present hostilities] *KKZ* 448, Sep., 4–9

Sugai, Shuichi (1937) 'Keisatsu no gainen' [The concept of police] *Hôgaku ronsô* 37, Oct., 590–602

——(1957) 'The Japanese police system' in Robert E. Ward (ed.) *Five Studies in Japanese Politics* Ann Arbor: University of Michigan Press, pp. 1–14

Sugimoto Moriyoshi (1952) 'Tokkô keisatsu no soshiki to unyô' [The organisation and use of the Special Higher Police] 2 pts *Jurisuto* 14, 15 July, 19–25; and 15, 1 Aug., 38–43

Sugimoto Seisaku (1933) *Keisatsu jitsumu mondô* [Questions and Answers about Practical Police Affairs] Tokyo: Shôkadô

Supreme Commander for the Allied Powers, Government Section (1949) *Political Reorientation of Japan, Sept. 1945–Sept. 1948* Washington, DC: United States Government Printing Office

Suzuki Eiji (1936) 'Keisatsu sôron' [An introduction to the police] pts 4 and 5 *Keisatsu kenkyû* 7, May, 77–98; and 7, June, 63–78

Suzuki Kisaburô Sensei Denki Hensankai (ed.) (1955) *Suzuki Kisaburô* Tokyo: Suzuki Kisaburô Sensei Denki Hensankai, originally 1945

Swanson, Glen (1972) 'The Ottoman police' *Journal of Contemporary History* 7, Jan.–Apr., 243–60

Swearingen, Rodger and Paul Langer (1952) *Red Flag in Japan: International Communism in Action, 1919–1951* Cambridge, Ma.: Harvard University Press

Tachibana Takendo (1929) *Shakai undô gaisetsu, hihan, torishimari* [Outline, Criticism and Control of Social Movements] Tokyo: Shôkadô

Taikakai (ed.) (1971) *Naimushô shi* [History of the Home Ministry] v.1 and 4, Tokyo: Chihô Zaimukyôkai

Takagi Takeo (1954) 'Nihon keisatsu zaiaku shi' [The history of Japanese police crimes] *Bungei shunjû* 32: 5, Apr., 110–19

Takahashi, Yûsai (1924) 'Pisutoru taiyô mondai' [The problems of being armed with pistols] *KKZ* 21–5

——(1927) *Keisatsu ronsô* [A Collection of Treatises on the Police] Tokyo: Daigaku Shobô

——(1930) 'Keisatsu kanbu no kyôkô' [Education of the police leadership] *KKZ* 359, July, 15–18

Takayanagi, Kenzo (1963) 'A century of innovation: the development of Japanese Law, 1868–1961' in Von Mehren (ed.) *Law in Japan* pp. 5–40

Takeno Takeji and Akaeda Kiyoshi (1946) 'Tokubetsu kôtô keisatsu shi' [History of the Special Higher Police] 4 pts *Chôryû* 1, Jan., 158–67; 1, Feb., 129–36; 1, Mar., 119–27; and 1, Apr., 124–32

Takeuchi, Sterling (1930) 'The Japanese civil service' in Leonard White (ed.) *The Civil Service in the Modern State: A Collection of Documents* Chicago: University of Chicago, pp. 515–55

Taki Shizuo (1974) *Keisatsu konjaku monogatari* [A Narrative of the Police Past and Present] Tokyo: Shin Jinbutsu Ôraisha

Tamaki Masayoshi (ed.) (1946) *Nihon kyôsantô kôhan tôsô hishi* [Secret History of the Japanese Communist Party's Struggle for a Public Trial] v.1, Fukuoka City: Kyûshû Rôdô Gakkô Shuppanbu

Tamuno, Tekena (1970) *The Police in Modern Nigeria, 1861–1965* n.p.: Ibadan University Press

Tamura Yutaka (1932) *Keisatsu shi kenkyû* [An Historical Study of the Police] Tokyo: Ryôsho Fukyûkai

Tanaka Sôgorô (1956) 'Dan'atsu to shinryaku to' [Repression and aggression] in Ôkochi Kazuo et al. (eds) *Nihon no shakaishugi* [Japanese Socialism] Shakaishugi kôza series, v.7, Tokyo: Kozu Shobô

Tatebayashi Mikio (1935) 'Keisatsu seishin sakkô undô no ninmu' [Duties of the movement for the promotion of police spirit] *KKZ* 418, May, 19–27

——(1936) ' "Ridô no shinshuku" to "keisatsu seishin no sakkô" ' ['Strict enforcement of the official's way' and 'promotion of police spirit'] *KKZ* 433, June, 7–15

Tateno Nobuyuki (1963) *Shôwa gunbatsu* [Shôwa Military Cliques] Tokyo: Kodansha

'Teikoku gikai ni okeru keisatsukan yûgû ni kansuru kengi' (1933) [Imperial Diet resolutions for improving the treatment of police officials] *KKZ* 393, May, 12–20; and 395, June, 7–17

Titus, David (1974) *Palace and Politics in Prewar Japan* New York: Columbia University Press

Tobias, J. J. (1972) 'Police and public in the United Kingdom' *Journal of Contemporary History* 7, Jan.–Apr., 201–19

Torigoe Jukuji and Matsuo Hidetoshi (1931) *Keisatsu jiten* [Police Dictionary] Tokyo: Shôkadô

Tosawa Shigeo (1965) 'Shisô hanzai no kensatsu jitsumu ni tsuite' [On the business of investigating thought crimes] in Yamabe (ed.) *Shakaishugi undô* pt 3, pp. 15–36

Totten, George (1966) *The Social Democratic Movement in Prewar Japan* New Haven: Yale University Press

Tottoriken (1928) 'Tottoriken keisatsu kaigi shorui tsuzuri' [Bound documents of Tottori Prefecture police meetings] in 'Japanese Rarities' Reel 10/Item 3.39

——(1932–41) 'Tottoriken Tokkô kankei shorui' [Tottori Prefecture Special Higher Police-related documents] in Naimushô, Keihokyoku 'Documents' Reel 15/Item 31E3

Toyama Fukuo (1933) *Keisatsukan no kyôyô oyobi taigû kaizen* [Improvement of the Education and Treatment of Police Officials] Tokyo: Shinkôkaku

Tsunajima Kakuzaemon (1937) *Keisatsu no jissai to risô* [The Reality and Ideal of the Police] Tokyo: Ryôsho Fukyûkai

Tsuneishi, Warren (1960) 'The Japanese emperor: a study in constitutional and political change' PhD thesis, Yale University

Tsunoda Chûshichirô (1956) *Kenpei hiroku* [Secret Memoirs of a Military Police Officer] Tokyo: Masu Shobô

Turner, Henry (ed.) (1975) *Reappraisals of Fascism* New York: New Viewpoints
United States, War Department, Office of Strategic Services, Research and Analysis Branch (1945) *The Japanese Police System under Allied Occupation* R and A Report No. 2758, Sep. 28 n.p.
Verba, Sidney (1965) 'Germany: the remaking of political culture' in Lucian Pye and Sidney Verba (eds) *Political Culture and Political Development* Princeton: Princeton University Press, pp. 130–70
Von Mehren, Arthur (ed.) (1963a) *Law in Japan: The Legal Order in a Changing Society* Cambridge, Ma.: Harvard University Press.
——(1963b) 'Commentary: part II' in Von Mehren (ed.) *Law in Japan* pp. 422–38
Wada Kanae (1920–21) 'Kiken shisô to keisatsu' [Dangerous thought and the police] *KKZ* 246, Dec. 1920, 1–10; and 247, Jan. 1921, 17–29
Wagatsuma Sakae (ed.) (1970) *Nihon seiji saiban shi roku* [Records of the History of Japanese Political Justice] v.4, Tokyo: Daiichi Hôki Shuppan Kabushiki Kaisha
Wakatsuki Reijirô (1950) *Kofûan kaikoroku* [Reminiscences of an Old-fashioned Hermit] Tokyo: Yomiuri Shinbunsha
Wald, Royal (1949) 'The Young Officers movement in Japan, ca 1925–1937: ideology and actions' PhD thesis, University of California
Ward, Harry F. (1925) 'Law and order in Japan' *Nation* 121, 9 Sep., 289–90
Watanabe Osamu (1976) 'Chian iji hô no seiritsu o megutte' [Centring around establishment of the Peace Preservation Law] *Gendai shi* no. 7, June, 18–37
Watanabe Sôtarô (1935) *Gyôseihô kôgi* [An Exposition of Administrative Law] v.2, Tokyo: Kôbundô Shobô
Watanabe Tetsuo and Ishikawa Shunsaku (1933) *Shumi no keisatsu jôshiki* [Interesting Police Common Sense] Tokyo: Keiseisha
Weed, Albert C. II (1970) *Police and the Modernization Process: Thailand* Princeton: Woodrow Wilson Association Monograph Series in Public Affairs.
Westley, William (1970) *Violence and the Police* Cambridge, Ma.: MIT Press
Westney, D. Eleanor (1982) 'The emulation of Western organizations in Meiji Japan: the case of the Paris prefecture of police and the Keishichô' *Journal of Japanese Studies* 8:2, Summer, 307–42
——(1987) *Imitation and Innovation* Cambridge: Harvard University Press
Wildes, Harry E (1925) 'Japan keeps the peace, new Peace Preservation Law aims at political agitators' *Nation* 120, 15 Apr., 418–19
——(1927) *The Press and Social Currents in Japan* Chicago: University of Chicago Press
——(1928) 'Japanese police' *Journal of Criminal Law and Criminology* 19, Nov., 390–8
Wilson, George M. (1968) 'A new look at the problem of "Japanese Fascism"' *Comparative Studies in Society and History* 10, 401–12
Wilson, James Q. (1967) 'Police morale, reform, and citizen respect: the

Chicago case' in Bordua (ed.) *The Police* pp. 139–60.
——(1968) *Varieties of Police Behavior* Cambridge, Ma.: Harvard University Press
Winant, T. T. (1971) 'The police of Tokyo' *Police Journal* 44, Apr.–May, 167–73
Wray, Harry (1973) 'Nationalism and internationalism in Japanese elementary textbooks, 1918–1931' *Asian Forum* 5, Oct.–Dec., 46–62
Yamabe Kentarô (ed.) (1965) *Shakaishugi undô* [Socialist Movements] pt 3, Gendai shi shiryô series, v.16, Tokyo: Misuzu Shobô
Yamagata Jirô (1921) 'Keisatsukan wa kokumin no daihyôsha nari' [Police officials are representatives of the people] *KKZ* 254, Aug., 20–37
Yamagata Tamezô (1968) *Shochô ichidai* [The Life of a Police Station Chief] Tokyo: Keisatsu Shôbô Tsûshinsha
Yamagataken, Tokubetsu Kôtôka (Oct. 1939) 'Yamagataken Tokkô kankei shorui: Shuppan keisatsu shitsumu yôkô' [Documents related to the Yamagata Prefecture Special Higher Police: main principles for the execution of publications police duties] in Naimushô, Keihokyoku 'Documents' Reel 15/Item 31F
Yamaguchi Kôzô (1933) *Kenkyo yori sôchi made* [From Arrest to Dispatch] Tokyo: Shinkôkaku
Yamamoto Katsunosuke and Mitsuho Arita (1950) *Nihon kyôsanshugi undô shi* [History of the Japanese Communist Movement] Tokyo: Seiki Shobô
Yamamoto Kazuo (1934) *Keisatsu jitsumu teiyô* [A Summary of Practical Police Affairs] Fukuoka City: Fukuokaken Keisatsu Renshûjo
——(1937) *Nihon keisatsu shi* [History of the Japanese Police] Tokyo: Shôkadô
Yashiro Kôji (1934) 'Parii keishichô no keisatsu ryoku to waga keishichô to no hikaku' [A comparison of the police power of the Paris Metropolitan Police Board with our Metropolitan Police Board] *KKZ* 405, Apr., 40–4
Yasko, Richard (1973) 'Hiranuma Kiichirô and conservative politics in prewar Japan' PhD dissertation, University of Chicago
Yokomizu Mitsuteru (1928) 'Tokkô keisatsu no tame ni' [For the Special Higher Police] *KKZ* 335, July, 18–25
Yokota Kisaburô (1949) *Tennô sei* [The Emperor System] Tokyo: Rôdô Bunkasha
Yokoyama Shinsaku (1928) *Junsa kara keishi made* [From Patrolman to Superintendent] Tokyo: Keigansha
Young, Arthur Morgan (1938) *Imperial Japan, 1926–1938* New York: William Morrow
Young, M. Crawford (1965) *Politics in the Congo: Decolonization and Independence* Princeton: Princeton University Press
Yuasa Kurahei (1924) 'Yûshû naru keisatsu' [An excellent police] *KKZ* 281, Jan., 8–11
Yubara Motoichi (1921) 'Keisatsukan no taigû mondai' [The problem of the treatment of police officials] *KKZ* 252, June, 14–17
Ziegler, Herbert (1989) *Nazi Germany's New Aristocracy* Princeton Princeton University Press

INDEX

Abe Genki 97, 100, 101, 120, 124, 178, 184
Administrative Enabling Law 31, 52, 60–1
Administrative Police Rules 58, 71
American police 6, 7, 8, 30, 37, 38, 81, 140, 165, 186
April 16 Incident 25
Arimatsu Hideyoshi 79

British police 6, 7, 37, 38–9, 81–2

Censorship 25, 27–8, 46, 57, 59, 61, 65–6, 67

Figaseusky, Emil 42
Fouché, Joseph 15, 45
French police 6, 15, 38–9, 45, 166
Fujinuma Shôhei 97, 110, 123, 183
Fukuzawa Yukichi 37

Gestapo 1, 4, 16, 25, 143–5
Go-Stop Incident 121–2, 141, 152
Gotô Shinpei 79
GPU (State Political Administration) 1, 4, 16, 25, 147

Great Treason Incident 19, 45

Hakamada Satomi 27
Hara Kei 43–4, 110
Himmler, Heinrich 68, 136, 143–5
Hibiya Park Incident 43, 50
Hiranuma Kiichirô 108, 110–11, 116, 152, 180
Höhn, Wilhelm 42–3
Honda Yoshinari 64, 169
Horikiri Zenjirô 66

Ishihara Tsunejirô 56, 115, 179
Itô Hirobumi 48, 56
Iwata Yoshimichi 133, 163
Izawa Takio 101, 111–12

Japanese Communist Party (JCP) 3, 4, 9, 17, 20, 21, 24–5, 26–7, 89, 97, 112–13, 127–9, 132–3, 143

Kamedo Incident 21
Kanai Noboru 108–9
Karasawa Toshiki 123, 179–80
Katayama Sen 18
Katsura Tarô 18–19, 61

Kawaji Toshiyoshi 10, 35, 36–8, 39, 40–1, 47–8, 81, 138, 167
Kawamura Teishirô 101–2
Kawasaki Takukichi 64, 101, 112, 114–15, 179, 181
Kiyoura Keigo 42, 59
Kobayashi Takiji 26, 133, 163
Kokutai 23, 24, 62–5, 69–70, 73, 74, 78, 83, 94–5, 109, 127, 129, 131–2, 137, 139, 141, 151, 153
Kôketsu Yazô 24
Kôtoku Shûsui 18–19
Kuwata Kumazo 108
Kyoto Gakuren 23, 114

Law for Protection and Observation of Thought Criminals 29
Law to Control Radical Social Movements bill 20, 111

March 15 Incident 23, 26, 69, 115, 182
Maruyama Masao 13
Maruyama Tsurukichi 88, 123, 179
Matsui Shigeru 67, 74, 79, 80, 81, 82, 83–4, 87, 95
Matsumoto Manabu 88, 101, 121–2, 179
May 15 Incident 27, 97
Minobe Tatsukichi 29, 64, 70–2, 170, 171–2
Mishima Michitsune 59
Miyashita Hiroshi 90, 94–5, 118, 171, 183
Môri Moto 23, 100, 118, 124
Morito Tatsuo 110

Nabeyama Sadachika 26
Nagata Tetsuzan 102, 179–80
Nanba Daisuke 21, 112
'New bureaucrats' 93–4, 102, 108, 123, 124–5, 150, 152, 179–80

Obata Tatsuo 27
Oizumi Kenzo 27
Ôkubo Toshimichi 37
Ôsugi Sakae 21

Pak Yol (Boku Retsu) 21, 112
Peace Preservation Law (1925) 3, 22–3, 25, 33, 52, 62–5, 107, 112–13, 128, 148–9
Peace Preservation Ordinance (1887) 59, 60
Police: brutality, 1, 25–6, 31, 132–3, 149–50, 163, 187; promotions, 78, 87–8, 99–101, 179; recruitment, 42, 77, 78, 86, 89, 139, 176; salaries, 42, 77, 87, 175; training, 79, 84, 86–7, 139, 140, 171, 175
Polizeistaat 14–15, 38, 41, 133, 142, 152
Public Peace Police Law 18, 22, 60, 66, 109

Rechtsstaat 39, 53, 55, 172
Regulations for Punishment of Violations of Police Ordinances 61
Regulations Governing Summary Decisions on Minor Offenses 61
Rice riots (1918) 19–20, 66, 81, 107, 110

Saigô Takamori 37, 40
Sano Manabu 26
Sasaki Sôichi 64, 70–1, 172
Shiono Suehiko 24, 115
Social movements 20, 29, 33, 88–9, 91, 101, 107–9, 114, 127, 141, 175
SS (Schutzstaffel) 143–6, 148, 149
Suzuki Kisaburô 24, 25, 108, 110–11, 115–16, 152, 180, 182

Tanaka Giichi cabinet 24, 115–16
Tenkô or *tenkôsha* 26, 28–9, 33, 55, 70, 73, 89, 116, 117–19, 133, 141, 150, 151, 168, 176, 183
Thought Countermeasures Committee 28–9
Thought procurators 23, 25, 116–17, 118, 148, 150, 152, 183
Toranomon Incident 21

Uesugi Shinkichi 64
Urakawa Hideyoshi 24

Wakatsuki Reijirô 63-4, 181, 164, 169

Yamagata Aritomo 40-2, 49, 58-9, 79
Yamamoto Kazuo 35
Yamaoka Mannosuke 63-4
Yuasa Kurahei 111-12, 181